MONEY AND SECRECY

MONEY
AND
SECRECY

*A Citizen's Guide to Reforming
State and Federal Practices*

Lawrence Gilson

Introduction by John W. Gardner

A COMMON CAUSE BOOK

PRAEGER PUBLISHERS
New York • Washington • London

PRAEGER PUBLISHERS
111 Fourth Avenue, New York, N.Y. 10003, U.S.A.
5, Cromwell Place, London SW7 2JL, England
Published in the United States of America in 1972
by Praeger Publishers, Inc.
© 1972 by Common Cause
Library of Congress Catalog Card Number: 72-88863

Printed in the United States of America

Contents

Preface   vii

Introduction   ix

I. THE PROBLEM: What You Don't See Is What You   1
   Get
   • Gives examples of the abuse of public trust: state
     and federal.
   • Identifies four key reform areas: open meetings,
     lobbying disclosure, conflict of interest, and cam-
     paign finance.

II. FEDERAL PRACTICES: Is This Any Way To Run a
    Government?   17
    • Summarizes existing federal laws, rules, orders, and
      customs in the four basic reform fields.

III. STATE PRACTICES: There Ought To Be a Law   33
     • Provides a state-by-state summary of existing laws
       in the four basic reform fields.

IV. ENFORCEMENT: There Ought To Be a Lawyer   183
    • Explains the tendency toward non-enforcement.
    • Describes the enforcement record for existing fed-
      eral laws.
    • Gives the results of a study of the degree to which
      state laws are enforced.

V. CITIZEN ACTION: How To Take Back Your
   Government   195
   • Suggests ways to promote enforcement of existing
     laws.

- Offers suggestions for when and how to seek new laws.
- Gives specific suggestions of where to begin in reforming government practices, state by state and at the federal level.

Appendixes   247
    A. Glossary
    B. Model Open Meetings Bill
    C. Model Lobbying Disclosure Bill
    D. Model Conflict of Interest Bill
    E. Model Campaign Finance Bill

The maps on pages 213 through 216 were drawn by Mauer, Fleisher, and Zon.

Preface

It is inevitable that a few laws will be changed between the time this book was researched and the time it is published. I apologize in advance for any inaccuracies that may result and hope that changes, if any, are to the benefit of the public.

I was very fortunate to have the assistance of many helpful, patient, creative people in the course of preparing this book. They include, but are not limited to: Lynn Bailets, David Bullock, Margaret Carroll, Lee Dolgin, Mitch Dorson, Bob Gallamore, Tim Gardner, Barbara Hanback, Helen Kaufman, Jim Krause, Katherine Lang, Mark Lefenfeld, Marylou Peterson, Steve Robin, Elie Robins, and Dave Tarr, as well as many other volunteers and staff members of Common Cause.

I give special thanks to Becky Cloud for helping to gather and interpret the data on the state laws and to my wife, Cathy, who lived with the ups and downs of the project as long as I did.

LARRY GILSON

August 1, 1972
Washington, D.C.

Introduction

by JOHN W. GARDNER
Chairman, Common Cause

This is a down-to-earth, practical book on a supremely important subject.

For almost two years now Common Cause has been saying something very simple to all who would listen: "The very instruments the people must use to solve their problems—the instruments of self-government—are themselves in need of repair."

Until the American people understand that, and act on it, we shall make little progress with the other problems that plague us—war, a deteriorating environment, inadequate schools and health care, a housing shortage, and so on.

Our constitutional framework is sound; the system of checks and balances is well conceived. Although the federal system, gradually refined and improved since 1789, may need further refinement and improvement, it has served America exceedingly well.

But over the years those office-holders whose chief concern is the preservation of their own power have devised rules and schemes and arrangements that have profoundly affected the way our government works and what the citizen can do about it. As a consequence, citizens do not have access to their own government. They cannot hold it accountable. It is not responsive to their needs. Behind a veil of secrecy, money dictates political outcomes.

These are the problems that underlie all the other problems of public policy. Until we tackle them, we will not solve the others. We can arouse citizen indignation, but it will somehow fail to affect policy. We can propose laws, but they will somehow get emasculated in secret committee sessions. We can appropriate billions of dollars, but they will somehow get spent without accomplishing their stated purposes.

The American people aren't in a mood to put up with that any longer. They have watched the charade with growing sourness, and that is, in part, the yeast of their discontent.

REVITALIZATION OF NATIONAL GOVERNMENT

Common Cause has focused its major effort on these issues of access and accountability in government. As a national organization, we have given primary attention to federal laws and rules on these subjects. Central among our many activities, we have helped enact a new national campaign finance law, exposed the frailties of the existing lobbying disclosure law, called on members of Congress to end their conflicts of interest, and opposed unnecessary government secrecy. These issues are discussed in this book. Facts and statistics document the record, and concrete, workable proposals for change are offered.

REFORM AT THE STATE GOVERNMENT LEVEL

Now Common Cause has embarked on a much larger task—seeing to it that this same job is carried out in every one of the fifty states.

In the past two or three years informed Americans have made —better late than never—a discovery of crucial importance. They have discovered that vast powers reside in their state legislatures. Actions are taken there that affect their pocketbooks, their jobs, and their safety.

And they have discovered that the breeze blowing from those state legislatures carries, all too often, the rich odor of corruption, the effluvium of decay, the din of mediocrity.

Until recently most citizen interest and concern focused on the federal government. Few Americans seemed to know or care what happened in the state capitals. And much of the present failure of state legislatures is traceable to that fact. An old farm proverb says, "The footprint of the owner is the best manure." The American citizen is the "owner" of his state legislatures, and he has been an absentee landlord. He has neglected these institutions, and now he's paying the price.

It is reasonable to expect citizens to participate actively in their state governments. But they need help in identifying the appropriate targets of reform. This book fills that void. It provides analysis, evaluation, and concrete suggestions for improvement of state laws as well as federal.

Not all state legislatures are in a pitiable condition. Only most of them. A number of them are too large to function effectively. A good many have sessions that are too short to too infrequent. Facilities are often inadequate. There is little or no office space and a lack of hearing rooms. Professional staff is often virtually nonexistent, or inadequate, underpaid, and poor in quality. Legislators themselves are often underpaid, and in some states there is a heavy (voluntary) turnover, especially among the younger and better-educated.

In many legislatures, there are grave shortcomings in the rules and procedures—shortcomings that make it easy for powerful legislators to sidetrack bills they don't like, shortcomings that make it difficult if not impossible for the ordinary citizen to get a fair hearing.

In most legislatures, there are multiple faults in the structure and functioning of the committee system—too many committees, poorly scheduled and conflicting committee meetings, inadequate notice of meetings and agenda, too many committee assignments per legislator, lack of adequate published rules and procedures, faulty allocation of committee functions, and so on.

One could add many other items to the list of problems that plague the legislatures. But this book wisely restricts itself to those problems that are creating the most serious ailments in the system, namely, secrecy and inadequacy of controls on lobbying, conflict of interest, and campaign spending. Money and secrecy are the crucial ingredients in corrupting the system.

They are the key to the whole question of citizen access and official accountability. They lie at the interface between the legislative process and the powerful outside interests that seek to influence and corrupt that process. For that reason, they involve the most controversial of legislative reforms and the ones most likely to arouse entrenched resistance. In other words, just the right targets for a citizen who wants to go to the heart of the matter.

CITIZEN ACTION

The most surprising political development of recent years is the emergence of a new kind of hard-hitting, relentless, and successful citizen action to "make our system work." The targets are politicians who ignore the people, unresponsive bureaucracies, and behind-the-scenes betrayals of the public interest.

In its brief two years of life, Common Cause and its more than 200,000 members have learned many of the secrets of success in the new style of citizen action. Those secrets of the trade are specificity, clear targets, concrete objectives, and lots of homework. The goal is tough-minded, professionally competent action by citizens who know precisely what they're talking about.

By itself, this book is only a guide. Its impact must come from the released energies of thousands of citizens intent on reform. But placed in the hands of a group of determined citizens —a local "good government" group, a handful of law school students, a political science department—this book can provide the springboard for effective action.

I · The Problem:

What You Don't See Is What You Get

> *The very essence of a free government consists in considering offices as public trusts, bestowed for the good of the country, and not for the benefit of an individual or a party.*
>
> JOHN C. CALHOUN

We have a problem. American government, both state and federal, is in disrepair. Few but the rich are assured access to elected officials. Campaign costs make politics a rich man's game. Lobbyists operate unobserved and unregulated. Legislators pass laws from which their friends derive personal financial gain. And all this goes on beneath a shroud of secrecy. The government is just not responsive or accessible to the people.

Money and secrecy are at the heart of the problem. This book is concerned with the four lines of citizen action that are essential to cope with the problem: open meetings laws, lobbying disclosure, prohibitions of conflicts of interest, and campaign finance regulation. It summarizes the existing laws, state and federal, bearing on these four lines of action. It tells which have been enforced. It tells what is wrong with each law and why most have been ignored. It provides models of good laws and tells how to work for their enactment and enforcement. It tells you how to make the government more accessible. Special emphasis is placed on the reform of state government, because that is a particularly neglected and crucial area.

Improving the state of American government is a task for us all. We must work together—we must mount concerted citizen campaigns—to improve the laws governing money and secrecy in politics and to seek their enforcement. The job of reform will not be easy, as the performance of our political system on these four issues is poor. Governments, like all institutions, respond most quickly and effectively to the demands they feel most forcefully and most persistently. As long as the greatest pressure comes from large corporations, major labor unions, and rich men, the government will operate most efficiently in their behalf.

Most elected officials are honest men and women, but the government practices they confront are both frustrating and potentially corrupting. Government rules and procedures stymie their efforts, and the special-interest benefits others are willing to accept make the honest men less competitive in office and at election time. To protect the public from those who succumb to

3

special interests and to insulate honest officials from ambiguous and potentially compromising situations, the law must provide clearer guidelines for the official conduct of elected and appointed representatives.

The way to keep the government from submitting to special-interest pressures is to apply a different kind of pressure, the pressure of citizen involvement. An informed, vigilant, involved citizenry can provide an effective counterforce to special interests. To do so it must have access to public officials and a knowledge of the process by which policy is made. The practices of the government in four key areas will determine whether the public will have the access and knowledge it needs. These four are open meetings, lobbying disclosure, conflicts of interest, and campaign finance.

Campaign finance laws determine the degree to which candidates will be forced into indebtedness to a few large contributors. Lobbying disclosure laws reveal the extent to which special interests, often the same ones that make the large contributions, are seeking to influence public policy. Conflict of interest laws prevent public officials from deriving personal financial gain at the public expense. Open meetings laws require that the process of decision-making be conducted under public scrutiny. In this way the public is better able to see the effect of pressures exerted by big campaign contributors, lobbyists, major corporations, and average citizens.

These four issues are at the root of the problem of declining responsiveness of our government institutions. Most laws dealing with open meetings, lobbying disclosure, conflicts of interest, and campaign finance are either ill-conceived or unenforceable, or both. The devastating result is that a minority of the American citizenry is able to wield disproportionate political power. Informed public involvement in the reform of government practices in the four areas will go a long way toward making the government work more effectively for a broader public good.

While many people are aware of the urgent need to reform certain federal government practices, few are committed to the same kind of practical reform effort at the state level. This despite the substantial impact of state government on our daily lives. As long as the United States remains committed to the concept of a federal union of states with a separation of powers, state governments must be made to work. Excluding defense expenditures, the states spend about 30 per cent of all money spent by governments in the United States, and that percentage is increasing. If we adopt some form of revenue sharing, federal monies disbursed by the states may increase even more dramatically, and state expenditures affect citizens' lives directly. States make half of all public welfare payments, pay for one-third of all health and hospital care costs, and pay for 66 per cent of all highway construction. Our federal system reserves to state governments the power to determine vast areas of public policy:

—to maintain a fair system of taxation
—to enact the laws necessary for the daily protection of life and property
—to ensure efficient delivery of public services by local governments and utility companies
—to participate with or act on a mandate from the federal government in regulating industry, maintaining roads, and funding schools
—to provide the great bulk of domestic law covering countless aspects of daily life
—to maintain penal institutions, mental hospitals, clinics, and other social agencies
—to establish, fund, and support a state judicial system, which handles the bulk of the nation's court cases
—to protect the environment and control pollution.

Considering then, that state governments are responsible for these and other areas of our life and our society, it is outrageous to find them so rife with conflicts of interest, secrecy, and outmoded rules of procedure. No longer can we ignore the nearly daily examples of abuse of public trust typified by men like Illinois Secretary of State Paul Powell, who allegedly collected over $800,000 and stored it in shoe boxes, to be discovered only after his death. No longer may we permit power companies in Colorado, mining interests in Montana, banks in Texas, lumber companies in Oregon, or chemical interests in Delaware to dominate our state governments. We can afford these practices no more than we can similar activities at the federal level. To place increased power or money in the hands of the state or federal government without at the same time taking steps to make them more responsive, more accountable, and more accessible to the citizen would be the worst kind of folly.

OPEN MEETINGS

In one of the ironic twists of modern politics, the New York State Assembly met in *closed caucus* to consider changes in their rules of procedure which would have required open meetings. This is not an isolated incident. In only seventeen of the fifty states are committee sessions of the state legislature held open to the public as a matter of course. At the federal level, according to the *Congressional Quarterly*, 36 per cent of all Congressional committee meetings in 1971 were held in secret session, down only slightly from the 41 per cent figure of 1970 and equal to the 36 per cent closed to the public in 1969. National security and personal privacy are legitimate reasons for closing some committee sessions, but such topics surely would not account for one-third of all sessions. More likely the secrecy serves to hide the fact that some legislators are busily deciding public business for the benefit of private interests.

A 1971 Texas grand jury investigated a stock manipulation scheme involving that state's former House Speaker, Gus Mutscher, and two fellow legislators. It found that, in exchange for getting stock at low prices, Mutscher and the others had agreed to rush a bill through the legislature exempting a bank from federal regulation. That grand jury statement concluded in part: "Some Texas lawmakers were too busy granting political favors and being influenced in exchange for turning a fast buck to be concerned about good government for the people." Mutscher and the others have since been convicted of enacting legislation favorable to special interests in exchange for a stock payoff. How many similar cases go undetected? It would be much more difficult for self-serving legislators in Texas or anywhere else to earn a private profit if the process were open to public scrutiny.

Secrecy in the U.S. Congress hides similar though sometimes more subtle special-interest dealings. The House Ways and Means Committee is among the most powerful committees in the Congress. It is responsible for drafting all federal tax legislation. Each January a majority of the committee's members vote to close *all* its deliberations for the entire year. So tight is security that even the staffs of congressmen on the committee and other congressmen who are not members of Ways and Means are banned from attending committee meetings.

The tax laws that the Ways and Means Committee drafts demonstrate vividly the kinds of interests at work in those closed sessions. The committee grants the oil industry an annual 22 per cent oil depletion allowance (until 1969 it was 27 per cent!). This tax break, which costs the Treasury more than a billion dollars a year, is extraordinary for an industry that ranks second only to pharmaceuticals in profitability. President Truman said of the oil depletion allowance, "I know of no loophole so inequitable." The oil industry contributes heavily to its "friends' " political campaigns. Secret meetings allow this game of "help your buddy" to be played, with virtual impunity, for astronomical stakes.

Nor are such secret meetings held only in the legislative branch. President Nixon appointed a board to advise him on how to combat industrial pollution. It is widely reported that this board, whose membership includes representatives of four of the nation's leading polluters, met secretly in late 1971 under the auspices of the Secretary of Commerce, Maurice Stans, to discuss ways of lobbying against the stringent provisions of an important Water Pollution Control Bill before Congress in 1971–72. We shall never know for sure what was discussed at this session or what advice the group gave the President, because a loophole in the federal Freedom of Information Act made public access to the meeting or to minutes of the meeting impossible.

LOBBYING DISCLOSURE

In the March 5, 1972, edition of the *New York Times Magazine*, a discussion of the recent history of the Florida legislature read in part:

> The legislative faction which controlled the state was called the Pork Chop Gang, a term that originally referred to their rural orientation but later also came to mean that they always got the best cut of the pig. The Pork Chop Gang ran Florida from the gray capitol in Tallahassee, meeting in one 90-day session every two years, voting in blocks to stifle reform and urban critics. Lobbyists infested the corridors and back rooms, so powerful they could name the membership of certain committees.

The Florida legislature has improved since then, but such a description may still fit other states.

At least until the mid-1960's, it was widely believed that the Arizona legislature was run from the Adams Hotel, Phoenix headquarters of the state's copper interests. The Sun Oil lobbyist in Pennsylvania has been called the state's "fifty-first senator." The Penn Central lobbyist was the fifty-second. In California, the onetime head of the liquor lobby was long considered the most powerful man in the state. These cases are exceptional, for lobbyists rarely flaunt their power so openly and so brazenly. But there is nothing exceptional about the grip that these special interests have on the state legislatures. The disproportionate power of special interests is a pervasive phenomenon in American politics. The inadequacy or complete absence of state lobbying laws has played into the hands of these special interests and has deprived the average citizen, who remains unrepresented by such lobbyists, from gaining control of, indeed from even influencing, what is supposedly his government.

The influence of special-interest lobbyists runs so deep that in some states these lobbyists have helped draft the laws by which lobbyists are regulated. Woodrow Wilson Musselman, a long-time lobbyist for the influential Pennsylvania Manufacturers' Association, openly contends that he wrote that state's lobbying registration bill a few years ago.

Whether the federal lobby law was written by special-interest lobbyists is less certain. What is certain is that it works in their favor. Its reporting requirements are weak, and by exempting individuals or organizations whose "principal purpose" is something besides lobbying it permits some of the most important lobbies to avoid reporting completely. General Motors, Ford Motor Company, the American Banking Association, International Telephone and Telegraph, and other huge corporations do not even bother to register as lobbying groups, although they maintain active "government liaison" offices in Washington, D.C.

One of the most active lobbying forces on behalf of supersonic transport (SST) development was Fairchild-Hiller, one of the project's subcontractors. This corporation was in regular contact with members of Congress. It encouraged a grassroots letter-writing campaign and chartered buses full of workers to lobby for the SST. Fairchild-Hiller never registered or filed lobbying reports.

The National Rifle Association takes pride in its ability to get half a million letters written by members in seventy-two hours. It was responsible for the largest single flood of mail to Congress on any issue during a debate on a gun control bill in 1965. A Senate subcommittee estimated the NRA's yearly spending on attempts to influence legislation at $2 million. The NRA itself has never reported spending a penny on lobbying. It often does not bother to register at all. Only occasionally does an NRA lobbyist register.

Some years ago the president of DuPont spent three full months walking the halls of Congress lobbying for a tax relief bill, which upon its passage gave DuPont and its stockholders a giant tax windfall. He did not register as a lobbyist.

Lobbyists who do file reports are often nearly as bad. In the first quarter of 1972, the Association of American Railroads ran a television commercial twenty times in prime time television spots. They also ran sixty radio advertisements, and on February 7 and 8 they ran newspaper ads in one hundred newspapers across the country. The huge publicity campaign urged Americans to support the Surface Transportation Act,

legislation which would benefit the railroad industry. The
cost of the television and radio spots was $808,100. The news-
paper ads cost about $110,000 more. Yet the AAR reported
its lobbying expenses for the first quarter of 1972 at $4,972.13.
What happened to the other $900,000? It fell through one of
the loopholes in the federal lobby law.

The American Medical Association is estimated to have
spent $1 million fighting Medicare in 1965. That year it reported
lobbying expenses of $45,000.

These glaring gaps in the law must be plugged, and the
clear failure to enforce the law, even so mild a one as the
current law, must end.

As with each of the four reform fields, however, it is not
enough to seek honest, representative, responsible legislatures.
There is ample evidence of "hard-sell" tactics directed against
the executive branch as well. The numerous meetings Harold
Geneen, President of International Telephone and Telegraph,
had with Justice Department, Federal Reserve Board, White
House, and Commerce Department officials prior to the 1971
approval of an ITT merger suggest that some high level
"lobbying" was going on. No average citizen could have the
access to executive-branch officials that Geneen enjoyed. Under
the present laws, the public has no means of discovering the
nature or extent of such executive lobbying.

CONFLICTS OF INTEREST

Millionaire oilman Russell Long, who chairs the Senate
Finance Committee, the committee responsible for initial Senate
approval of the oil depletion allowance, was once asked whether
he had any financial holdings that could give rise to conflicts
of interest. He replied, "I have no conflicts of interest. I have
an identity of interest." Such open admissions on such a subject
are rare among United States senators, but that does not mean
that instances of conflict of interest are rare. Weak conflict of
interest laws, especially when they do not require public disclosure of financial holdings, make it virtually impossible for
the public to have the facts needed to determine whether one

of their senators is voting for his private interests or the public good.

The slightly more meaningful disclosure requirements in the House of Representatives provide some revealing facts. Eight members of the House Banking and Currency Committee and six members of the House Ways and Means Committee are known to have holdings in banks and other financial institutions. Five of these members are bank directors. Those two committees make decisions critical to the banking industry.

Other members of the House who have similar holdings face conflict of interest problems when legislation dealing with financial issues comes to the floor for a vote. There are eighty-eight other House members who have holdings in banks or other financial institutions, including thirty-four who serve on their boards of directors.

Legislators associated with law firms have ample opportunity to dispense personal favors. It is not illegal for a corporation or labor union to pay large sums of money to a senator's or congressman's law firm. The legislator may not handle the corporation's case, but he nonetheless profits from the fees the law firm receives. He may feel a divided loyalty when his firm's client seeks a legislative favor.

As of mid-1972, fifty-nine members of the Congress of the United States are actively associated with a law firm or otherwise involved in the practice of law. Two of these are on the Senate Judiciary Committee, eleven on the House Judiciary Committee.

Maintenance of private holdings that give rise to conflicts of interest is so widespread and the federal laws so weak and unenforced that we need a major overhaul of federal laws in this area. All the reform efforts proposed in this book are in part designed to combat potential or existing conflicts of interest among public officials. Whether this is done by requiring that all meetings be open, or that lobbyists make themselves known, or that campaign contributions be limited, the goal is a more representative, responsive, accountable public official.

Frequently, state legislatures assign members to committees covering activities in which they have a financial interest. This practice, rationalized on the grounds of expertise in the field to be regulated, in fact provides opportunities for financial windfalls to members whose scruples are outweighed by their greed. Even if the legislator does not himself benefit from his official position, it is difficult for him to maintain an "arm's-length" objectivity when his friends and former colleagues will benefit or lose as a result of committee action.

The *Louisville Courier Journal*, discussing just this issue with respect to the Kentucky legislature, noted recently that the House Banking and Insurance Committee is chaired by State Representative Charles S. Wible, a lawyer who numbers "at least five insurance companies, banks, and other financial institutions among his clients." To provide back-up "expertise," other members of his committee include a manager of a savings and loan association, a bank vice-president, an assistant cashier of a bank, the son-in-law of a bank president, six present or former insurance agents, and the executive secretary of the Kentucky Bankers Association, who is himself a former banking lobbyist. Not to be outdone, the Senate Banking and Insurance Committee is headed by a bank president, and the vice-chairman is a lawyer who represents at least eight insurance companies and financial firms. The Kentucky House Agriculture and Natural Resources Committee, which handles strip mining and reclamation bills, has a new chairman, a lawyer whose firm has as clients three coal miners' associations and several coal companies.

The problem is not merely that financial interests, big business, and small groups of rich men benefit by either being on legislative committees themselves or having friends on such committees. The problem is that these financial windfalls are subsidized by the average citizen. If banks go unregulated, strip mining is unsupervised, and insurance companies are unscrutinized, the social costs are paid by the society as a whole, not by the special interests who are the prime beneficiaries of this extreme form of *laissez faire*.

Examples of legislators using their official positions for personal gain are abundant. In 1971 State Senator Al Song, a lawyer who also is chairman of the Senate Judiciary Committee in

California, wrote to ninety-nine lobbyists, many representing labor whose bills he had pushed. The chairman described the letter to a *Los Angeles Times* reporter: "I chided them. I told them I was one of labor's champions and now where's the law business you guys were talking about. . . . I was trying to point out to them that you guys have got to come across with more dough."

American history texts tell of quaint old-time political corruption, citing examples like the Teapot Dome scandal and Credit Mobilier. Highly publicized scandals surrounding former Secretary to the Senate Democrats Bobby Baker, former Congressman Adam Clayton Powell, and former Senator Thomas Dodd have been reported, as they should be, as extreme examples of corruption and conflict of interest. Yet a great many federal and state public officials who are neither quaint nor extreme maintain financial holdings that conflict with the need for official objectivity.

Such problems are not the exclusive domain of the legislative branch. The Antitrust Division of the Justice Department recently approved a merger of two of the nation's largest pharmaceutical firms. The merger was negotiated by Mudge, Rose, Guthrie, and Alexander, the former law firm of John Mitchell and Richard Nixon. The inclination of executive-branch officials to help their former associates and current friends may have been as great in this instance and others as it appears to be in the legislative branch.

The law now on the books and the enforcement of that law present a discouraging picture, but there is still some room for optimism. While it is premature to evaluate the degree to which the law will be enforced, a new Arkansas statute may serve as a model of one that can be enacted. The new law provides a comprehensive definition of conflict of interest. It requires annual disclosure of financial holdings of public officials in all branches of government as well as disclosure by candidates. Enforcement procedures and penalties for violation are strong, and a citizens' standing provision is included to help ensure that the law is enforced. Similar legislation should be actively pushed in the other forty-nine states and at the federal level.

The job of ensuring broad adherence to the law then begins. This is the citizen's as well as the government's responsibility.

CAMPAIGN FINANCE

No single part of the political process is more responsible for making public officials indebted to special interests than the need to solicit enormous campaign contributions. In 1968, according to the best available estimates, $100 million was spent on the Presidential campaigns and $200 million more on all other elections. These figures show an increase of 50 per cent over 1964. The experts predict a total of $400 million will be spent in the 1972 elections. In the Congressional elections of 1970 a number of senators spent $1 million each, and a number of candidates for the House of Representatives $250,000 each.

Huge sums of money are also spent in state and local campaigns. In 1970 Carter Burden spent at least $80,000 to gain a seat on the New York City Council. Andrew Stein expended $258,000 to win election to the New York State Assembly. Milton Shapp, who spent $2 million to $3 million in an earlier, unsuccessful bid for the Pennsylvania governorship, laid out at least $1.5 million the second time around. Texas Governor Preston Smith raised a similiar amount during his re-election campaign, mostly on the strength of 8,000 phone calls he made to Texas businessmen. Winthrop Rockefeller expended an estimated $4 million in his unsuccessful bid for a third term as governor of Arkansas. When a student asked how much he was spending on the campaign, Rockefeller snapped, "It's none of your damn business."

Unless a candidate has great personal wealth, the high cost of campaigning usually forces him to solicit massive campaign contributions. Such contributions frequently are provided with a *quid pro quo:* Take the money, but don't forget my legislative needs.

We can ill afford a government that responds to its citizens in proportion to the thickness of their wallets. A single incident demonstrates the risks of such a calculus. Early in 1972 the Department of Agriculture decided to decrease its subsidy to milk producers. A few days later a delegation of milk producers met with the President at the White House. This chat was followed in quick succession by a large political contribution from the milk producers to the Republican Party and an announcement by the Secretary of Agriculture, Clifford Hardin, that, on the basis of new facts, the Department had reconsidered. The Department, said Hardin, would raise, not lower, the subsidy. One hopes that "new facts" dealt with milk production not campaign contributions.

There is no question that money makes a difference in elections. It can be as crucial on state referendums as in a Presidential race. In 1970, a proposed constitutional amendment on the California state ballot would have permitted diversion of part of the state gasoline tax into pollution research and mass transit, instead of spending it all on roads and highways. Pollsters had figured that the amendment, Proposition 18 on the ballot, might carry by 3 to 1 in the increasingly environment-conscious state. But a $300,000 publicity blitz mounted by what many Californians refer to as the "Road Gang"—made up of oil companies, tire producers, contractors, and the state's two AAA auto clubs— overwhelmed proponents of the measure. Proposition 18 was defeated by half a million votes.

The public had no prior knowledge of exactly who had mounted the publicity campaign or of who was contributing funds to the effort. Members of the California AAA, for instance, had no role in deciding that their organization would disburse funds to fight the proposition, and most of them learned of its donations only after the election was over. Let us not put to the test further the creativity of big donors in finding ways to make personal gains through investments at election time.

Most politicians are honest, but they fight an uphill battle. And most campaign donors give for honorable and civic-minded reasons. But much campaign giving is a flagrant and often successful attempt to buy influence. Former Senator Albert Gore said, "Any person who is willing to sell his soul can have handsome financing for his campaigns." For the good of the candidates as well as the country we must enact and enforce new state and federal laws that set limits on campaign contributions and expenditures. Until such laws are enacted, the cartoons of Thomas Nast that depict rich contributors controlling help-less politicians will be as accurate today as they were when they first appeared in the late nineteenth century.

There are other problems facing our government and other reforms that would contribute to the survival of American democracy. None, however, is as fundamental as those dealing with open meetings, lobbying regulation, conflict of interest, and campaign finance. Every citizen must have the information to evaluate intelligently the motivations and actions of his public officials. All citizens should have roughly equal access to their representatives. Effective laws and vigorous enforcement in these four fields will help guarantee that the preconditions for effective democracy are met.

To the degree that there are grave shortcomings in state and federal practices as instruments of a responsive and honest government, the responsibility rests not with the politician alone but with the American public as well. We have all neglected our government.

II · Federal Practices:

Is This Any Way To Run a Government?

Let everyman make known what kind of government would command his respect and that would be one step toward obtaining it.
HENRY DAVID THOREAU

In 1946 Congress enacted the Legislative Reorganization Act. It included a section establishing federal regulations for groups and individuals while lobbying the Congress. Within two years the lobbying section was shown to be so ill-conceived that discussions began about amending it. Nothing happened. In the 1950's, Senator John Kennedy called the provisions "worthless." Later, Senator William Proxmire described them as "a farce." Yet that 1946 law remains the only statute governing federal lobbyists' activities.

The most recent conflict-of-interest statute aimed specifically at members of Congress was passed in 1964. The status of open meeting legislation is little better. Only in the area of campaign finance has a new law been enacted, and even in that field there is much room for improvement.

What follows is a description of the maze of laws, rules, executive orders, and voluntary procedures that determine the practices of the federal government in the fields of open meetings, lobbying disclosure, conflict of interest, and campaign finance.

OPEN MEETINGS

Rules and customs determine which meetings of the United States Congress and its committees shall be open to the public and which votes taken at such meetings will be publicly available.

Long-standing House and Senate rules state the general principle that the Congress shall conduct all meetings in public unless special conditions require secrecy. Unfortunately the rules do not spell out what constitutes "special conditions." As a result, the general principle has had little if any effect on the practices of either house of Congress.

The Legislative Reorganization Act of 1970 makes it somewhat more difficult for a Congressional committee or subcommittee to go into executive (closed) session. Prior to its passage, the decision to go into executive session was an informal matter, arrived at by consensus of the committee or by the chairman of the committee acting alone. The 1970 law requires that committee or subcommittee sessions be closed only upon a majority vote of the committee's members. The major weakness of the law is that a majority vote of the committee at its initial session each year is enough to close all sessions for the rest of the year. The House Ways and Means Committee has consistently used this loophole to keep the public in the dark on the discussions and the deals that result in such critical legislation as tax reform, welfare, and national health insurance. In fact, Ways and Means rules prevent other congressmen, not on the committee, from attending committee sessions.

Even committee sessions that are open to the public are often poorly attended and poorly reported. No doubt this is partly a result of public apathy, but it is equally because House and Senate rules require only that committee hearings be announced one week in advance. This is insufficient time to request permission to appear as a witness and to prepare testimony. It does not even give committee members themselves the time they need to prepare for the session.

While the Legislative Reorganization Act of 1970 requires that all votes taken in standing committees of the legislature be recorded by individual member and open to the public, there is no requirement that committee decisions be made by vote (as opposed to consensus), and no provision makes it possible for committee members to demand that a vote be taken. As a result, some House and Senate committees continue to operate with little or no public scrutiny. For example, the records of the House Appropriations Committee's consideration of the important Defense Appropriations Bill in 1971 shows no record of any votes. Until recently no law required the full House of Representatives to take recorded teller votes. House procedures are such that many key decisions on legislation are made in committee. In the case of bills coming from the Ways and Means and Appropriations committees, practice frequently results in bills reaching the floor in an unamendable form. In the case of bills from these and all other committees, House parliamentary rules on the "germaneness" of amendments, sometimes coupled with a Rules Committee "closed rule" by which amendments are not permitted at all, seriously circumscribe House floor action and make committee procedures all the more important. Thus, on much important legislation the full House membership has little opportunity to amend bills or vote on them section by section. For this reason most key votes take place in committee. Obstacles to getting a recorded vote on such key floor amendments as were taken were virtually insurmountable. As a result of these practices no House member was on record, for example, as favoring or opposing the American involvement in Vietnam until 1971.

In 1971 a new House rule was adopted that allows one-fifth of a quorum of the Committee of the Whole House to obtain a recorded roll call vote on any matter the House of Representatives considers. The new rule has already made an important difference in the responsiveness and accountability of the House to the electorate. On the other hand, Senate rules permit any senator to obtain a recorded roll call on any matter before that body. Senate rules have long permitted freer discussion and more numerous votes on bills that have reached the Senate floor. If these votes had not been recorded, senators would have felt less pressure to be responsive to the public.

Certain key meetings of the Congress are unaffected by any of the rules or laws discussed above and, as a result, are always closed. Committees composed of representatives of the two houses meet to work out compromise language on bills that have passed both houses in differing forms. These groups, called conference committees, have the power to draft new language in areas where the two versions differ. Only rarely does the Congress reject language adopted by the conference committee. Yet, despite their substantial power, conference committees always meet in secret. As a consequence, the public often loses on the compromise struck. Indeed, the secret meetings frequently result in compromises that do not even reflect the views of the majority membership of one or both of the houses of Congress. Conference committees convened to resolve House and Senate defense appropriations differing in size have sometimes decided on dollar figures larger than either the Senate or the House version. In 1971, a conference committee reinstated funds to develop the SST after both houses had voted down such funds. Subsequent House votes overturned the conference "compromise." While a variety of factors contribute to such results, the fact that such decisions are reached in closed meetings no doubt gives legislators the feeling they can act with impunity.

Party caucuses are also closed. They are made up of all the senators or all the representatives belonging to the same political party. While some congressmen contend that these caucuses are private party matters and therefore not an appropriate matter for public scrutiny, the fact remains that many matters of importance to the public are decided there. All committee chairmen are in effect selected in caucuses of the majority party, and under current House and Senate rules chairmen wield tremendous power. The power of party caucuses seems to be increasing. In April, 1972, the House Democratic Caucus voted to instruct the Democratic members of the House Foreign Affairs Committee to report out a bill setting a date certain for the termination of American involvement in Indochina. The majority of the Democrats on the Foreign Affairs Committee followed this instruction and voted such a bill out of committee in early June. A precedent for similar future instructions by the caucuses may thus have been set. Since caucus votes can directly affect the course of legislation, it is all the more important for such meetings to be open and for votes taken in them by each congressman to be recorded.

Mark-up sessions, in which a committee actually drafts the language of the bill they will vote on and send to the full House or Senate, are also generally closed to the public. Only the House Education and Labor Committee holds open mark-up sessions as a matter of course. No senate committee at all has regular procedures by which all meetings are open.

Rules affecting open meetings of the executive branch are contained in the Freedom of Information Act (5 U.S. Code 552), the basic law determining the extent of the public's right of access to information in the files of federal agencies. Such written materials will certainly include the minutes or transcripts of agency and interagency meetings.

Agency materials designated as public information include, among other things:

–organization descriptions and procedures whereby the public
　　may obtain information
–statements of the general cause by which an agency functions
–substantive rules of general applicability and statements of
　　general policy
–final opinions and orders made in the adjudication of cases
–administration staff manuals and instructions to staff that
　　affect a member of the public
–final notes of each member in every agency proceeding.

While these categories appear sufficiently broad to guarantee
public access to the records of agency meetings, a series of
exemptions provide virtually limitless opportunity for agency
secrecy. The categories of information that may be kept secret
include:

–national security matters
–matters related solely to internal personnel rules and practices
–trade secrets and confidential commercial/financial information
–matters specifically exempted from disclosure by statute
–inter- or intra-agency memoranda or letters that would not
　　be available by law to a party other than a party in
　　litigation with the agency
–personnel and medical files
–investigatory files compiled for law enforcement purposes,
　　except to the extent available by law to a party other than
　　an agency
–assessment data used by agencies responsible for supervision
　　of financial institutions
–geological and geophysical information.

Such seemingly understandable exemptions as that excluding
some intra-agency memoranda have been regularly used to justify
unreasonable secrecy. In an interpretation based on the intra-
agency exemption, Attorney General Ramsey Clark wrote that
"internal communications which would not routinely be available
to a party to litigation with the agency, such as internal drafts,
memoranda between officials or agencies, opinions and interpreta-
tions prepared by agency staff personnel or consultants for the
use of the agency, and records of the deliberations of the agency

or staff groups, remain exempt so that free exchange of ideas will not be inhibited." This interpretation provided the rationale by which the transcripts and minutes of the Department of Health, Education, and Welfare's 432 advisory bodies are regularly withheld from the public. The public is thus prevented from learning of available documentation about such things as the environmental effects of nuclear testing or the health hazards inherent in certain consumer products. Aside from permitting the withholding of factual data that would be useful to the public, the exemptions in the act allow bodies supposedly created to represent the public to meet behind closed doors to plot their personal gain. Meetings of the presidentially appointed industrial pollution advisory board appear to fit this description. Created to advise the President on how to fight industrial pollution, the board appears to have met to set strategy for weakening a water quality bill then before Congress. The public deserves to know who takes what positions and what decisions are reached at such meetings. The exemptions in the Freedom of Information Act make such public knowledge virtually impossible.

LOBBYING DISCLOSURE

One law, the Legislative Reorganization Act of 1946, regulates those who lobby in the United States Congress. There is no law at all governing attempts to lobby any other branch of the federal government.

The act defines a lobbyist as any person or organization who is hired for pay by someone else for the principal purpose of lobbying Congress. All such persons are required to register with the Clerk of the House of Representatives and the Secretary of the Senate at the commencement of lobbying activities. The weakness of this definition of a lobbyist is that many individuals and the organizations that hire them claim that their "principal purpose" is something other than lobbying Congress. They may claim that their principal purpose is information dissemination or education or whatever, but not lobbying. By this device such powerful Washington policy-influencers as the American Bankers Association, International Telephone and Telegraph,

General Motors, and the National Rifle Association avoid register-ing as lobbies. Moreover, no provision of the act empowers the clerk or the secretary to interpret the principal purpose clause (Sec. 207) in order to determine which groups and individuals should be required to register.

Both the registered lobbyist and his employer must file quarterly statements with the clerk and the secretary detailing income received and expenses incurred in relation to lobbying. The infor-mation required on such statements includes:

–an accounting of every contribution of $500.00 or more made to the lobbyist and the total sum of contributions

–each expenditure of $10.00 or more made by the lobbyist and the sum of all such expenditures

–the duration of the lobbyist's employment

–the amount and manner of a lobbyist's payment from each employer

–a list of publications in which lobbyist or employer has had published any articles or editorials

–the proposed legislation the lobbyist is employed to support or oppose.

The Clerk of the House and the Secretary of the Senate are responsible for compiling this information and having it presented on a quarterly basis in the *Congressional Record*. There is no re-quirement, however, that the reports be published within any set period. As a result the public and the Congress often do not get the Clerk or Secretary's report until well after the date when the information would have been most useful. The reports for the last quarter of 1971 were not made public until May 25, 1972.

Any person who is convicted of violating a provision of the act is subject to fine and/or imprisonment and is prohibited from attempting to influence legislation for a period of three years from the date of conviction. It is unlikely that violators will be convicted, however, since the clerk and secretary are not required to evaluate the reports they receive or to name as delinquent anyone who fails to file a report. This absence of any enforcement mechanism is one of the glaring weaknesses in the act.

The act exempts from its coverage those persons who merely

appear before Congressional committees to testify, as well as public officials acting in their official capacity and newspapers and other regularly published periodicals that in the ordinary course of business print news items, editorials, or paid advertisements on issues. When the Act was passed, it was thought that regulation of lobbying might infringe on the Constitutional guaranteed right of free speech and the right to petition the government. Those questions were resolved in the 1954 case of the *United States v. Harriss*, 347 U.S. 612, 75 S. Ct. 808 (1954). In his majority opinion, Chief Justice Earl Warren wrote:

> Full realization of the American ideal of government by elected representatives depends to no small extent on their abilility to properly evaluate such pressures. Otherwise the voice of the people may all too easily be drowned out by the voice of special interest groups seeking favored treatment. . . .
>
> We believe that Congress, at least within the bounds of the Act as we have construed it, is not constitutionally forbidden to require the disclosure of lobbying activities. To do so would be to deny Congress in large measure the power of self-protection.

Thus, the right of the Congress to pass legislation regulating lobbyists was affirmed. Unfortunately, by the date of the *Harriss* decision, lobbyists had easily discovered the weakness in the act and rendered it ineffective in giving Congress or the public the information they need to identify those who try to influence public policy. The public must know who is attempting to influence its representatives so that it may more effectively evaluate the degree to which Congressional action reflects public good or private interests. Similarly, legislators have a right to know who is generating pressures so that they may more accurately gauge real public sentiment.

CONFLICT OF INTEREST

A variety of federal laws, executive orders, and Congressional rules bear on the subject of conflict of interest. The most comprehensive, if not the strongest, of these is the Congressionally approved Code of Ethics (H. Con. Res 179—passed the House August 28, 1957; Senate, July 11, 1958). Passed in 1958, it applies to all employees of the federal government, including members of Congress. Among its broadly worded provisions, the code forbids all federal employees from dispensing favors for money (Rule 5). The code is so broadly worded that Senator Clifford Case labeled it a mere "oratory exercise" in an article in the 1964 *Federal Bar Journal.*

Existing statutes, all of which were general and largely unenforceable, were drawn together and slightly strengthened by an act of Congress in 1962 (PL 67–649).

Members of Congress are prohibited by sections of the United States Criminal Code (Title 18 USC) from accepting bribes or otherwise misusing public office for personal financial gain.

None of the above laws result in any real inhibition to those who wish to make personal gain from public office nor do any of the laws guarantee the public the information it needs to decide whether a conflict exists. The only way such goals can be accomplished is by requiring that public officials make full public disclosure of their financial holdings. Neither the House nor the Senate has completely adequate rules requiring disclosure. House Rule 44, adopted on April 3, 1968, and amended on May 26, 1970, requires House members to file annual statements with the Committee on Standards of Official Conduct. Members must list any financial interest maintained in a firm that has contracts with the federal government, the name of any professional organization (such as a law firm) from which the member derived income of $1,000 or more in the preceding year, honorariums of $300 or more, and the names of creditors to whom the member was indebted for ninety consecutive days or more, or for $10,000 or more. All of the above information is available to the public. Additional, more detailed information is provided to the committee but is kept secret and may be used only in the course of a committee investigation. Senate Rule 44, adopted on March 22, 1968, requires only that a senator or candidate for the Senate report his income from speeches and writing.   .

Enforcement of any rules regulating the conduct of representatives and senators is the Constitutionally guaranteed right of Congress itself. While each house has the power to censure or

expel its members and each house has established an ethics
committee, only the most flagrant abuses have been punished.
The House committee is the Committee on Standards of Official
Conduct. The Senate version is the Select Committee on
Standards and Conduct.

The record of the executive branch on the question of disclosure
is only slightly better. President Lyndon Johnson issued an
executive order on May 8, 1965, requiring all federal employees
above a certain salary level or in sensitive positions to fill out
financial statements disclosing stock and bond investments, home
mortgages, furniture debts, and real estate interests. These statements are reviewed by a member of the White House staff. Since
neither the statements nor actions taken by the reviewing agent
are made public, it is impossible to know if the procedure in
any way limits conflicts of interest. The statements should be
made public and suspension should be in the hands of an
objective, independent agent, not left to a White House political
appointee. The order could be further improved by requiring
all public officials to disclose the same set of facts. Current
procedure allows separate agencies to use their own discretion
as to what information its employers and officials disclose.

Laws regulating members of the judiciary include no disclosure
requirement. In addition to the standard practice by which judges
disqualify themselves from hearing cases in which they have
an interest, they are governed by a resolution of the Judicial
Conference of the United States. Passed in 1963, the resolution
forbids any judge from serving as an officer, director, or employee
of a corporation organized for profit.

Each of the above rules, orders, or laws deals specifically
with some aspect of conflict of interest on the part of federal
public officials. Like all other Americans, public officials are
subject to federal income tax statutes. Any official who attempts
to conceal income derived from a conflict of interest, bribe, or
any other source would be subject to prosecution under these
statutes.

It has become a parlor game for Americans to complain about
high taxes and unresponsive public officials. Public complaints
are not without foundation. Part of the fat could be skimmed

from the budget if the public were able and willing to evaluate the degree to which government—that is public—funds are being spent to benefit a few, when coupled with strong laws in the other three reform fields. Comprehensive conflict of interest statutes could go a long way toward making such an evaluation possible.

CAMPAIGN FINANCE

The Federal Election Campaign Act of 1971 took effect on April 7, 1972. It applies to candidates for President, Vice President, and the United States Congress.

The key requirement in the new Act is that each candidate and each political committee supporting one or more candidates must file periodic reports. Reports listing both contributions and expenditures are due in Washington, D.C., and in the office of the Secretary of State of the home state of the candidate or committee. Candidates for the House of Representatives file with the Clerk of the House; candidates for the Senate file with the Secretary of the Senate; and candidates for President and general political committees file with the General Accounting Office.

Reports are due on specified days in June and September of election years, as well as fifteen and five days prior to each election (including primary, run-off, and general) for which a candidate or committee receives or spends money. All reports are cumulative and must cover the period from the closing date of the previous filing to seven days before the date the reports are due. A report covering the last twelve days before an election is due on the last day of January of the year following the November general election.

Information that must be disclosed at the time of each filing includes:

1. The cash on hand at the beginning of the reporting period
2. The sum of all contributions of $10 or less received during the reporting period
3. The sum of all dinner ticket sales and proceeds of other fund-raising events

4. The details of each loan over $100 made or received
5. The sum of all receipts during the reporting period
6. The name and address of each political committee or candidate involved in any transfer of funds to or from the reporting committee or candidate, plus the amount and dates of all transfers (Note: this provision covers all contributions received from "political committees," as opposed to individuals, and it is not subject to the $100 cutoff.)
7. The amount and nature of debts and obligations owed by or to the candidate or committee
8. The full name, mailing address, occupation, and principal place of business (if any), for each person to whom expenditures have been made in an aggregate of more than $100 during the year. Also, the date, the amount, and purpose for which each such expenditure was made
9. The sum of all expenditures made during the year.

In addition, each candidate and committee must list the full name of every person contributing more than an aggregate amount of $100 during the year, as well as the contributor's complete mailing address, occupation, and principal place of business, if any, plus the amount and date of the contribution.

Any person who makes a contribution or expenditure in excess of $100 during the year, other than by contributing to a candidate or political committee, must file a separate statement revealing this information.

The new law sets a limit on the amount of money that may be spent on behalf of a candidate for communications media. The term "communications media" includes television, radio, newspapers, magazines, billboards, and paid telephone banks. Not included are mailing expenses, especially the increasingly popular "personalized" computer letter-writing services.

A candidate's spending on specified communications media is limited to ten cents for each eligible voter in the potential constituency or $50,000, whichever sum is greater. Of this amount, no more than 60 per cent may be used for radio and television expenditures.

No over-all spending limit is set. A candidate may spend as

much money as he can raise on such campaign expenses as air-
fare, hotels, office space, and campaign staff.

A candidate and his immediate family may spend no more
than specifically designated amounts in the candidate's behalf.
These amounts are: $50,000 for a Presidential or Vice-Presidential
candidate, $35,000 for a Senatorial candidate, and $25,000 for
a candidate for the House of Representatives.

The new law sets no limit on individual contributions by anyone other than the candidate and his family. Prior to the passage
of the 1971 act, the legal limit on individual contributions was
$5,000. That limit was never enforced. The absence of any indi-
vidual limit is one of the most serious weaknesses of the law.

Direct political contributions by corporations or labor unions
are prohibited. Employees of a corporation or members of a labor
union can contribute voluntarily to a fund, which the union or
corporation would dispense to such candidates or committees as
it might select.

Any person who believes a violation of the disclosure requirements may have occurred may file a complaint with the agent
responsible for receiving the disclosure statement. If the appropriate supervisory agent has reason to believe a violation may
have occurred, he must make an investigation. If he becomes
convinced a violation has occurred, he shall inform the Attorney
General, who is supposed (but not required) to institute legal
preceedings to prevent further violation of the act.

III · State Practices:

There Ought To Be a Law

Good laws lead to the making of better ones; bad ones bring about worse. As soon as any man says of the affairs of the State, "What does it matter to me?" the State may be given up for lost.
JEAN JACQUES ROUSSEAU

Because of the way state governments currently operate, few citizens have ready access to key public officials. Fewer still can afford to make the campaign contributions by which one may purchase such access and, thus, influence. Average citizens must earn their access, and this is best done by being diligent in pursuit of the knowledge they need to gain access to and influence on the public officials who can reform the system.

While it is one thing to know that the "system isn't working" and to have an image of how it should work, it is quite another to know the practical nuts-and-bolts reasons why the system is inadequate. One must know existing laws to reform them.

Following is a state-by-state summary of current statutes and constitutional provisions, executive orders, and legislative rules that make up the law on open meetings, lobbying disclosure, conflict of interest, and campaign finance. It tells us where we are now so that we may more knowledgeably decide where we should go next.

ALABAMA

Open Meetings

• Committee meetings of the state legislature are never open to the public, nor are conference committee sessions. Indeed, no announcement is made in advance of conference committee sessions. Executive sessions are frequently held, as the only requirement that must be met before convening such a session is approval of a majority of the committee members. The University of Missouri Freedom of Information Center lists Alabama as the state that holds such executive sessions most frequently among the fifty states. Committee votes are never held in open session, nor are they recorded in any way, either by aggregate or by individual. This applies to votes in committee not only on procedural motions and amendments, but on final passage of bills as well.

• An Alabama state statute provides that certain categories of state commissions, boards, and courts are prohibited from holding executive or secret sessions. However, this category includes only such boards as the Alabama Public Service Commission, the School Commission of Alabama, and state or county tax commissions. The provision does not apply either to the state legislature or to the offices of the executive branch.

LOBBYING DISCLOSURE

• The only regulations covering the activities of lobbyists in Alabama are found in the rules of the Senate of Alabama and apply only to attempts to lobby that chamber of the state legislature. Lobbyists are defined in the Senate rules as all persons except members of the Alabama legislature who seek to encourage the passage, defeat, or modification of any legislation in the Senate or before its committees who are compensated by any person, firm, corporation, or association other than the news media by which they are employed. All of the individuals thus described as lobbyists are required to register prior to each legislative session in which they expect to lobby. Such registration is with the Secretary of State.

• Information required at the time of registration is the name and business address of the lobbyist, the name and business address of its principal or principals, the general and specific areas of his legislative interests, and the duration for which he was hired.

• No statement listing the lobbyist's income or expenditures is required, nor is any financial statement required of the employers (principals) of lobbyists.

• A Committee on Rules of the Senate itself is empowered to supervise and enforce the provisions of this statute. Enforcement takes the form of recommendations from this committee to the full Senate, which then has permission to censor, reprimand, or place on probation any lobbyist who appears to have violated the provisions of this rule.

CONFLICTS OF INTEREST

No law.

CAMPAIGN FINANCE

• This law applies to candidates for public office in all primary and general elections. The law requires the disclosure of both receipts and disbursements by campaign committees. Candidates are required to file affidavits supporting committee statements. Filing dates are fifteen days after the primary and thirty days after general elections. Statements are filed with the Secretary of State.

• Expenditure limits exist and are computed so that disbursements for primary and general election together do not exceed limitation. Limit is $50,000 for Governor or United States Senator, making them the highest among the states setting limits, except Florida. Candidates for U.S. Representative may spend $10,000. Several states have limits around $10,000 for the House.

• Corporations are prohibited from making campaign contributions. No similar prohibition exists for labor union contributions. There is no limit on individual contributions.

• Successful candidates who violate the law are not permitted to take office. Unsuccessful candidates are guilty of a misdemeanor. No law designates any single person responsible for the enforcement of the provisions.

ALASKA

OPEN MEETINGS

Committees of the state legislature generally vote and discuss public business in open public sessions. Legislative committees and executive boards do have the right on majority vote to close such meetings as deal with information whose public disclosure would have a deleterious effect on the finances of the governmental unit involved or that deal with subjects that might tend to prejudice the reputation or character of any person. When meetings are held at which such accepted subjects are to be discussed, the meeting must first be convened as a public meeting, the question of holding an executive session must be discussed openly, and the majority vote must be taken in public session. Conference committees operate on the same basis as do other legislative committees. When committee sessions are closed, the votes taken in closed session are recorded by individual and are available from the clerk or the secretary after the end of the session. The same provisions for closing meetings apply not only to legislative committees but to all governing bodies of the state and local subdivisions of the state.

LOBBYING DISCLOSURE

• "Lobbyist" is not specifically defined in the statute but can be interpreted to mean anyone employed either with or without additional compensation as agent to promote/advocate legislation in either house or the executive approval/veto of legislation. Both the lobbyist and his employer are required to register with the Department of Administration of the State of Alaska. This registration with a relatively impartial administrative body is far preferable to registering with the much more politicized Clerk of the Assembly or Secretary of the Senate, as is the custom in most states. Two legislative dockets are maintained. One lists legislative counsels, that is, individuals who appear only before legislative committees. The other lists legislative agents, those who fit more general descriptions of lobbyists. Each of these dockets is open to public inspection as a matter of law.

• At the time of registering, the lobbyist and his employer must list the following in addition to his name and, in the case of the employer, in addition to the name of his employee:

1. the principal contributor by way of salary, fee, or otherwise for the work done by the lobbyist in attempting to influence legislation
2. the amount and manner of payment made to the lobbyist
3. the type of legislation or particular bills for or against which the lobbyist intends to work
4. the names and addresses of other than the major employer and the contribution or consideration made by such minor employers.

• Both the lobbyist and his employer must file an itemized statement of receipts and expenditures related to lobbying within thirty days after the final adjournment of the session with the

Department of Administration. This requirement applies to all expenditures or receipts related to lobbying activities except for professional services rendered in drafting bills or expenses or receipts of accredited counsels or agents of municipal corporations, public boards, or public institutions. Also exempted are individuals who appear before the legislature or legislative committees only in response to an invitation from such committees.

• It is the responsibility of the Department of Administration to identify potential violators of this statute and to inform the Attorney General of suspected violations.

• Contingent payments are specifically prohibited.

• There is a registration fee of $10 for resident lobbyists and $100 for nonresident lobbyists, who must additionally pay $5 per resident contributor and $25 per nonresident contributor. This registration fee is good from the time of payment until the beginning of the following session of the legislature.

Conflicts of Interest

No law.

Campaign Finance

No law.

ARIZONA

Open Meetings

• Votes of legislative committees are always open, recorded, and available from the Clerk of the House or the Secretary of the Senate. All official meetings at which any legal action is taken by any governing bodies of the State of Arizona or of any of its political subdivisions are required to be open and public meetings. Note that the phrase "official meetings" provides a potential loophole in that meetings that are informal, casual, and therefore not official may be used as a means of circumventing this law. There are certain exceptions to this apparently blanket

open meetings requirement. The primary among these exceptions is that executive sessions may be called by a majority of the members of the body involved. It is true, however, that no votes, appointments, or other official actions may be finally approved at such executive sessions.
• Conference committee sessions are usually announced in advance but are never open to either the public or the press.

Lobbying Disclosure

• "Lobbyist" is defined as any person employed or retained to influence actions of the House of Representatives of the State of Arizona. Only the lobbyist is required to register. There is no similar requirement regarding employers of lobbyists. Lobbyists must register with the Rules Committee of the House. Such registration is permanent. No renewal is required after the initial registration.
• Information required of the lobbyist at the time of registration includes his name and address, the names of his employers, and the general subject of his legislative interest.
• No requirement is made with respect to the filing of financial statements of either expenditures or income of any lobbyist.
• Enforcement is left to the Rules Committee of the House of Representatives.
• Exempted from the above registration requirements are legislative agents. The legislative agent is defined as any attorney, agent, or representative of any person, firm, association, or company desiring to appear before the House or any committee of the House. Such agent must first make application to the speaker or to the relevant committee chairman. Granting of such permission gives the legislative agent the right to file written or printed briefs, arguments, or statements or to make oral arguments before the appropriate committee or the House as a whole without filing any registration statement.

Conflicts of Interest

No law.

CAMPAIGN FINANCE

• This law covers primary, general, and special elections; however, there are some provisions that apply only to primary elections. The law applies to candidates for state, county, city, or town offices. "Special election" is not defined, and no mention is made of initiative, referendum, or other issue campaigns. References to special elections specifically indicate "special election at which candidates . . . are to be elected."

• A campaign committee cannot receive or spend money until after a chairman and treasurer have been chosen. The treasurer is responsible for keeping a detailed and exact account of all receipts and expenditures. There must be a receipt for each payment or disbursement exceeding $5, and receipts must be kept for fiften months after the election. A detailed account of monies received must be given to the treasurer within five days after it is received.

• Before any primary election, a candidate must file a report with the name and address of every person authorized to expend money in defraying the expenses of his campaign *or* a statement that he will personally account for all expenses. A candidate's name will not be placed on the ballot unless this information is filed. In primary elections both candidates and campaign committees are required to file a statement of expenditures. Campaign committees are also required to report money collected. (Committee statement is signed by treasurer and chairman.) In general or special elections, both candidates and campaign committees are required to file statements of expenditures and contributions (each aggregate of $10 or more listed). Preprimary report is due with nomination petition. Primary election expenditure and/or contribution statements are due no later than ten days after the election. They are filed with the same officer with whom nomination petitions were filed. Statements of contributions and expenses for general and special elections are due within thirty days after the election. They are filed with the Secretary of State for state offices and members of the legislature, with the clerk of the board of supervisors for county offices, and with the city or town clerk for city or town offices.

• Corporations are prohibited from making campaign contributions. No limit is set on individual contributions.
• Expenditure limits apply only to primary elections and are exclusive of stationery, postage, printing, media, and necessary personal travel or subsistence expenses.

U.S. senator	$3,500
Congressman or governor	2,500
Statewide offices	1,500
Superior Court judge or state senator	250
Countywide election	500
State representative, unless more than one per county	250
County or district subdivision	150
Mayor (pop. 5,000 or over)	350
City or town	250

• If a candidate fails to file or files fraudulent required reports or statements, his name will not appear on the ballot, nor will he receive the certificate of nomination or election, as the case may be. A losing candidate failing to file is guilty of a misdemeanor and subject to fine. No enforcement provisions are included in the act.

ARKANSAS

OPEN MEETINGS

• "The Freedom of Information Act" of 1967 declares that public business should be performed in an open and public manner. This covers meetings of any agency of the state or its political subdivisions except grand juries supported wholly or in part by public funds or expending public funds. All public records required to be kept or maintained shall be open to inspection and copying by any citizen. These regulations apply to all meetings, formal or informal, special or regular.
• The time and place of each regular meeting is to be furnished to anyone who requests this information. The news media may request notification of emergency or special meetings. The person

calling such meetings is responsible for notifying news media making such general requests.

• Executive sessions are permitted only for discussing or considering the employment, appointment, promotion, demotion, disciplining, or resignation of any public officer or employee. No resolution, contract, regulation, or motion considered or arrived at in executive session will be legal unless the public body reconvenes in public session and presents and votes on that matter.

• Any person denied the rights granted in this Act may appeal immediately to the appropriate circuit court. The circuit court must assign a day when the petition will be heard within seven days of the date of application and must hear and determine the case. Anyone who violates this Act is guilty of a misdemeanor and punishable by a fine of not more than $200 and/or thirty days in jail.

• The provisions of this Act apply to the state legislature as well as to all other public meetings.

LOBBYING DISCLOSURE

• A lobbyist is defined as any person who, by his acts as a representative of any recognized group or organization, or for compensation, seeks to influence in any manner the vote of any member or members of the General Assembly or any of its committees on any pending bill, resolution, or other measure.

• All lobbyists must register before commencing their lobbying activities. No similar registration requirement is made of employers of lobbyists. Registration is with either the Chief Clerk of the House or the Secretary of the Senate. Registration with one or the other of these supervisory agents is sufficient to permit lobbying in both houses of the legislature. At the time of registration, the lobbyist must list the name and place of business of his employer and any organizations he represents, and the nature of legislation in which such person is interested.

• The statute includes no provision whatever requiring financial statements of either lobbyists or their employers, dealing with either expenditures or incomes of lobby-related activities.

• No provision dealing with enforcement or penalties is included in the statute.

CONFLICTS OF INTEREST

• The Arkansas Code of Ethics for public officials was established by Act 313 of the 1971 session of the Arkansas Legislature. The definition of a public official is "every person holding a position of public trust in or under any executive, legislative, or judicial office of the state, including judges, members of the General Assembly and the Chief Clerk and Sergeant-at-Arms of the House and the Secretary and Sergeant-at-Arms of the Senate, and all constitutional officers, and all appointive officers charged with administration of laws or engaged in supervisory, policy making, or public enforcing work." It also includes anyone who files as a candidate for election to an office and any division head within an agency or department of the government. The Code of Ethics applies to all above-defined public officials.

• A written statement is required of every public official on or before December 31 of each year and is to be filed with the Secretary of State. This written statement, that is, public disclosure, must include:

1. the name of any corporation, firm, or enterprise under the jurisdiction of a regulatory agency (any state board, commission, department, or officer authorized to make rules or adjudicate contested cases except in the legislative or judicial branch) in which he has a direct financial interest in excess of $1,000 (insurance policies are not considered a financial interest)

2. every official position or directorship held by him or his spouse in any corporation, firm, or enterprise under jurisdiction of a regulatory agency

3. each type of business or business activity from which he received compensation in excess of $1,500 during the preceding twelve months

4. the name of any agency or agencies and the name of any firm, partnership, or association with which he is associated, such as an attorney and his law firm, an accountant and his

business establishment, and others practicing before regulatory agencies during the preceding twelve months.

A candidate must file the above four categories of information
within thirty days after the deadline for filing for the office for
which he seeks election.

• No requirement is made that any potential conflict be divested
by any public official. Full disclosure of holdings, and therefore
possible conflicts, is considered an adequate substitute for divestment.

• No public official or state employee shall accept employment
or engage in any public or professional activity that might cause
him to disclose any information acquired by reason of his position, nor shall he otherwise use such information for his personal
gain or benefit. No public official or state employee shall use his
position to secure special privileges or exemptions for himself, his
immediate family, or those with whom he has a substantial financial relationship. No public official or state employee shall pay to
or receive from any other public official or state employee any
compensation in addition to his salary.

• The Secretary of State is responsible for enforcing the provisions of this act and for maintaining the disclosure statements
required for at least five years. During that five-year period, such
disclosures are a matter of public record. Violators of this Act are
guilty of a misdemeanor punishable by a fine of between $50 and
$500 and/or imprisonment of ten to ninety days. Any person who
misrepresents or conceals any information to be disclosed in the
written statement must forfeit his public office or position of
employment.

CAMPAIGN FINANCE

• This law applies to any candidate seeking election to a public
office in any primary, general, or special election. No mention is
made of attempts to promote or defeat measures voted on by the
people.

• Only the candidate is responsible for expenditures; he must
report expenditures of more than $25. Statements of expenditures
are to be filed by the candidate within sixty days after the elec-

tion. In county and local races, this statement is filed with the secretary of the respective party county committee in party primaries and with the County Clerk in any general election. In district or state races, the statement is filed with the secretary of the respective party state committee in party primaries and with the Secretary of State in the general election.

• There are no individual contribution limits. There are no campaign spending limits. There are no prohibitions of corporate or labor contributions.

• Failure to comply with the statement of expenditures is a general misdemeanor.

CALIFORNIA

OPEN MEETINGS

• Sessions of legislative committees are always open to the public, and votes taken in such committees are open. They are, however, recorded only by aggregate. No records of committee votes by individual legislator are kept. Aggregate records are available from the committee chairman, the Clerk of the Assembly, or the Secretary of the Senate. Conference committee sessions are never open to the public.

• All meetings of state agencies must be open and public, and all persons shall be permitted to attend any meeting of a state agency. Executive sessions are permissible only when the agency is considering the appointment, employment, or dismissal of a public officer or employee, or is hearing complaints or charges brought against such an officer or employee by another public officer, person, or employee, unless such accused officer or employee requests a public hearing. The same exceptions that permit executive sessions of state agencies apply to executive sessions of legislative committees.

LOBBYING DISCLOSURE

• Any person engaged for pay or other consideration for the purpose of influencing the passage or defeat of legislation by the legislature, or its signature or veto by the governor, must first register with the Clerk of the Assembly and the Secretary of the Senate. Such person is considered a lobbyist. The registration is given in writing and under oath. A lobbyist must register at the beginning of each general session of the legislature as long as he is employed and must include a written authorization from each employer he lists on his registration forms. Information on the registration form should include the lobbyist's name and business address, the name and address of the lobbyist's employer or the person in whose interest he appears or works, the duration of his employment, how much he is to be paid, including expenses, and by whom the payment is to be made. Employers of lobbyists are not required to file separate reports.

• All lobbyists are required to file financial statements on the first and fifteenth day of each calendar month. These statements, given under oath to the Clerk of the Assembly and the Secretary of the Senate, should include all monies received and each expenditure made over $25, to whom paid and for what purposes, total expenditures, the names of any publications in which the lobbyist has caused to be published any articles or editorials, and the proposed legislation the lobbyist is employed to support or oppose. Any violation of the above provisions is a misdemeanor punishable by a fine of not more than $1,000 and/or imprisonment of not more than twelve months. Any person so convicted is prohibited from attempting to influence legislation for three years. Anyone who violates the three-year period is guilty of a felony punishable by a fine of not more than $10,000 and/or imprisonment for not more than five years. Committees of each house of the state legislature are empowered to grant certificates of registration, revoke or suspend such certificates, investigate complaints filed by any citizen, and recommend changes in the statute described above. Where legal action is called for, the committees are empowered to report suspected violations to the appropriate law enforcement officers.

• Neither the registration nor the financial statement requirement is applicable to any person who appears only before a legislative committee for the purpose of giving testimony in support of or opposition to legislation, nor to any state official acting in his official capacity, nor to any representative of the news media, nor to any person representing a bona fide church solely for the purpose of protecting the public right to practice the doctrines of such church.

• Contingent payments are specifically prohibited by this statute.

• A lobbyist has the following obligations, the violation of any of which is cause for suspension or revocation of a certificate of registration:

1. not to engage in lobbying activities unless registered
2. not to place a legislator under personal obligation to him or his employer
3. never to deceive a legislator
4. never to cause the introduction of a bill for the purpose of later being employed to secure its passage or defeat
5. to abstain from soliciting employment as a lobbyist except on the basis of his experience or knowledge of his proposed employer's business
6. to abstain from creating a fictitious appearance of public favor or disfavor of any legislative proposal
7. not to encourage the activities of, or have business dealings relating to legislation with, any person whose registration has been suspended or revoked
8. not to represent that he can control or obtain the vote or action of any legislator or the approval or veto of any legislation by the governor
9. not to represent an interest adverse to his employer.

CONFLICTS OF INTEREST

• Three California statutes deal with conflict of interest. Statutes 8920 and 3600 bear on legislators and legislative employees and executive officials and employees. Statute 1090 deals with all the above categories except executive employees. No law bears on judicial conflicts.

• Legislators and legislative employees and executive officials and employees are all prohibited from acquiring conflicting interests. Only legislators and legislative employees are prohibited from maintaining conflicting employment or from receiving gifts, loans, or favors or receiving compensation from nonstate sources. Both legislators and executive officials are regulated as to their transactions with or on behalf of the state or employer agency. The nature of that regulation is unknown. Lawyer-legislators are severely limited in the ways they are permitted to appear before state agencies.

• All state officials and employees, both legislative and executive, as well as employees and officials in the judiciary, are required to make public disclosure of their financial interests.

CAMPAIGN FINANCE

• Candidates and their campaign committees are required to file expenditure and contribution statements thirty-five days after primary and general elections. It is unclear whether special elections or committees established to promote or oppose initiatives, referendums, or recalls are included. Only a list of contributors of $500 or more need be filed twenty to twenty-five days prior to the election. Statements are filed with the Secretary of State.

• There is no expenditure limit for either candidates or campaign committees in either primary or general elections. No law regulating campaign contributions exists, except one provision granting a $100 tax deduction for individual contributions. Only nine states have such a provision.

• Violations of the above campaign laws are misdemeanors. Violation prevents the issuance of a certificate of nomination or election or, for losing candidates, entails possible fine or imprisonment.

COLORADO

OPEN MEETINGS

• All meetings of boards, commissions, committees, or authorities of the state, including the state legislature, or any political subdivision of the state created by law, must be held openly and in public, except for such sessions as are closed by majority consent in order to consider documents or testimony given in confidence. Such closed executive sessions shall in no way be used to make final policy decisions, nor shall any resolution, rule, ordinance, regulation, or formal action or any action approving a contract or calling for the payment of money be adopted or approved at any session that is closed to the general public. By permitting meetings to be closed in order to consider testimony given in confidence, the Colorado law provides an opportunity to circumvent the general intent of the Open Meetings Statute in a way not available in most other states. If all that is required to close a session is a request by the witness testifying that he wants the session closed, most special-interest hearing and testimony would never be witnessed by the public.

• The votes of legislative committees are not recorded either by aggregate or by individual. Conference committees of the legislature are never announced in advance and never open to the public or the press. No procedure exists by which a committee member may force a recorded committee vote. The legislature as a whole votes in a recorded manner only on the third reading of legislation. It meets on some occasions as a Committee of the Whole, and in those instances no roll call votes are taken.

LOBBYING DISCLOSURE

• Lobbying regulations for the State of Colorado are found in the House and Senate rules. No statutory provisions distinct from these rules exist. Senate rules are limited in scope and deal only with prohibitions against lobbyists' attempts to unfairly influence legislators or misrepresent clients or the facts. Such minor matters as the rights of lobbyists to appear on the floor of the Senate are also discussed, but, in general, no provisions requiring financial statements by either the lobbyist or his employer and no comprehensive registration requirements apply.

• House rules are only slightly more inclusive. A lobbyist is defined in the House rules as any person other than a member of the General Assembly who by his acts seeks to influence in any manner the vote of any member or members of the House or the actions of any of its committees upon any bills, resolutions, or other measures pending before the House or any of its committees. Note that the definition does not state that to be a lobbyist one must receive compensation from another person, a standard qualification in lobbying definitions in most other states. While the Colorado definition appears to be more comprehensive, it is likely that it is so as a matter of oversight rather than intent. Lobbyists who wish to appear before the House must make the fact known with the Sergeant-at-Arms and must register with the Chief Clerk of the House. At the time of registration the lobbyist must indicate his name and address and the interest or interests he represents as well as the bill or bills upon which he desires to be heard. No separate registration is required of the employers of lobbyists.

• Neither the lobbyist nor his employer is required to make any financial statement at any time indicating his sources of income or the nature or amounts of his expenditures.

• While the Chief Clerk of the House is generally charged with the responsibility of maintaining order and reasonable conduct with respect to House activities, no specific person is responsible for enforcing the provisions or the rule on lobbying.

CONFLICTS OF INTEREST

• No state statute covers conflict of interest of state legislators as a group. What regulations do exist are found in the Senate and House rules. These provisions vary substantially between the Senate and House. Senate rules will be discussed first.

• A Senate Committee on Legislative Conduct is created by Senate Rule No. 5. Every senator must file a financial disclosure statement on or before January 15 of each year in written form to this committee. The rule does not indicate, however, that such written financial disclosure statements are to be made public, so it may be assumed that such statements as are filed are kept privately by the committee.

• The Committee on Legislative Conduct is composed of two committee members appointed by the majority floor leader of the Senate and two appointed by the minority floor leader. All

substantive votes of the committee are to be determined by a
majority, that is, at least a three-to-one vote.

• It is the primary purpose of this committee to investigate and
make recommendations as well as set general guidelines for
potential or real conflicts of interest of state senators. The senator
is not required by law to abide by the recommendations of the
Senate committee, but if he fails to do so, the committee
has the prerogative of publishing its opinion in the journal of
the state legislature. The committee has the power to subpoena
witnesses, take testimony under oath, and assemble records and
documents in the same manner as would a court of the State of
Colorado. Any information gathered in any of these manners
may be used in a court of law in any subsequent enforcement
of the provisions of this rule.

• None of the rulings of the Committee on Legislative Conduct
are binding. Such rulings merely take the form of recommendations. The Senate as a whole appears to retain the right to
discipline its own members with respect to conflict of interest.
Individual senators who violate provisions of this Senate rule
may be found in contempt of the Senate and are to be punished
as the Senate provides.

Following is a summary of the regulations contained in the
Colorado House Rules of Procedure that apply to conflicts of
interest of state House members:

• Any House member who has an immediate personal or financial
interest in any bill or measure, proposed or pending, before the
General Assembly shall disclose the fact to the House and shall
not vote upon such bill or measure. Any member of the House
who wishes to be excused from voting shall make this fact known
before the beginning of the roll call. The statement of the desire
to be excused from voting should be accompanied by a brief
indication of the reasons for such desired exclusion.

• No supervisory agent or penalties are specifically provided for
in this House rule. It may be assumed, therefore, that the House
as a whole retains responsibility for overseeing and enforcing
this rule and that violators of any of the provisions of this
House rule would be subject to a charge of contempt of the
House.

CAMPAIGN FINANCE

• The law applies to every candidate in any primary, general, or special election and committees in support of or opposition to such candidates. Each must file an itemized statement under oath of all monies contributed to or expended by him in aid of his election, within ten days after the primary and within thirty days after a general or special election. The chairman and secretary of the state, Congressional, judicial, senatorial, representative, and county central committees of each political party presenting candidates shall file such a statement, under oath, within thirty days after each general or special election.

• The candidate is responsible for filing statements detailing campaign expenditures and receipts. No mention is made of a political treasurer. Both expenditures and contributions must be reported.

• Candidates for office to be filled by the electors of the entire state, or any division or district thereof greater than a county, and candidates for either house of the General Assembly, for district judge, and for district attorney shall file their statements with the Secretary of State. Candidates for county offices and all other offices not otherwise provided for above shall file their statements with the county clerk of the county where election occurs. Statements of state, congressional, judicial, senatorial, and representative central committees shall be filed with the Secretary of State, and those of county central committees with the county clerk. All statements are to be preserved by the officers with whom they are filed until the next general election and shall be open to inspection by the public.

• No limit is set for individual contributions. No limit is set on campaign expenditures. No prohibition is made with respect to corporate and labor union political contributions.

• Violation of any of the provisions of the law is a misdemeanor punishable by a fine of not more than $1,000 or imprisonment in county jail for not more than one year, or both. Both the district attorneys and the Attorney General have the power to prosecute. Any person may file an affidavit with a district attorney or the Attorney General stating the name of any suspected violator and facts bearing on the alleged offense. Upon the filing, an investigation shall be made, and the district attorney or Attorney General is required to take appropriate action.

CONNECTICUT

Open Meetings

• Committees of the legislature hold deliberations and vote in open session. Executive sessions may be convened by the chairman of the legislative committee. Votes taken in the full legislature on final passage of bills, procedural, motions and amendments are all open and recorded.
• A comprehensive open meetings law in Connecticut applies to administrative and executive boards, commissions, agencies, bureaus, committees, and other bodies of the state or any of its political subdivisions but does not include either the legislature, its committees, or the judiciary. Meetings of bodies covered by this state statute must be open to the public when in session unless the majority of the members of the body present and voting vote to close the meeting and cause it to be an executive session. While some state statutes permit executive sessions only to discuss certain categories of business, no such requirement is included in the Connecticut law. A majority vote may close any meeting for whatever reason. The votes of each member of any body covered by this statute must be made available in writing to the public within forty-eight hours, excluding weekends and legal holidays, after the vote was taken and shall be recorded in the minutes of the session, which shall be available for public inspection at all reasonable times.

Lobbying Disclosure

• Each person retained or employed for compensation to promote or oppose, directly or indirectly, the passage of any legislation or to promote or oppose executive approval of any legislation is considered to be a lobbyist.
• All lobbyists must register with the Secretary of State before the commencement of their lobbying activities. Registration forms

must include the name or names of the employer or principal by whom or on whose behalf the lobbyist is retained or employed, together with a brief description of the legislation in reference to which such service is to be rendered.

• Each person, firm, corporation, or association in whose behalf a person has been employed or authorized to promote or oppose legislation shall file within two months after the adjournment of the General Assembly, in the office of the Secretary, an itemized, verified statement showing in detail all items paid, incurred, or promised directly or indirectly in connection with the legislation pending at the last previous session with the names of the payees and the amount paid to each, or, if no compensation has been paid or promised for the services rendered, such statement shall so indicate. Notification must also include the names of all persons hired to render services on behalf of the employer in the form of lobbying.

• The Secretary of State, who receives reports when filed, is responsible for notifying the Attorney General of any violation of this statute that may occur. The Attorney General is responsible for verifying suspected violations and prosecuting violators.

• Contingent payments are specifically prohibited.

Conflicts of Interest

• The conflict of interest statute applies to members and employees of the General Assembly, members and employees of the executive branch, and members of the judicial department.

• No provision requires the public disclosure of financial holdings of any public official. No requirement is made that public officials divest themselves of financial holdings that represent real or potential conflicts of interest.

• The statute requires that no member of the General Assembly shall participate in proceedings concerning matters in which he has a financial interest. Financial interest is not specifically defined, however, in this provision. Throughout the statute the term "substantial conflict with duties" serves as a general description of a potential conflict of interest, but this term is not adequately defined.

• Enforcement of the statute is the responsibility of the General

Assembly. The statute calls for the creation of a special committee of the legislature to be made up of four members of the House and four members of the Assembly. The committee would have the power to investigate any allegations of violation of the law that are brought to its attention and to hold a hearing. After the hearing, the committee's findings are to be referred to the General Assembly as a whole for appropriate action if the violator is a member of that General Assembly or an employee thereof. If the violator is a member or an employee of the judicial or executive branch, such findings will be turned over ot the appropriate authority. While no general disclosure requirement appears in the statute, the committee does have the power to request reports of the economic interests of persons included under this act and of their spouses and children pursuant to any investigation based on an allegation of violation.
• No specific penalties are written into this statute. Penalties are up to the discretion of the appropriate enforcing authority. In the case of a legislator, this may include impeachment, censure, suspension, or dismissal from employment. In no case, however, are the courts involved in either the determination of guilt or the setting of penalties. The law states that the committee has a "power," upon receipt of a written complaint alleging violation of the act, to investigate such a complaint. It is unclear whether this "power" would serve as an adequate guarantee that a citizen filing the complaint will be able to generate a legislative hearing and investigation.

All of the above provisions are included in a new Connecticut statute, which takes effect on January 3, 1973. Several conflict of interest–related statutes are and will continue to remain on the books in the State of Connecticut. The major provisions of those additional statutes are as follows:
• Under a separate law, enacted in 1969, municipalities are empowered to prohibit any member or employee of a municipal board or agency from having any interests or receiving any gift which might have an effect on the purchase orders or contract orders of that municipality. This statute grants such municipalities the power to make such a prohibition; it does not itself prohibit such potential conflict.

• Under a separate law, enacted in 1961, salaried commissioners or deputized commissioners of the state, county sheriffs, or any persons receiving salary or pay for services rendered at Hartford, were prohibited from accepting any emolument or any other valuable thing in return for influencing any legislation. It was also made illegal for any party to make such an offer to such individuals for the purpose of influencing legislation.

• Complaints directed at identifying suspected violators should go to the state's attorney for Hartford County, who, upon proof, shall cause the arrest of any offender and cause him to be presented for trial before the Superior Court in and for Hartford County. This statute is confusing because of its reference to "services rendered at Hartford." It is not clear whether individuals rendering comparable services in Connecticut but not in Hartford County would be required to meet the provisions of this statute whether they were public employees or not.

CAMPAIGN FINANCE

• This law applies to all elective public offices at all levels in campaigns for election and preliminary primaries.

• Every candidate and political committee is required to have a campaign treasurer. The campaign treasurer is responsible for expenditures. The candidate is allowed to receive funds and make expenditures only for personal expenses—postage, travel, lodgings, phone bills, and so forth.

• Campaign treasurers are required to file reports of contributions and expenditures. Statements are due within thirty days following the election and are filed with the Secretary of State. If a candidate is not nominated, his statement is due within thirty days after the primary. If reports show a deficit or surplus, supplemental reports must be filed every ninety days until the deficit is eliminated or the surplus distributed. In local elections, statements are filed with the town clerk.

• There are no limits on individual contributions. There are no campaign spending limits. Corporations are not permitted to make contributions. Anonymous contributions are not permitted.

• Penalties are imprisonment or fines, or both. But no provision is made to prohibit offenders from subsequently appearing on a ballot or taking public office. In the case of election of local officers, any state referee, any judge of the superior court, or any judge of the circuit court may, upon the written request of any state's attorney or of any prosecuting attorney of the circuit court, conduct an inquiry as to whether any crime has been committed.

DELAWARE

OPEN MEETINGS

• Voting in legislative committees is usually open to the public, although technically the matter is left up to the chairman of the relevant committee. The decision about whether votes on procedural motions and amendments taken in the full legislature are to be open and recorded or if only votes on final passage are to be recorded is left to the Speaker's discretion.

• The meetings of all boards and commissions of the State of Delaware or any political subdivision thereof at which any business is transacted are to be open to the public and to representatives of the press. However, the law specifically states that meetings of boards and commissions of the state where no public business is transacted, that is, where final decisions are not made, need not be open. This provides an opportunity for substantial dealing in private and convening of open sessions merely for pro forma ratification of decisions made in such private sessions.

LOBBYING DISCLOSURE

• No statewide statutes or constitutional provisions bear on the registration of lobbyists. Indeed, no regulations cover attempts to lobby the state Senate at all. The only regulations that exist are found in the Rules of the House of Representatives of the State of Delaware. In those House rules, any person who is employed for compensation paid by others than the legislature, and whose employment calls for or includes activity in or about the House of Representatives in regard to legislation, must register with the Chief Clerk of the House of Representatives. The use of the term "activities in or about the House of Representatives" is a vague way of describing lobbying activities, and its vagueness undoubtedly leads to a lack of enforcement.

• Information required at the time of registration includes the name and address of the registrant; the name and address of the registrant's employer, including any association, organization, state agency or office, or labor union and, in cases of multiple employers, a sufficient number so identified as to indicate the class or classes registered with whose interest the registrant is connected; and the subject or subjects of legislation to which his employment relates. The requirement that only "a sufficient number" of contributors to the lobbyist's employment be listed is a major weakness of this bill. It permits a specific contributor to the lobbyist's salary to be totally anonymous while still obeying the provisions of the law. All contributors to the salary and expenses of all lobbyists should be known.

• No requirement is made that either the lobbyist or any of his employers file financial statements indicating either expenditures or incomes relating to lobbying activities.

• No specific person is responsible for enforcing the provisions of this House rule, nor are there any penalty provisions in the rule.

CONFLICTS OF INTEREST

No law.

CAMPAIGN FINANCE

No law.

FLORIDA

OPEN MEETINGS

• All meetings of any board or commission of any state agency or authority or of any agency or authority of any county, municipal corporation, or political subdivision must meet in open session at all times; no resolution, rule, regulation, or formal action shall be considered binding unless taken at such a meeting. This statute applies to the state legislature as well as to independent agencies and executive branch groups. The minutes of meetings of such boards, commissions, or committees are to be promptly recorded and such records are to be made available for public inspection. The circuit courts of the State of Florida have jurisdiction to issue injunctions to enforce the provisions of this statute.

• Any person who is a member of a board or a commission and who violates the provisions of this act by attending a meeting not held in accordance with its provisions is guilty of a misdemeanor and upon conviction shall be punished by a fine or imprisonment or both.

LOBBYING DISCLOSURE

• Lobbyists are defined as all persons except members of the Florida legislature or duly authorized aides designated in writing by such members who seek to encourage the passage, defeat, or modification of any legislation in the House or before the committees of the House. All persons so defined as lobbyists must register with the Clerk of the House prior to the commencement of lobbying activities.

• Information required at the time of registration includes the name and business address of the registrant, the name and business address of the principal or principals whom he represents, and the general and specific areas of his legislative interest. In addition, each registrant is required to state the extent of any direct business association or partnership with any current member of the legislature. Employers of lobbyists are not required to file separate registration forms.

• Thirty days after the conclusion of the regular legislative session, each lobbyist must file a signed statement listing all lobbying expenditures and the sources from which funds for making such expenditures have come. Lobbying expenditures shall not include personal expenses for lodging, meals, or travel. Thereafter, so long as an individual continues to be a lobbyist, he must file interim financial statements in the first week of each regular session of the legislature to cover expenses incurred while the regular legislature was out of session. The legislative committee on Standards and Conduct is responsible for supervising this act and recommending disciplinary action where necessary to the full legislature.

CONFLICTS OF INTEREST

• This statute applies to officers and employees of state agencies, to officers and employees of counties, cities, or other political subdivisions of the state, and to members of the legislature and legislative employees.

• If any of the individuals regulated by this statute maintains a substantial business interest in any business regulated by or having dealings with the state or any of its political subdivisions, such individual must file a sworn statement disclosing that interest with the Department of State if he is a state official or employee; if he is an officer or employee of a county, city, or any political subdivision of the state, he shall file the sworn statement with the clerk of the circuit court of the county in which he is principally employed. No individual covered by the provisions of this statute is required to divest himself of any financial interest.

• All individuals covered by this statute are prohibited from making financial gain on the basis of special knowledge or confidential information gained in the course of official responsibilities. They are also prohibited from accepting any gift, favor, or service that might reasonably tend to improperly influence the discharge of official duties. Note that this is not an outright prohibition, that the phrase "might reasonably tend" leaves the matter open to individual interpretation.

• In the event that any individual who may be covered by the provisions of this statute is unsure about its applicability to himself, he may submit to the Attorney General a full written statement of the facts and the questions to which he requires answers. The Attorney General may then render an opinion to such person.

• Violation of any of the provisions of this statute constitutes grounds for dismissal from employment or removal from office or any other penalty as provided by the law and shall constitute a misdemeanor and upon conviction shall be punishable by a fine not exceeding $1,000 or imprisonment not exceeding one year.

• Note that substantial discretion is given to individuals covered by the provisions of this statute in almost every instance. In contrast to the provisions of other states, in which all individuals covered by the conflict of interest statute are required to make public financial disclosures, in the State of Florida only those who believe they may have a conflict are required to do so. Similar discretion on the part of the individual covered by the statute is granted with respect to receiving gifts and maintaining supplemental employment and income aside from that received from the performance of official public functions.

CAMPAIGN FINANCE

• This Florida law applies to candidates for public office at all primary and general elections.
• Candidates or treasurers file as follows:

  a. Treasurers file on the first Monday of each calendar quarter from the time appointed until the candidate files papers and fees—
    after that (1) for statewide office—Monday of each week preceding the election; (2) for all other offices—the first and third Monday of each month preceding the election.
  b. The candidate must file a statement of receipts and expenditures for the last twelve months after the last election in which he was a candidate, within thirty days of the end of that twelve month period.

Committees file as follows:

  a. If no general election—January 1, April 1, July 1, October 1.
  b. If general election—January 1, April 1, July 1, and the first Monday of each month following the closing date of qualifications of candidates until the month following the general election. Depositories must file statements forty-five days after the election. Statements are filed with the Secretary of State.

• While many states impose no limits whatever on campaign expenditures by candidates seeking either federal or state office, Florida does impose such a limit, but it is one that is unbelievably high. Candidates for governor or U.S. Senator may spend $350,000. Candidates for U.S. Representative may spend $75,000. It is difficult to understand how such high limits could have been set, since in all other respects Florida campaign finance and contribution limits are within relatively reasonable bounds.

• Corporations are prohibited from making contributions. No similar prohibition exists for labor unions. Individual contributions are limited to $3,000 for statewide offices and $2,000 for Congressional races.

• Knowing violation of requirements to file is a misdemeanor with the penalty of fine or imprisonment. Willful violation voids nomination or election. Electors may file a petition with a circuit court. The Attorney General must act as counsel for the state. If the state attorney refuses to file pleadings, the petitioner may file pleadings in the name of the state against the person alleged to have committed the violation.

GEORGIA

OPEN MEETINGS

In 1972, the Georgia legislature passed HB 1283, opening the meetings of virtually all legislative, executive branch, and independent agency sessions at which "official actions are to be taken." Excluded are conference committees of the Senate and House and committees of either house whose duty it is to fix the calendar for each house. Executive sessions are still permitted to deliberate public business as long as no final decision is reached and no official action is taken at such executive sessions. This law took effect on July 1, 1972.

LOBBYING DISCLOSURE

• The Georgia Constitution defines lobbying as any personal solicitation of a member of the General Assembly during a session

by any person who misrepresents the nature of his interests or
who is employed for consideration by a person or corporation
for the purpose of procuring the passage or defeat of any bill,
resolution, report, or claim. In one of the oddities of all state law,
the Georgia constitution specifically prohibits lobbying as defined
above. Rather than seeking the straightforward remedy of a
constitutional amendment, the Georgia legislature has been
satisfied to enact contradictory and confusing regulations with
respect to lobbyist registration. Carefully avoiding the word
"lobbyist" or "lobbying," the legislature requires that every person
representing, with or without compensation, any person, firm,
corporation, association, or organization for the purpose of aiding
or opposing actions of the General Assembly, must register with
the Secretary of State, stating whom he represents.

• Individuals required to register under Georgia law must do so
at the beginning of each legislative session. The docket on which
such registration is recorded is open to public inspection. No
financial statements dealing with either expenditures or income
of those registering in accordance with this act are required.

• Members of the General Assembly are responsible for reporting
violations of this statute to the Rules Committee, which, in
turn, reports suspected violators to appropriate law enforcement
officials. Violation of this law is a misdemeanor. Contingent
payments are specifically prohibited.

CONFLICTS OF INTEREST

There is no standard conflict of interest statute included in
the Georgia codes. All that exists is a general code of ethics
for government service, which applies to any person employed
in government service in the State of Georgia. Among its ten
broad principles is one that prohibits individuals from discrimi-
nating unfairly by dispensing special favors or privileges to anyone,
whether for remuneration or not. It is also prohibited for
individuals in government service to accept for themselves or
their families favors or benefits under circumstances that "might
be construed by reasonable persons as influencing the performance
of his governmental duties." This is as close as the State of

Georgia comes to a statute regulating conflict of interest of public officials.

CAMPAIGN FINANCE

No law.

HAWAII

OPEN MEETINGS

The law applies to agencies, boards, commissions, authorities, and committees of the state or its political subdivisions, whether those bodies are legislative or executive. It does not apply to such bodies of the judicial branch. While open meetings are generally required, they may be closed by a recorded two-thirds vote of the membership of the committee. No ordinance, ruling, regulation, contract, appointment, or decision shall be finally acted upon at such executive sessions. However, substantial deliberations may be conducted in such sessions, and final votes taken in open meeting may be little more than a pro forma ratification of decisions hammered out in private.

LOBBYING DISCLOSURE

No law.

CONFLICTS OF INTEREST

• The law applies to every nominated, appointed, or elected officer or employee of the state—including members of boards, commissions, and committees, and employees under contract to the state, and *excluding* justices, judges, and magistrates.
• Only legislators and executive employees are required to make disclosure of financial interests, and only in cases where a conflict exists need a report be filed. Such reports are confidential. Of the eleven states requiring some disclosure, only Hawaii and Washington make the reports confidential. No disclosure is

required if the interest concerned is not a controlling interest.
• There is no requirement for public officials to divest themselves
of private holdings in order to avoid possible conflict of interest.
Executive officials and employees are prohibited from acquiring
conflicting interests, but legislators are not so prohibited.
• The law does not require legislators to disqualify themselves
from official dealings because of a conflict of interest. However,
employees are prohibited from participating as agents or representatives of state agencies in any official actions in which they
have an interest. Nor shall any employee appear in behalf of
private interests before any state agency for compensation that
is contingent upon action by a state agency.
• The law prohibits legislators and employees from using special
knowledge for personal gain or for the benefit of any private
interests. It prohibits legislators and employees from accepting
or receiving any gifts that could reasonably be interpreted as
intended to influence the performance of their official duties.
It prohibits a state agency from entering into contracts with
legislators or employees or with businesses in which any legislator
or employee has a controlling interest unless the contract is made
after public notice and competitive bidding. The law also prohibits
any state agency from entering into contracts with persons or
businesses that are represented or assisted by a person who has
been an employee of the agency within the preceding two years
and who participated while in state office or employment in the
matter with which the contract is concerned.
• Enforcement and administration are the responsibility of an
ethics commission, which shall hold hearings on alleged violations. After such a hearing, when the ethics commission determines that there is sufficient cause to file a complaint against
a legislator or employee removable only by impeachment, it
shall issue a complaint and refer the matter to the legislature.
If the legislature does not act on the complaint within thirty
working days, the commission shall then make the charges
public, though making it clear that the charges have not been
determined to have merit. With respect to employees who are
removable by means other than impeachment, the commission
shall refer the matter and make its complaint to the civil service

commission or other authority having the power to discipline the employee.

• In addition to any other penalty provision, the appropriate authority may reprimand, put on probation, demote, suspend, or discharge an employee found to be in violation.

CAMPAIGN FINANCE

• This law covers all elections—primary, general, and special— including any measures presented to the people. It applies to candidates at all levels except Presidential candidates who reside in other states.

• Committee statements are signed by an authorized person, but that person is not required to appoint a treasurer. The candidate is responsible for his expenses. Candidate and committee statements must list all expenditures and the names of contributors of an aggregate amount of $500 or more.

• Candidates for state and national offices and their committees file with the chief election officer. Others file with the clerk of the county. Presidential committees are required to file, even though their candidates are not. If a candidate is not nominated at the primary, his committee's statement is due within twenty days after the primary. For those nominated and on the ballot at the general election, the statement is due twenty days after the general election.

• No limit is set on individual contributions.

• No limits are set on campaign spending.

• Contribution of corporate funds is prohibited.

• No effective enforcement or penalty provisions are included in the law.

IDAHO

OPEN MEETINGS

Idaho has no legislation dealing specifically with open meetings of any body either in the legislative, executive, or administrative branch of the government. Certain legislative rules do cover some aspects of open meetings. Legislative committees always conduct discussions in open session. Votes are usually conducted in open session. Conference committee sessions, while always announced in advance, are never open to the public or the press. When legislative committee votes are not open to the public, votes are available by individual and by aggregate from the speaker of the appropriate house of the legislature.

LOBBYING DISCLOSURE

No law.

CONFLICTS OF INTEREST

No law.

CAMPAIGN FINANCE

No law.

ILLINOIS

OPEN MEETINGS

Legislative committee votes are generally open to the public and the press, are recorded by individual, and are available from the Clerk and Secretary. Such committee meetings may be closed by a two-thirds vote of the relevant committee at the discretion of the committee members, if in their judgment the public interest requires a closed meeting. No limiting definition of public interest is provided to serve as a guideline to legislators. Votes of the legislature as a whole on final passage of bills are recorded and open to the public. Votes on procedural motions and amendments are required if requested by two members of the Senate or by five members of the House.

Meetings of legislative, executive, administrative, and advisory bodies of the state and its political subdivisions must be open to the public except under certain specified conditions. They include:

1. personnel or collective negotiating matters between public employers and their employees or representatives
2. executive sessions of the Illinois Crime Investigation Commission in which investigations are discussed
3. deliberations concerning decisions of the Illinois Commerce Commission, the Illinois Parole and Pardon Board, and the Illinois Youth Commission.
4. meetings regarding the acquisition of property by the state
5. grand or petit juries
6. other such places in which the Constitution may provide for secret meetings.

The provisions of the act described in this paragraph do not apply to the General Assembly or to its committees or commissions. Those bodies are covered by the provisions described in the first paragraph of this open meetings section.

LOBBYING DISCLOSURE

• A lobbyist is defined as any person who, for compensation or on behalf of any person other than himself, attempts to influence action on legislation before the General Assembly or any of the General Assembly's committees, or attempts to influence the passage or veto of such legislation by the Governor, or any person, any part of whose duties as an employee of another person includes attempting to influence action on legislation.
• All individuals meeting the above description are required to register annually with the Secretary of State. The employers of such registering individuals are not required to make separate registration.
• At the time of registering, a lobbyist is required to indicate his name and address, the name and address of his employer, a brief description of the legislation with which he is concerned, and his picture.
• A financial statement dealing with a lobbyist's expenditures must be filed with the Secretary of State between the first and the twentieth of July of the years in which the General Assembly is in regular session, and between the first and twentieth of

January each year for the preceding year or part of the preceding year in which the General Assembly was not in session. The report must show in detail the person or legislator to whom or for whose benefit such expenditures were made. Expenditures of $25.00 or less may be reported in aggregate. Expenditures of more than $25.00 must be reported in detail.

• Any person violating this statute is subject to fine of up to $1,000 and/or imprisonment from one to ten years. Any corporation violating this act is subject to fine up to $10,000. In addition, anyone convicted of violating this statute may be prohibited from further lobbying activities for three years. A violation of the three-year prohibition carries the penalty of a fine of not more than $10,000 or imprisonment of from one to ten years or both. It is the responsibility of the state's attorney of the appropriate county or of the Attorney General to prosecute violations of this act.

• Contingent payments are specifically prohibited.

• Notice of the termination of employment of a given lobbyist must be provided to the Secretary of State within thirty days of that termination. This written notice must include a report of expenditures since the previous report.

• The following categories of individuals are exempted from compliance with the above statute:

1. persons who appear without compensation only as witnesses before committees
2. employees of a bona fide news medium who meet the definition lobbyist only in the course of their professional duties
3. persons performing professional services such as drafting bills
4. employees of departments, divisions, or agencies of the state government who appear before committees only to explain the effect of legislation related to their departments, divisions, or agencies
5. employees of legislators, agencies, and commissions of the legislature
6. persons with expertise who appear at the written request of a member of the General Assembly
7. any full-time employee of a bona fide church or religious

organization appearing solely to protect the right to practice the religious doctrines of such church.

Conflicts of Interest

• The Illinois Governmental Ethics Act, which took effect on January 24, 1972, applies to conflicts of interest of legislators and legislators-elect.
• In addition to the general conflict of interest provisions included in this act, Article 4A, titled "Disclosure of Economic Interests," has a broader scope. It deals not only with legislators and legislators-elect also but with the following categories:

1. persons holding an elected office in the executive branch of the State of Illinois or on the board of trustees of the University of Illinois and candidates for nomination or election to these offices

2. members of a commission or board created by the Illinois Constitution and candidates for nomination or election to such commissions or boards

3. persons whose appointment to office is subject to confirmation by the state Senate.

4. holders of and candidates for nomination or election to the office of judge or associate judge of the circuit court and the office of judge of the Appellate Court or Supreme Court

5. persons (except those primarily employed by the state in teaching, as distinguished from administrative duties) who are compensated for services to the state as employees and not as independent contractors at the rate of $20,000 per year or more and are employed by any branch of the government of the State of Illinois

6. persons who are elected to an office in a school district or in a unit of local government as defined by the Illinois Constitution, and candidates for nomination or election to such an office.

7. persons appointed to the governing board of the school district or to a special district, and persons appointed to a

zoning board or zoning board of appeals or to a regional county or municipal plan commission

8. persons who are employed by a school district or by any unit of local government as defined by the Illinois Constitution and are compensated for services as employees and not as independent contractors at the rate of $20,000 per year or more.

The scope of the disclosure section of this statute is perhaps the most extensive in the country. It is particularly notable for the inclusion of office-seekers, whether appointed or elected, and of office-holders and seekers on a sub-statewide level.

• For the purposes of the disclosure requirements of this statute, the economic interests and holdings of the spouses of the individual making the statement are considered to be his own economic interests. Campaign receipts are not considered to be applicable to the disclosure provisions of this statute.

• The statement of economic interest to be filled with the Secretary of State must include the following information:

1. the name, address, and type of practice of any professional organization or individual professional practice in which the person making the statement was an officer, director, associate, partner, or proprietor, or in which he served in any advisory capacity from which income in excess of $1,200 was derived during the preceding calendar year

2. the nature of professional services (other than services rendered to the unit of government in relation to which the person is required to file) and the nature of the entity to which they were rendered if fees exceeding $5,000 were received during the preceding calendar year from that entity for professional services rendered by the person making the statement

3. the identity (including the address or legal description of real estate) of any capital asset from which a capital gain of $5,000 or more was realized in the preceding calendar year

4. the name of any unit of government that has employed the person making the statement during the preceding calendar

year other than the unit of government in relation to which
the person is required to file

5. the name of any entity from which a gift or gifts, or honorarium or honorariums, valued singly or in the aggregate
in excess of $500 was received during the preceding calendar
year

6. additional information serving to round out the relevant
financial holdings of the person filing the statement. Generally, the receipt of $1,200 worth of income or the posses-
sion of $5,000 worth of assets or more constitutes cause for
the inclusion of an explanation on the disclosure statement
required.

• The statute includes a series of recommended ethical principles
for legislators, but none of the provisions of this section, most of
which deal, in part or in whole, with recommended divestment
or self-disqualification where potential or real conflicts occur, may
be used as the basis for disciplinary action. The statute recom-
mends, however, that a legislator avoid accepting or retaining any
economic opportunity that presents a substantial threat to his
independence of judgment. Also, in the event that an individual
holds an economic interest that may bear upon his legislative
decision-making, it is recommended that he consider first eliminating by divestment such financial interest or, short of such
divestment, consider the possibility of abstaining or disqualifying
himself from such official action. At a minimum, these recommended rules of ethical behavior suggest that the individual legislator announce the fact of the possible conflict even if he
proceeds to vote without having either divested himself or disqualified himself.

• While the legislator is not prohibited from receiving supplemental compensation besides his legislative salary, he is prohibited
from accepting income, gifts, loans, discounts, favors, or other
things of value having an aggregate value of $100 or more in any
calendar year from any person known to have a legislative interest. Such person is not clearly defined, and, in large part, compliance with this and other related prohibitions is left to the
discretion of the individual legislator.

• Except for the disclosure provision, which is to be supervised by the Secretary of State, no other provisions or prohibitions in this act are linked to specific enforcing agents, and, while penalty provisions are included with each section, it is not clear who is likely to bring charges that would lead to the utilization of such provisions.

CAMPAIGN FINANCE

No law.

INDIANA

OPEN MEETINGS

• The legislature holds its deliberations and votes in open session. Legislative committees sometimes vote in open session. When meetings are closed to the public, records of the proceedings and votes taken during closed sessions are kept by the committee. They are not recorded in the journal and not made readily accessible to the public.

• An Indiana statute requires open meetings but does not supersede statutes permitting closed or executive sessions, which were enacted prior to the open meetings statute. Therefore it is quite possible that whole categories of closed meetings are still permitted despite the apparently broad language of the open meetings provision.

LOBBYING DISCLOSURE

• A lobbyist is defined as any person, firm, corporation, or association employed to promote, advocate, or oppose, in any manner, any matter pending before the General Assembly or any matter that the General Assembly is legally permitted to consider.

• Any person, firm, corporation, or association that employs a lobbyist must register. No specific requirement is made that the lobbyist himself file a separate registration. The practice of requiring the employer but not the employee to register is the reverse of the standard state statutes. The employer of a lobbyist is required to register with the Secretary of State within one week after such employment.

• The registering employer must provide the following information:

1. if an individual, his full name, place of residence, and place of business
2. if a firm, the correct firm name, place of business, and the full name and place of residence of each partner
3. if a corporation or association, its full name, principal place of business, whether domestic or foreign, and names and residences of each of its officers
4. whether the employer is an individual, firm, or corporation, the nature of its employment
5. the full name, residence, and occupation of each person, firm, corporation, or association employed as legislative counsel or legislative agent, and the full period of that employment
6. the exact subject matter pending or that might legally come before the General Assembly, with respect to which the employed legislative counsel or legislative agent shall deal
7. any change in the information provided must be reported within one week of that change.

• All employers who are required to register must file financial statements within thirty days after adjournment of the General Assembly. Such statements, filed with the Secretary of State, must include a complete and detailed statement of all expenses paid or incurred by those employed by the registering employer. Such statements shall include salaries paid to legislative agents or legislative counsel. These reports are open to public inspection. Violation of this statute is a felony. Punishment is a fine of $200 to $1,000 or imprisonment of three months to one year. It is the duty of the Attorney General to prosecute violators of this statute.
• It is unlawful for any unincorporated association or combination of two or more persons to collect, receive, keep, or expend money for the purpose of promoting or opposing legislation unless they first appoint a treasurer and report such to the Secretary

of State. The treasurer must be a resident of Indiana. All financial transactions must pass through the treasurer. He must file a report of receipts and expenditures within thirty days after the adjournment of the General Assembly. Within one week from the date of his employment, he must file a statement of the following information:

1. name, occupation, and address of each person comprised by such association or contributing to its funds. Name and address of each member of the governing body
2. the exact matter of interest
3. the name, address, and occupation of each employed legislative counsel or agent.

• Contingent payments are specifically prohibited.

CONFLICTS OF INTEREST

No law.

CAMPAIGN FINANCE

• This Indiana law applies to candidates for public office in primary and general elections. Candidates and political committees are required to file statements. Committees must include receipts and disbursements; candidates need include only disbursements. Reports are not due until forty-five days after each primary or general election. They are filed with the clerk of the circuit court.

• A candidate's combined aggregate total expenditures in both primary and general elections cannot exceed $25,000 for governor of U.S. senator and $10,000 for U.S. representative.

• Both corporations and labor unions are prohibited from making campaign contributions. Indiana is one of four states prohibiting labor union contributions.

• There is no limit on individual contributions.

• Violators of these laws are subject to fine and/or imprisonment and disenfranchisement for five years or disqualification from office or the ballot. The clerk of the circuit court notifies the prosecutor, who shall take appropriate action. Defeated candidates or any ten electors may petition to prevent a candidate who is alleged to have violated the Corrupt Practices Act from taking office.

IOWA

OPEN MEETINGS

• All committee votes are open to the public and the press and are available from the Clerk of the House or the Secretary of the Senate. Votes are recorded by individual. Conference committee meetings are always open to the public and the press. A separate Iowa statute requires open meetings of all boards, councils, commissions, and governing bodies, as well as public agencies, unless two-thirds of the members of the agency, body, or board vote to close such session. The vote of each member on the question of holding the closed session and the reason for the closed session are to be entered in the minutes and made publicly available. The only legitimate reasons for closing such sessions relate to the premature disclosure of information relating to real estate or possible injury to the reputation of an individual.

LOBBYING DISCLOSURE

• No definition of lobbying is given. The legislation refers alternately to people who lobby and to people who "attempt to influence legislation on a regular basis." It may therefore be assumed that a lobbyist can be defined only in this quite general way.
• Every lobbyist must register prior to the commencement of lobbying activities with the Chief Clerk of the House. At the time of registration he must list his name and the name and address of each firm, company, corporation, union, association, or cause for which he wishes to lobby, as well as the numbers of the bills with regard to which he intends to lobby. No requirement is made that the employers of lobbyists register. Neither the lobbyist nor his employer is required to file any financial state-

ments listing income or expenditures related to lobbying activities.
• No specific individual is charged with the responsibility of enforcing the provisions of this act, and no penalty provisions are included.
• Contingent payments are specifically prohibited, as is any attempt on the part of a lobbyist or the employer of a lobbyist to offer economic or investment opportunities to any member of the House with the intent of influencing his conduct in the performance of his official duties.

CONFLICTS OF INTEREST

• Iowa statute 68B.10 covers conflict of interest of legislators, legislative employees, and executive officials and employees.
• No state law prohibits the acquisition of conflicting interests or the maintenance of conflicting employment.
• Legislators, legislative employees, and executive officials and employees are all prohibited from receipt of gifts, loans, and favors. All those categories except legislators are regulated with regard to any additional or extra compensation from nonstate sources.
• State law limits the circumstances under which lawyer-legislators may represent legal clients before state agencies. This regulation includes a postemployment limitation.
• No law requires the public disclosure of financial interests.

CAMPAIGN FINANCE

• This Iowa law applies to candidates for public office in primary and general elections.
• Candidates and political committees must file contribution and expenditure statements. Candidates must file thirty days after both primary and general elections. Political party central committees must file only after general elections. Statements are filed with the secretary of state.
• Expenditure limits are figured at 50 per cent of the annual salary of the office sought. Separate limits apply to primary and general elections. Only candidate expenditures are included; no

mention is made of limits on political committee expenditures.
• Corporations are prohibited from making contributions. No
similar prohibition covers labor union contributions. There is no
limit on individual contributions. A $100 tax deduction is possible
for individuals making contributions.

KANSAS

Open Meetings

• Votes of legislative committees are generally open to the public.
This is a matter of practice, however, not a matter of law. When
votes are not open, vote totals by aggregate are available from the
clerk or the secretary. After the end of the legislative session, the
vote totals are available from the Secretary of State. Conference
committee sessions are never open, nor are their votes available
either in aggregate or by individual.
• The meetings of all policy-making bodies of the executive
branch and the state administrative agencies and departments
must be open to the public unless the business to be discussed
bears on the reputation of an individual. Specific provisions of the
open meetings statute have recently been worked out and enacted into law in the 1972 legislative session as House Bill 1699.

Lobbying Disclosure

• The term "lobbyist" is not explicitly used. Instead, legislative
counsels and agents are defined. These two categories are to include any person employed, appointed, or retained by any person,
firm, association, organization, or corporation having an interest
in any measure or measures pending before, or to be introduced
in, either branch of the legislature, who attempts at any time to
influence the act or vote of any member of the legislature. Legislative counsel is to include persons who appear before legislative
bodies or legislative committees or seek to influence legislative
bodies or committees by the making of oral arguments or by the
submission of briefs. All others who attempt to influence legislation are considered legislative agents.

• Both legislative counsels and legislative agents are required to register. No separate registration requirement applies to employers of counsels or agents. Registration is required prior to each annual session of the legislature. Such registration is to be filed with the Secretary of State.

• Information required of registrants includes the name or names of employers whom the agent or counsel represents, and a brief description of legislation of interest. The dockets on which such information is recorded are to be maintained by the Secretary of State and open to the public. Any changes or additions in the areas of interest in legislation by a counsel or agent must be reported by that counsel or agent.

• Financial statements by all registrants must be filed after January 1 and before January 15 of each year. Statements are required for each legislative counsel or agent whose total compensation in the preceding year was $1,000 or more, or who incurred expenses in the performance of his duties of at least $1,000. These financial statements should be filed with the Secretary of State and should include the following:

1. the manner in which the registrant's compensation was determined and by whom it was paid
2. the manner in which he was reimbursed for expenses and by whom.

It is unlawful for any legislative counsel or agent to accept payments in cash as compensation for his services or as reimbursement for expenses incurred in the performance of his duties.

• The Attorney General is responsible for prosecuting violators of this statute. In addition, a group of legislators made up of the President pro tem of the Senate, the majority and minority floor leaders of each house, and the Speaker of the House is responsible for keeping close surveillance on anyone influencing or attempting to influence actions or decisions of the legislature. Whenever a group determines that the activities of any person conflict with the public interest, they can deny or revoke the privilege of registering and instruct the Secretary of State to make a record of such action. The same group of legislators can reverse such action. Any person whose privilege is denied or revoked may appeal to the District Court of Shawnee County within twenty days. Violators of this act are subject to punishment by a fine of not more than $5,000 or by imprisonment of not more than a year, or both. They may also be disqualified from acting as legislative counsel or agent for a period of three years. Any corporation convicted of violating provisions of this act can be punished by a fine of not more than $5,000.

• Contingent payments are specifically prohibited.

CONFLICTS OF INTEREST

• The provisions of this statute apply to all candidates for elective office in Kansas or all public officials and employees appointed or employed to serve as board members or executive officers of any state agency, department, board, bureau, office, institution, council, or commission of the executive, legislative, or judicial branch of the state government, and every public official or employee exercising supervisory authority over a primary division or subdivision of the State of Kansas.

• All above-named categories must make public disclosure of all substantial financial interests. Candidates for elected public office must make such financial disclosures at the time they file a declaration of candidacy or at the time of their appointment as a candidate. All other categories covered by this statute must file financial disclosure statements at the time of taking office. The Secretary of State of Kansas is responsible for receiving such disclosure statements and making rules and regulations dealing with the receipt, maintenance, and completeness of such statements.

• No provision of this statute requires that any public official or employee divest himself of any potential or real conflicts of interest. A Committee on Governmental Ethics is established by this statute. It is the duty of the committee to render advisory opinions on the interpretation or application of the conflict of interest law. Such opinions may be requested by any public official or employee or any person who certifies his intention to become a candidate for elective public office. Any person who requests and receives such advisory opinion and who acts in accordance with that provision shall be presumed to be in compliance with the statute. All requests for opinions must be filled within thirty days of their receipt. The opinions of this committee are merely advisory and are not legally enforceable.

• No public officer or employee shall in his official capacity make or participate in the making of a contract with any person or business by which he is employed or in whose business he has a substantial interest.

• If for some reason a public official or employee is not required to file a financial disclosure statement by any other provision of this statute, he is required to do so in the event that he stands to make personal financial gain as a result of one of his official decisions.

CAMPAIGN FINANCE

• This law applies to every committee, club, organization, municipality, or association designed to promote or engage in promoting the success or defeat of any party, election or candidate or candidates to political office, or adoption or defeat of any proposed constitutional amendment or other question submitted at any election. It also applies to every candidate for nomination or for election to any city, school district, community junior college, township, county, or state office. (The wording appears to exclude campaigns for national office, which is why the language has been reproduced almost verbatim here.)

• Committees, clubs, and so forth are required to have treasurers. A candidate is not required to have a treasurer and is required to file campaign financial statements personally.

• Both candidates and organizations (through their treasurers) must file statements covering both expenditures and receipts as follows:

—Committees, etc., must file annual statements with the county election officer and, in cases where the election or defeat of any candidate for state office or of a constitutional amendment was involved, shall also file with the Secretary of State. The accounts of the state committee of each political party shall be audited and a copy of the audit filed with the Secretary of State.

—Candidates for nomination or election to local office shall file with the county election officer, and candidates for state office with the Secretary of State, within thirty days after each primary, general or special election.

• No limit is set on individual contributions.

• The expenditure limit is 10 per cent of the first year's salary of the office sought. Those limits do not include traveling and hotel expenses. If the annual salary is less than $1,000, the limit is $500. *Note:* Candidates owning any medium of advertising must compute all expenditures related to such advertising at the same rate charged other candidates.

• There is no prohibition on corporate or labor union campaign contributions.

• Violation of any provisions of the law is a misdemeanor punishable by fine. Additionally, any office-holder convicted of any violation shall vacate the office held and be disqualified from holding public office for two years. This last penalty does not apply to candidates for office in cities of the third class or for township offices.

KENTUCKY

Open Meetings

• Kentucky has no comprehensive open meetings statute that applies to either the legislative, executive, administrative, or judicial branches of the government. Meetings of legislative committees and votes held at such meetings are seldom open to the public. When votes are held in closed session, they are recorded by individual, however, and are available in the committee reports. It is unclear, though, whether this means that all votes taken in committee or only final votes bearing on the reporting out of a final version of the bill must be recorded by individual. Conference committee sessions are never open to the public or the press.

• While no over-all statutory provision requires that meetings of the executive or administrative branches be open to the public, by practice and as a matter of policy many of these boards are open on a regular basis. This is not sufficient, however, in that it relies on the goodwill of the individual members of the agency or department involved; it should be a matter of law, not a matter of custom.

LOBBYING DISCLOSURE

• A lobbyist is defined as any person employed as legislative agent or legislative counsel to promote, oppose, or act with reference to any legislation which affects, or may affect, private pecuniary interests as distinct from those of the whole people.
• Both the person employing a lobbyist and the lobbyist himself must enter the lobbyist's name on the legislative docket.
• Such registration by lobbyist and employer is required before the commencement of lobbying activities. Registration is with the Attorney General of the State of Kentucky.
• At the time of registration, lobbyist and employer must indicate the name, residence, and occupation of each lobbyist, the name and address of his employer, the date of employment, the length of time such employment is to continue, and the legislative topics on which the lobbyist will be involved. When new subjects of legislation arise that the lobbyist is to promote or oppose, his employer must make additional entries opposite his own name on the legislative docket and opposite the name of his lobbyist as well. Each lobbyist must file with the Attorney General, within ten days after his registration, a written authorization to act as a lobbyist signed by his employer. All employers and lobbyists who are required to register with the Attorney General must make a full statement of expenses paid or incurred within thirty days after the adjournment of the General Assembly. Such statements are to be open to the public.
• If an employer fails to register a lobbyist or file a statement, he can be fined not more than $1,000 for a first offense and not more than $5,000 for the second and each subsequent offense. If a corporation is involved in a violation, its charter may be for-

feited at the discretion of the court. If an officer of a corporation or an association fails to file the required registration form or the required financial statement, he can be fined not more than $1,000 or confined in prison for not more than one year. If any lobbyist violates any of the provisions of this statute, he can be fined not more than $5,000 and/or confined in prison not more than five years. The Attorney General is responsible for enforcing the provisions of this statute.

• Contingent payments are specifically prohibited.

• No lobbyist shall attempt by coercion, intimidation, bribery or any other improper method to influence any member or officer of the General Assembly in the discharge of his duties.

CONFLICTS OF INTEREST

• This law applies to members of the General Assembly or officers or employees of the General Assembly and to officers or employees of any department of the state government; any division, board, bureau, commission, or other instrumentality within any department of the government; or any independent state authority, commission, or instrumentality.

• There is no requirement in this statute that any individual covered by its provisions make any disclosure of financial interests that may result in conflict of interest.

• No requirement is made that any official or employee covered by the provisions of this statute divest himself of any private holdings in order to avoid possible conflict of interest.

• Individuals covered by the provisions of this statute are prohibited from participating in any decision-making, in the course of their official responsibilities, that may result in a possible financial gain as a result of private holdings.

• No member of the General Assembly or officer or employee of the General Assembly or of any government agency may act in any transaction between the Commonwealth of Kentucky and a business in which he has a substantial interest.

• No penalty or enforcement provisions are included in this statute, and it is not explicitly clear who is responsible for enforcing the statute.

CAMPAIGN FINANCE

• The law applies to all candidates and political committees involved in any primary, regular, or special election for state or federal office from Kentucky.
• Each candidate and political committee must appoint a treasurer. A candidate may appoint himself as treasurer. The treasurer is responsible for filing required financial reports.
• Financial reports must include an accounting of both campaign expenditures and contributions.
• Reports of candidates for the Congress of the United States, all statewide offices, Judge of the Court of Appeals, circuit judge, Commonwealth's Attorney, circuit court clerk, and the Kentucky General Assembly and their campaign committees shall be made thirty days prior to an election, ten days prior to an election, and within thirty days following an election. Reports of candidates for other public offices and their campaign committees shall be made ten days prior to the election, and within thirty days following the election. State and county executive committees are required to file within thirty days after the regular primary and general elections. All reports are filed with the Kentucky Registry of Election Finance.
• No limits are set on individual contributions.
• No limits are set on campaign expenditures.
• No law prohibits campaign contributions by corporations or labor unions.
• Violation is a misdemeanor punishable by fine or imprisonment or both. Nomination or election of a candidate found to be in violation shall be void. An action to declare a vacancy under the above may be brought by the registry or by another candidate for the office sought. The Attorney General, the Commonwealth's Attorney, or the Registry may sue for injunctive relief to compel compliance with the provisions of the law. *Note:* Before the law was amended, any registered voter could sue.
• If a candidate runs unopposed, he is not required to file financial reports. This is a poor exemption, since a candidate may still expend money even if running unopposed. Indeed, expenditures made early in the campaign may scare off opposition and result

in an unopposed candidacy. Such expenditures should be reported.
• Candidates making no expenditures and receiving no contributions are required to file a signed statement to that effect.

LOUISIANA

OPEN MEETINGS

• The open meetings law applies to councils, governing bodies, boards, or authorities of the State of Louisiana. The law specifically excludes the state legislature, and no other statute requires open meetings of the legislature.
• Open meetings are required of all the bodies to whom the statute applies except that each of these bodies may go into executive session upon a two-thirds majority vote of its members. While some states permit executive sessions by vote of the committee only in relation to certain matters, no such limitations exist in Louisiana, and meetings apparently may be closed by that majority vote for whatever reasons the committee may propose. While no law requires that the legislature meet in open session, by custom it has met openly in *most* but certainly *not all* cases. As a matter of rule the legislature meets in closed session to consider and vote on the confirmation of gubernatorial appointments. At the federal level, such hearings on executive appointments are matters of great public concern, and open debate is an important feature of confirmation hearings. Clearly the need is no less great at the state level to have such public scrutiny at the time of advice and consent on an executive appointee.

LOBBYING DISCLOSURE

No law.

CONFLICTS OF INTEREST

• This statute covers all elected and appointed officials and any state employee who acts in an official capacity. It does not, however, include judges, educators, or officials or employees of any political subdivision of Louisiana. (Therefore, officials or employees of towns, local school boards, etc., would not be included under the statute.)

• No provision of this statute requires public disclosure of financial holdings by any elected or appointed official.

• No provision requires the divestment of any potential or real conflict of interest by any elected or appointed official.

• The statute provides that a public official should excuse himself from official proceedings in which he or his spouse or children have an economic interest. The fact that the statute says "should" and not "must," however, leaves open to question just how automatic such disqualification is. It also makes it virtually impossible to bring suit against any public official who fails to disqualify himself on any matter in which he has a personal economic interest.

• The statute does prohibit public officials or their spouses or children from accepting personal gain from an interested source. No limit on the amount of gifts a public official may receive from a so-called disinterested source is set, however, and the line between interested and disinterested is a vague one. Public officials other than elected officials are prohibited from accepting employment related to their duties in public office for two years after the termination of their state employment.

• Provision is made for a commission on governmental ethics consisting of five persons appointed by the governor, responsible for enforcing such parts of this act as apply to all state officials *except* those in elective office. Regulation of those in elective office is by a board consisting of three members, one appointed by the governor, one by the House, and one by the Senate. No member of the House or Senate may serve on the latter board.

• Any registered voter of the State of Louisiana has the right to file a complaint with the proper commission or board about any public official concerning a conflict of interest. This complaint must be investigated by that commission or board, which, in turn, has access to the courts. While this is quite strong, it is not clear that the commission or board must inform the appropriate legal authorities if it does discover what it believes to be violations of the statute.

• Penalties exacted by the commission regulating public officials *other than* elected officials may include dismissal, demotion, and the cancelation of a state contract made in violation of the law. In addition the state may collect a civil penalty through the courts of up to $5,000.

• Penalties exacted by the courts against an elected official in violation of this act, or against a person who participates with him in violation, may include a fine of up to $2,000 and imprisonment of up to one year.

CAMPAIGN FINANCE

No law.

MAINE

OPEN MEETINGS

Any transactions affecting any and all citizens of the state by any administrative or legislative body of the state or of its political subdivisions must be open to the public. These sessions may, however, be closed by a majority vote of the members of the body or agency. No ordinances, orders, rules, resolutions, regulations, contracts, appointments, or other official actions shall be finally approved at such executive sessions. It is possible, however, that the bulk of the compromising and politicking go on in such closed sessions, with only a pro forma ratification of predetermined compromises taking place in open session after the conclusion of such closed meeting.

LOBBYING DISCLOSURE

• While the term "lobbyist" is not generally used in the Maine statute, the terms "legislative counsel" and "legislative agent" do apply. "Legislative counsel" means any person who, for compensation, appears at any public hearings before committees of the legislature in regard to proposed legislation. "Legislative agent" means any person, firm, association, or corporation that for hire or reward acts to promote or oppose proposed legislation except to appear before committees, and includes all persons who, for compensation, approach members or members-elect of the legislature to influence their decisions.

• Within forty-eight hours of employment to act as legislative counsel or agent, both the employer and the employee must place their names on the legislative docket. The docket is maintained by the Secretary of State's office and is open to public inspection. Information required at the time of registration includes the names and addresses of legislative counsels or agents and the names and addresses of their employers, the date and subject matter of employment, and the designation of whether an individual meets the definition of legislative counsel or agent or both.

• Neither the legislative agent or counsel nor the employer of either one is required to file financial statements listing either expenditures or incomes related to lobbying activities.

• Violators of these provisions are subject to fines of not less than $100 nor more than $500. The Attorney General is responsible for prosecuting suspected violators of these statutes. Any person, firm, or corporation that falsely enters names on the docket is subject to a fine of $100 and is answerable in damages to persons whose names are falsely entered.

• Contingent payments are specificially prohibited.

Conflicts of Interest

• The conflict of interest statute applies to state legislators only. No provision of the law requires members of the legislature to make regular or public disclosure of their financial holdings. Only in the event that a legislator is under investigation by the Committee on Legislative Ethics may he be required to disclose such financial holdings as may be revelant to that investigation.

• No requirement is made that members of the legislature divest themselves of potential or real conflicts of interest.

• The Committee on Legislative Ethics is responsible for supervising any possible conflict of interest among state legislators. It is empowered, however, only to give advisory opinions and guidelines; the individual state legislators are not obliged to act in accordance with such guidelines. If the committee has determined that a legislator has a conflict, he is not allowed to vote on any questions in connection with the conflict.

• In a provision designed to protect members of the legislature against malicious and unjustifiable accusations regarding conflict of interest, persons making false accusations are subject to fine and/or imprisonment.

• It is not considered a conflict of interest for any legislator to serve on a public board, authority, or commission created by the legislature so long as he receives no compensation other than his actual expenses.

Campaign Finance

• The Maine campaign finance law applies to candidates for public office in primary and general elections. Candidates and political committees are required to file contribution and expenditure statements with the Secretary of State thirty days after primary and general elections. No explicit legal provisions require that the Secretary of State report to the prosecutor failures to file.

• Maine has no law setting expenditure limitations for candidates or committees or regulating campaign contributions. Neither corporate nor labor union contributions are prohibited. No ceiling is set for individual contributions.

• The penalty for failure to file is a daily assessment of fines up to $5 a day. If the assessment is not paid, the person is disqualified and his name may not appear on the official ballot used for any election during the same calendar year. Failure to file is also a misdemeanor punishable by fine or imprisonment, or both. The Attorney General must prosecute offenders. Any person may make a written application to the Campaign Reports Committee or the legislature requesting an investigation.

MARYLAND

Open Meetings

• The open meetings statute applies to executive and administrative departments only and requires only that those bodies meet in open session to determine final decisions affecting public policy. They are permitted to go into executive session under any other circumstances. This means that for all practical purposes all business of the executive and administrative departments could be conducted in private closed session with the public excluded except for pro forma ratification of decisions previously agreed to in such closed sessions.

• The legislature under legislative rules holds all its deliberations and votes in open session. The only exception is that the Democratic caucus meets in closed session to select its officers in the legislature. Legislative committee hearings are always open to the public, but votes of legislative committees are only sometimes open, with the decision to close left to the committee's discretion. All committee votes that are open to the public are recorded in aggregate and are available from the committee chairman, the Clerk of the House, or the Secretary of the Senate at the end of the session.

LOBBYING DISCLOSURE

• In lieu of the word "lobbyist," Maryland statutes refer to "legislative agent." Such agents are any persons who, for compensation, appear before the General Assembly, committees of the General Assembly, or its members for the purpose of influencing any matter pending before that body.

• Everyone employed as a legislative agent must register. All registration is with the Secretary of State and must be accompanied by a written authorization from the agent's employer. At the time of registering, the legislative agent must file a written authorization from his employer. The authorization includes the full and legal name and business address of both the employer and the legislative agent, the period of time of employment, and the proposal or subject upon which the employer is represented. A separate registration form is required for each employer whom the legislative agent represents. It is the additional responsibility of the legislative agent to report to the Secretary of State any changes in the extent of his employment immediately as they occur so that they may be entered appropriately on the docket. While the legislative agent has responsibility for updating the registration form and authorization form, he is not obliged to file a statement distinct from that required of his employer.

• On or before May 15 of each year, a legislative agent who has appeared before the General Assembly, any committee of that assembly, or any individual member of that assembly during the previous twelve months must file an itemized account of all salaries, fees, expenses, or other compensation paid, or to be paid, in connection with his employment. This report is filed jointly with his employer, a separate report being required for each employment. If his salary includes services other than those performed as a legislative agent, such salary must be prorated so that the value of time and efforts spent in activities as a legislative agent may be known. The governor of the State of Maryland has the prerogative to require that these financial reports be filed any time prior to the April 15 standard deadline.

• Violations of the provisions of this statute are a misdemeanor punishable by a fine of not more than $1,000 and/or imprisonment for not more than six months. The Secretary of State, upon receiving information that may lead to the suspicion of a violation, may refer to the appropriate state's attorneys any apparent violation.

• Certain categories of individuals are exempted from compliance with this statute. They include persons performing professional services in drafting bills and other legislative services, persons appearing at the specific request or invitation of a committee who engage in no further lobbying activities, and persons appearing solely on matters pertaining to their official duties.

• Contingent payments are specifically prohibited.

CONFLICTS OF INTEREST

• Maryland statute C.19A is the only existing statute in the state dealing with conflict of interest. It is quite limited in scope, regulating only transactions with or on behalf of the state or employer agency.

• No Maryland statute deals in a comprehensive way with potential or existing conflict of interest among legislators, legislative employees, executive officials or employees, or members of the judiciary. No law requires the public disclosure of financial interests of any public official.

• While Maryland law permits agencies to promulgate codes of ethics for executive officials and employees, such permission does not ensure that such codes will be either enacted or enforced. This is, in fact, a minor provision in relation to the substantial areas of conflict of interest on which the law is silent.

CAMPAIGN FINANCE

• This law applies to all general, primary, and special elections and to candidates at all levels, excluding Presidential candidates. Initiative and referendum elections are not covered.
• Each candidate and each state central committee or political committee must have a treasurer who is responsible for all contributions and expenditures. A candidate cannot act as his own treasurer. The treasurer of a state central committee may appoint one subtreasurer for each voting precinct. The treasurer designated by a candidate must file a report or statement of contributions and expenditures. The chairman and treasurer of a committee are responsible for filing its statement of contributions and expenditures.
• Statements of candidates for statewide office or U.S. senator or representative are to be filed with the State Administrative Board of Election Laws. Others are filed with the board of the county or city in which the candidate resides. Statements are to be filed no later than noon on the seventh day preceding any election and again no later than noon on the thirtieth day after the election, or before a candidate takes office, whichever comes first. Until any unpaid bills or deficits are cleared, subsequent reports are required sixty days after the election, six months after the election, and one year after the election.
• A limit of $2,500 is placed on individual contributions in any primary or general election.
• Candidates can spend the following amounts in each of the primary and the general elections

Statewide office or U.S. Senate	$20,000
Citywide office in Baltimore	15,000

Representative in Congress	10,000
Office in voting district with voting registration not less than 200,000	10,000
Office in district with registration from 100,000 to 200,000	7,500
Office in district with registration from 40,000 to 100,000	5,000
All other offices	2,500

• Anonymous contributions are prohibited. Corporation contributions are limited to $2,500. Associations and unincorporated associations are also limited to contributions not greater than $2,500.
• No person is deemed elected to any office until the required statements are filed. Any willfully false, fraudulent, or misleading statement constitutes the crime of perjury and is punishable as such. Every person guilty of any prohibited practices under this law is subject to fine and/or imprisonment and is ineligible for any public or party office for a period of four years. State's attorneys in each county are responsible for prosecution.
• At any time within thirty days after the election, any defeated candidate or any ten duly qualified voters may present to any county circuit court a petition setting forth that prohibited practices were committed by the successful candidate or his agent. If the candidate petitioned against is found guilty, the election is void. He is then ineligible for public or party office for a period of four years. Any violation of this law is a misdemeanor carrying the punishment of fine and/or imprisonment.

MASSACHUSETTS

OPEN MEETINGS

• While a statute requires that state administrative boards and commissions meet in open session, they are permitted to call executive sessions when they believe that matters to be discussed might adversely affect the public security the financial interests of the commonwealth or its political subdivisions, or the reputation of any person. The language is sufficiently broad to permit virtually any committee to justify a closed meeting in terms

of one of the three legitimate justifications provided in the law.
• Legislative committees never vote in open session. Records are kept of all votes held in private and are theoretically available by aggregate in the Journal. In practice, however, such totals are available only for committee votes on final passage of bills. There are very few exceptions to this. Votes taken on procedural motions or on amendments to bills in committee are rarely recorded.
• Separate open meetings titles apply to counties, county commissions, and municipal governments. These separate titles are similar to those which apply to the state administrative boards and commissions.

Lobbying Disclosure

• In lieu of the word "lobbyist," "legislative counsel" and "legislative agent" are used. A legislative counsel is any person who, for compensation, appears at any public hearing before any committee of the General Court in regard to proposed legislation but commits no other acts in regard to the same except as are incidental to such appearance before a committee. A legislative agent is any person who for hire or regard does any act to promote or oppose legislation except to appear at a public hearing before a committee of the General Court as legislative counsel.
• The employer of such legislative counsel or agent must register, as must the employee himself. Such registration is required within one week after the commencement of employment and is filed with the Sergeant-at-Arms.
• Registration requires that the employer enter the names of both himself and his employee and include additionally the business address of each, the residence and occupation of the employee, and the subjects of legislation engaged in by specific title and number of each bill. As additional subjects of legislative interest are engaged in by the legislative agent or counsel, his employer must make additional entries in the appropriate docket under the names of both the employer and the employee.
• Within thirty days after March 31, June 30, September 30, and December 31 of each year, every legislative counsel or agent

shall supply the Attorney General with a statement of all expenses incurred in furtherance of the objectives of any employer in dealing with the legislative branch or with the executive branch for purposes of seeking passage or veto of a legislative act, or in dealing with any authority created by that legislature in promoting or opposing legislation or enforcement or interpretation of the general laws. Such statements shall include, but should not be limited to, such things as meals, gifts, and campaign contributions. Also included in this financial statement shall be the total salary or retainer paid by every employer of a legislative counsel or agent and the percentage of such salary or retainer as is allocated to his lobbying function as counsel or agent. The General Court may disqualify a legislative counsel or agent after a hearing held before a committee of that General Court or in such other manner as is determined by that Court. Such disqualification shall be in effect until the termination of the third regular session of the General Court following such disqualification.

• Every group or organization of more than five people with expenditures of more than $100 that attempts to influence matters under consideration by the executive or legislative branch or pertaining to any authority empowered by that legislative branch shall, within thirty days after the prorogation of the General Court, submit to the Attorney General a statement of all expenditures related to such efforts to promote or oppose legislation or enforcement or interpretation of the general laws. The statement shall include names and addresses of the principals of the group and every expenditure of $10 or more, including, but not limited to, such items as meals, campaign contributions, gifts, and advertising. In addition, the statement shall include names and addresses of every individual or group who contributed $100 or more during the year for the purposes stated above.

• Within thirty days after March 31, June 30, September 30, and December 31 of each year, every direct and indirect employer of any legislative agent or counsel shall submit a statement to the Attorney General of all expenditures of $10 or more incurred separately by the employer and not listed under the employee's financial statement. Items listed must include, but need not be limited to, such expenditures as meals, gifts, campaign contributions, and advertising. The employer must also report the total salary or retainer paid to legislative counsels or agents and the percentage of such salary or retainer allocated for the function of lobbying.

• Required statements are to be retained by the Attorney General for ten years. On receipt of a written complaint of violation of the requirements the Attorney General shall investigate and hold hearings, using his powers of subpoena if necessary. Violation is punishable by a fine of not less than $100 nor more than $1,000, and any legislative agent or counsel who acts in violation shall also be disqualified until after the termination of the third regular session of the General Court following the disqualification. The Attorney General has the power of enforcement.

• Contingent payments are specifically prohibited.

CONFLICTS OF INTEREST

• Massachusetts Statute C.268A governs potential conflict of interest by public officials.

• Massachusetts law specifically prohibits the maintenance of conflicting employment by legislators, legislative employees, executive officials, executive employees, and members of the judiciary.

• The same groups are specifically prohibited from receiving gifts, loans, or favors. This prohibition includes a postemployment limitation.

• The same groups are also regulated in regard to the receipt of extra or additional compensation from nonstate sources.

• No state law requires the public disclosure of financial interests, but Massachusetts is the only state to require that executive or legislative employees divest themselves of conflicting interests.

CAMPAIGN FINANCE

• This law applies to candidates for public office in primary and general elections.

• Candidates and treasurers of committees and depositories are required to file contribution and expenditure statements with the Secretary of State.

- Candidates and committees must file fourteen days after either primary or general elections. Treasurers of depositories must file on the fifth and twentieth day of each month. Failure to file must be reported by the Secretary of State to the prosecutor.
- All campaign expenditure limitations were repealed by amendments in St. 1962, c.444, Sec. 2.
- Corporate contributions are specifically prohibited. No similar prohibitions exist for labor union contributions. Individual contributions during any given year are limited to $3,000 to one candidate, $3,000 to one party, and $3,000 to nonelected political committees not organized on behalf of any candidate.
- The penalty for failure to file the required statements is fine or imprisonment. The Attorney General or district attorney is responsible for prosecution of violators. Any five qualified voters can apply to a justice of the Superior Court to bring an election petition against a candidate. The election is declared void if the justices find that a corrupt practice was committed.

MICHIGAN

Open Meetings

- The law on open meetings with respect to the state legislature reads as follows: "The doors of each house shall be open unless the public welfare requires secrecy." Clearly the scope for individual discretion on what requires secrecy is so vast as to make this provision of the Constitution virtually meaningless. No separate statutory regulations regarding open meetings outside the Constitution apply to the legislature. Most legislative committees meet in open session, but as a matter of custom rather than a matter of law. Committees that deliberate in open session frequently vote publicly as well. The Constitution requires that only votes on final passage of legislation be opened for the legislature as as whole. One-fifth of the members present may request a roll call vote on amendments or procedural motions, however.

Separate chapters of the Michigan statutes require that meetings of townships, fourth-class cities, home-rule cities, and supervisors and auditors, as well as school boards, be held in open session.

LOBBYING DISCLOSURE

• In lieu of the word "lobbyist," the term "legislative agent" is used, defined as any person employed by a person, firm, association, or corporation or by any board or agency of the State of Michigan, or any political subdivision thereof, to engage in the promotion or advocacy of, or opposition to, any matter pending or which might legally come before either house or the legislature or its committees. In the above definition, the terms "advocating," "promoting," and "opposing" mean any act or acts directly undertaken with a member of the legislature for the purpose of influencing him or urging him to use his influence for or against any pending matter.

• The legislative agent must register before the commencement of lobbying activities. Such registration is filed with the Secretary of State in a separate statement. No separate statement is required of employers of legislative agents. Information required at the time of filing statements includes:

1. the full name, residence, and business address of the registrant
2. the name of the firm, association, or governmnetal agency of which he is an employee, partner, or owner; the position held, business interests, and principal occupation of the firm
3. If employed by more than one person, firm, or association, the names, business addresses, and principal occupations of each employer
4. the name and address of persons and firms who will keep custody and control of the accounts and records required as a part of this statute
5. any change or modification in or addition to such employment, which must be reported by the applicant within one week of such change to the Secretary of State.

• Every legislative agent or his employer, or an agent appointed by either, must keep a record of all expenses incurred pursuant to his employment as a legislative agent and must keep records of all compensation payments to him for his services. These records must be kept for a period of six years immediately following the final adjournment of each legislative session in which the legislative agent was employed. They must be produced upon subpoena issued by a court of competent jurisdiction or by legislative committe created and authorized by a concurrent resolution of that legislature. Thus no specific financial statement is required to be filed, although full records must be kept.

• Any person acting as a legislative agent who has any financial transactions with any member of the legislature shall within five days of that transaction file a sworn statement with the Secretary of State giving in detail the nature of the transaction and the name of the legislator. A copy of the statement is furnished to the legislator mentioned therein. Failure to file such a statement is a felony.

• Violations of the provisions of this act are a felony punishable by fine or imprisonment. The Attorney General is responsible for enforcing this statute.

• Contingent compensation is specifically prohibited.

• Not covered by the provisions of this statute are individuals who confine their activities to written communications or to formal appearances before committees of the legislature and who in writing clearly identify themselves and each person, firm, corporation, association, or other interest they represent. Nor does the statute apply to any person who furnishes information at the request of a legislator or committee regarding any pending matter.

CONFLICTS OF INTEREST

• Michigan Statute 4.1700 governs potential conflict of interest with respect to legislators, legislative employees, executive officials, executive employees, and members of the judiciary. This law deals exclusively with state officials regulating, assisting, or representing themselves in transactions with the state.

• No state law prohibits the receipt of gifts, loans, or favors, nor does the law regulate the receipt of extra or additional compensation from nonstate sources, prohibit the acquisition of conflicting interests, prohibit the maintenance of conflicting employment, or require the public disclosure of financial interests.

CAMPAIGN FINANCE

• This law applies to candidates in all primary, general, and special elections, including any proposal submitted to the voters.
• Every candidate and committee are required to file contribution and expenditure statements. Reports are filed with the candidate's county clerk, who forwards a duplicate copy to the Secretary of State for any candidate for statewide office or an office covering more than one county.
• Reports are due ten days after primary elections and twenty days after general elections.
• Campaign expenditure limits are determined on the basis of $40 for each 1,000 votes cast for Governor in the last Presidential election year in the state or political subdivision in which the candidate is running; but no candidate shall be restricted to less than the 25 per cent of one year's compensation, or $100. A candidate may spend up to these limits in primary and general election campaigns. The limit applies to expenditures by or on behalf of the candidate with his knowledge and consent.
• Corporate contributions are specifically prohibited. No similar prohibition exists on labor union contributions. There is no limit on individual contributions.
• No person can take office, collect salaries, or receive a certificate of nomination of election until he has filed the required statements. Violators are also subject to fine and/or imprisonment. Either the prosecuting attorney or the Attorney General is responsible for prosecution.

MINNESOTA

OPEN MEETINGS

• Legislative rules require that votes of all committees be taken in open session and be recorded by aggregate and individual. These vote totals are available from either the Clerk or the

Secretary or, after the session, from either the Secretary of the Senate or the State Archives. Conference committee sessions are seldom announced in advance and are never open to the public.
• A separate state statute applies to meetings of executive departments. It requires that, except as otherwise expressly provided by the law, whenever any agency, department, board, or commission in the executive department of government is required or permitted by law to transact business in a meeting, such meeting shall be open to the public. This law does not apply to the deliberations of any quasi-legislative or quasi-judicial body or to the meetings of the Board of Pardons, the Adult Correction Commission, or the Youth Conservation Commission.

LOBBYING DISCLOSURE

The following regulations are found in Rule 68 of the 1971 Permanent Rules of the Minnesota House of Representatives and apply only to that house:
• A lobbyist is defined as any person employed for compensation by others than the legislature whose employment requires him to be in or about the House and to deal with legislation.
• Such individuals must register before the commencement of their activities. Employers of lobbyists are not required to make separate registration or to file separate financial statements at any time.
• Such registration as is required is to be filed with the Chief Clerk of the House.
• Sufficient information shall include the name and address of the registrant, the name and address of the registrant's employer, including any association, organized group, state agency or office, or labor union that participates in or contributes to payment of the expenses or salaries of the lobbyist. In the event that there are multiple employers of a specific lobbyist, a sufficient number of such employers must be identified as to describe the class or classes that the lobbyist represents. Note that this manner of filing does not require all employers of a given lobbyist to register or to indicate the amount of their contribution or interest. This makes it possible for a given employer or contributor to a

lobbyist's income or salaries, or a given employer whom the
lobbyist may represent, to be totally anonymous.
• All registrants must file with the Chief Clerk of the House,
within fifteen days after the end of each month in which the
legislature has been in session and within thirty days after the
adjournment of any session, a sworn statement of all expenditures
for the preceding period in connection with his lobbying activities.
Such statements may exclude salaries or personal living and
travel expenses incurred as a result of lobbying activities.

The House of Representatives, acting through its agent, the
Chief Clerk, is responsible for the enforcement of this House
rule.
• The Senate of the State of Minnesota has its own rules govern-
ing lobbying activities with respect to that body. They are
incorporated in Rule 80 of the 1971 Permanent Rules of the
Minnesota Senate. They are similar to those included in the House
Rules described above, except that the Secretary of the
Senate has the responsibilities therein entrusted to the Chief
Clerk of the House, although enforcement is not solely the
prerogative of the Secretary of the Senate. Rather, the Lobby
Registration Committee is empowered to investigate any complaints by a member of the Senate with regard to lobbying
activities of any lobbyist registered with the Secretary of State.
This committee consists of four members appointed by the
Committee on Committees of the Senate. The Senate rules are
more complete in their description of prohibitions of certain
lobbying activities and in spelling out the penalties for violators
of this rule. Any person judged guilty by the Senate upon
recommendation by the committee shall be barred from acting
as a lobbyist until reinstated by the Senate. The name of anyone
so barred shall be recorded in the Journal of the Senate.

CONFLICTS OF INTEREST

• Minnesota Statute 3.88(4) governs conflict of interest among
legislators and legislative employees only. This is the major state
statute in this field.
• These two categories are specifically prohibited from main-

taining conflicting employment or receiving extra or additional compensation from nonstate sources.
• The law contains no prohibition against the acquisition of conflicting interests or the receipt of gifts, loans, or favors. No form of public disclosure of financial interests is required of any public official.
• Appearances of lawyer-legislators before state agencies also are unregulated.

CAMPAIGN FINANCE

• The law covers primary, general, and special elections, including elections on measures brought before the people. It does not include elections for President or Vice-President of the United States.
• The candidate is responsible for the disbursements allowed by law. He may appoint a political treasurer who then shares that responsibility.
• Candidates and committees (personal, political, or party) are required to file financial statements in all state elections and in all municipal elections in municipalities with more than 20,000 population. All reports must include a listing of expenditures and receipts.

Statements are due eight days before the primary, on or before the tenth day after the primary, eight days before the general election, and ten days after the general election. The statements of candidates and their personal campaign committees must be filed with the officer authorized to issue a certificate of nomination or election or, if there is no such officer, with the clerk of the town, city, or village in which the candidate resides. The statements of state and Congressional campaign committees must be filed with the Secretary of State. Political committees must file financial statements within thirty days after any primary or general election. If the committee is supporting a candidate for federal or statewide office, the report is filed where the candidate files. If the committee relates to a candidate for the state legislature, the state judiciary, or county office, reports are filed with the county auditor. If the committee is established

to support or oppose a constitutional amendment, reports are filed with the Secretary of State.
- No limit is set on individual contributions.
- Expenditure limits are set as follows:

1. for governor, $7,000 and, in addition, five cents for each of the total number of persons who voted in the state at the last general election
2. for other state officers, $3,500 and, in addition, five cents for each of the total number of persons who voted in the state at the last general election
3. for state senator, $800 and, in addition, five cents for each of the total number of persons who voted in the district at the last general election
4. for members of the House of Representatives, $600 and, in addition, five cents for each of the total number of persons who voted in the district at the last general election
5. for federal elections, no expenditure limits.

MISSISSIPPI

OPEN MEETINGS

Mississippi has neither constitutional nor statutory provisions dealing with open meetings. There are certain legislative rules, but these are very limited. Votes of legislative committees are never open to the public, nor are records kept of such votes in any form. While conference committee sessions are frequently announced in advance, they are never open to the public or the press.

No rules, statutes, or constitutional provisions apply to any decision-making body other than the legislature, and in that case only the rules referred to above are relevant.

LOBBYING DISCLOSURE

- The term "lobbyist" is defined as any person or firm attempting to influence actions on any matter pending or any matter that might legally come before either house of the legislature, its committees, or any individual member of the legislature.

• Any person, firm, corporation, or association that employs a lobbyist must file a registration form. No separate form is required of the employee, that is, the lobbyist himself.

• Such registration forms are to be filed with the Secretary of State within five days of the commencement of employment of a lobbyist.

• Registration forms should include the following information:

1. if an individual, his name, place of residence, and place of business
2. if a firm, its full name, its place of business, and the full name and place of residence of each partner
3. if a corporation or association, its full name, principal place of business, whether domestic or foreign, and names and places of residence of each of its officers and directors
4. the nature and kind of his, their, or its business, occupation, or employment
5. the name, residence, occupation, and period of employment of each person employed as a lobbyist
6. the exact subject matter with respect to which the lobbyist is employed.

Within five days of any change, modification, or addition to the above six points, the employer must furnish a statement indicating such change to the Secretary of State.

• Within thirty days of the final adjournment of any legislative session, each person, firm, etc., that has employed a lobbyist and has registered, has paid or expended, or has promised to pay or expend any money or thing of value in relation to any matter pending, or which might legally come before such session, shall file with the Secretary of State a detailed and complete statement of expenses. Every person who receives money to be expended on lobbying activities must also file a statement. Such statements are kept as public records and are open to public inspection. Note that while the individual lobbyist is not required to register at the commencement of his activities, he is required to file a separate financial statement form distinct from that filed by his employer.

• Any person who violates any provision of this act is subject to imprisonment for not more than three years or a fine of not more than $1,000 and imprisonment for not more than six months, or both. Any corporation or association violating this law can be fined not more than $5,000. Prosecution of any individual does not bar the prosecution of a corporation that may have hired that individual.

• Contingent payments are specifically prohibited.

• This statute does not apply to representatives of the news media who meet the definition of lobbyist only in the course of pursuing their professional function, nor does it apply to those who are employed for the purpose of rendering legislative services such as drafting, nor does it apply to any persons who appear before the legislature only in response to a written invitation from that legislature or its committees, nor to representatives of state institutions, nor to individuals acting in their behalf, nor to representatives of subdivisions of the state.

CONFLICTS OF INTEREST

• No comprehensive conflict of interest statute exists in the Mississippi codes.

• The only provisions that do exist are constitutional provisions prohibiting bribery or the accepting of bribes and requiring that all laws granting a donation or gratuity in favor of any person or object shall be enacted only with two-thirds of the members of the legislature voting in favor.

CAMPAIGN FINANCE

• This law applies to any candidate for state, county, or district office at any time when such candidate's name is presented for consideration by the electorate.

• Only candidates are responsible for expenditures, and they are required to file contribution and expenditure statements.

• Reports of contributions of $500 or more are required on the

fifth day of every month during the campaign and on the Saturday before election day. Reports of expenses over $250 must be filed within sixty days after the election. Statements are filed with the Secretary of State or with the circuit clerk.
• There are no limits on individual contributions. All expenditure limits were repealed in a new election law of 1971.
• Corporate as well as most other contributions to judicial candidates are prohibited during the primary elections. No other prohibition exists on corporate or labor union contributions.
• There are no penalty or enforcement provisions.

MISSOURI

OPEN MEETINGS

Missouri has no statutes dealing with open meetings. A constitutional provision, however, requires that votes on final passage in the legislature be open to the public and that roll call votes be taken on constitutional amendments. No requirement is made, however, that votes on procedural motions or amendments in the legislature be open. Committee votes are never open to the public. Votes are recorded by aggregate only, not by individual. Conference committee sessions are never announced in advance and are never open to the public or the press.

No constitutional provisions, statutes, or rules require any open meetings of the executive, administrative, or judicial branches of government.

LOBBYING DISCLOSURE

• The term "lobbyist" is not specifically defined in the statute but is generally interpreted to mean any person who engages himself for pay or any other valuable consideration for the purpose of attempting to influence the passage or defeat of any legislation by the General Assembly, or who expends money for such purposes.
• All lobbyists must register. No separate registration requirement is made of employers of lobbyists. Registration is with the

Chief Clerk of the House and the Secretary of the Senate and must be filed within ten days after the commencement of lobbying activities.

• Such registration must include the name of the lobbyist registering and his business address, the name and address of his employer or employers, and the expected duration of his employment.

• Each person registered must, within ten days after each regular or special session of the General Assembly, file with the Chief Clerk and Secretary a detailed report showing expenses involved in carrying out his work; to whom payments were made by the lobbyist; for what purposes those payments were made; the names of any publications in which he has caused anything to be published; and the proposed legislation he is employed to support or oppose. A report containing the same information, covering the period from the day the regular session closes until the convening of the next regular session, must be filed within thirty days after the convening of any regular session. All this information is open to public inspection until the convening of the next regular session.

• The Clerk of the House and the Secretary of the Senate are responsible for supervising and enforcing this statute. Failure to comply with provisions of this statute is a misdemeanor punishable by fine of not more than $500 and/or imprisonment for not more than one year.

CONFLICTS OF INTEREST

• The conflict of interest statute applies to the governor, the lieutenant governor, and any legislator. Separate statutory provisions apply to any officer or employee of an "agency." An agency is defined as any department, office, board, commission, bureau, institution, or any other agency except the legislative and judicial branches of the state or any political subdivision of the state.

• If the governor, lieutenant governor, or any legislator has a substantial interest in any measure or bill, proposed or pending before the General Assembly, he must, before passing on the bill or measure, file a written report of the nature of that interest with the Chief Clerk of the House and the Secretary of the Senate, and that statement is recorded in the Journal. Rather than filing a statement on each measure or bill, these individuals may file a statement disclosing their "substantial" financial interest at any time during the legislative session. Substantial interest is defined as holding a 10 per cent or greater interest in any business entity, or having an interest whose value is $10,000 or more, or an interest that results in a compensation or remuneration of $6,000 or more in a given year. No similar disclosure requirements apply to officers or employees of any agency of the State of Missouri.

• No officer or employee of an agency shall transact any business in his official capacity with any business entity with which he is associated or owns a substantial interest; nor shall he make an investment that might create a substantial conflict; nor shall he or any business entity with which he is associated sell any goods or services to any business entity licensed or regulated by the agency in which the officer or employee serves. Note especially the prohibition against the acquisition of conflicting interests. Such prohibition, which here applies to officers or employees of an agency, is not extended to apply to either members of the executive or members of the legislative branch.

• No officer or employee of an agency shall transact business with any person or entity that has a matter upon which the officer or employee will be called to render a decision or pass judgment. If he is already involved in the business transaction when the matter arises, he shall be disqualified from rendering any decision. Note especially here the requirement that an individual be disqualified if a conflict of interest exists. No similar mandatory self-disqualification exists with respect to members of the legislative or executive branch of the Missouri government.

• No person who has served as an officer or employee of an agency shall, within a period of two years after the termination of the service or employment, appear before the agency or receive compensation for services previously rendered.

• While penalty provisions are included with each section of this statute, no particular enforcing agent is identified. It must be assumed, therefore, that violations of this statute will be dealt with in the same manner as would be violations of any other portions of the Missouri State Codes.

CAMPAIGN FINANCE

Chapter 129 of the Revised Statutes of Missouri is entitled "Corrupt Practices and Offenses Relating to Registration and Elections."

• This law applies to candidates in state elections at all levels and to candidates for Congress. All primary, general, and special elections are covered, including measures submitted to the vote of the people.

• Both candidates and campaign committees are responsible for expeditures. Each campaign committee must appoint a treasurer to receive and disburse money.

• Candidates and treasurers of political committees are required to file contribution and expenditure statements. Committee statements include both receipts and disbursements; candidate statements must only include disbursements.

• Reports are due thirty days after each election. Statements are to be filed with the officer required by law to issue certificates of election or commissions as the result of elections. Each candidate must file a duplicate with the recorder of deeds for the county in which he resides.

• No limit is set on individual campaign contributions.

• Expenditure limits are set at $25 for each 100 votes cast for all candidates for President in the state, county, district, or municipality in the last Presidential election. Expenditures up to the limit may be made in both the primary and the general election campaigns.

• Corporations are specifically prohibited from making contributions. No similar prohibition exists for labor unions.

• Any person failing to file the required statements is liable to a fine, to be recovered in action brought by the Attorney General or by the prosecuting attorney of the county of the candidate's residence. No person will be allowed to take office until the required statements are filed.

MONTANA

OPEN MEETINGS

• Voting in the legislature is never open; conference committees are always closed; committees never vote in open session; and votes are not recorded by individual, nor are they available in aggregate. The Constitution provides only the weakest kind of antisecrecy provisions with respect to the legislature. Article 5, Section 13, sets the requirement for open meetings as follows: "The session of each house and of the committees of the whole shall be open unless the business is such as requires secrecy." Clearly this is no open meetings provision at all.

• All meetings of public or governmental bodies, boards, bureaus, commissions, or agencies of the state or any political subdivision of the state are covered by a separate house statute. These bodies must be open to the public except as otherwise specified in law or except in cases where the meetings involve or affect any of the following:

1. national or state security
2. the disciplining of a public officer or employee or the hearing of any complaint with respect to an officer or employee
3. the employment, appointment, promotion, dismissal, demotion, or resignation of any public officer or employee
4. the purchasing of any public property, the investing of public funds, or other matters involving competition or bargaining
5. the revocation of a license of any person licensed under the laws of the state
6. law enforcement, crime prevention, probation, or parole.

Clearly these exemptions are sufficiently broad and may be interpreted sufficiently liberally to effectively dilute the intent of the open meetings statute.

LOBBYING DISCLOSURE

• A new Montana law requires that all lobbyists register before the commencement of lobbying activities. Information required at the time of registration includes the name and address of the lobbyist and his employer and the nature of the issues on which the lobbyist will be active.

• The lobbyist, but not his employer, is required to make a financial statement listing income and expenditures related to lobbying activities. Failure to file such a report results in possible forfeiture of lobbyist registration. Delinquent lobbyists may re-register as soon as the necessary past due statements have been filed.

CONFLICTS OF INTEREST

No law.

CAMPAIGN FINANCE

• This law applies to any candidate whose name is printed on an official ballot for public office, with his consent, for nomination or election. Special elections are not specifically mentioned.

• Candidates, political committees, and political agents are all responsible for expenditures. Current law requires that candidates, committees, and others file statements of contributions received and expenditures disbursed. This requirement applies to both primary and general elections.

• Candidates must file reports fifteen days after each election. Statements are filed with the Secretary of State.

• No limit is set on individual contributions, although all those contributing in excess of $50 must file statements describing such contributions.

• Campaign expenditure limits are set as a percentage of the annual salary of the office sought: 15 per cent of the annual salary is the limit for primary elections and 10 per cent for general elections. This sets campaign limits at an unreasonably low level and encourages violations.

• Corporate contributions to campaigns are prohibited. No prohibition exists on contributions by labor unions.

• Deprivation of nomination or office and, in some cases, a

monetary fine are the penalties for failure to file or for illegal or excessive expenditures. No citizen standing provision exists in the law, so state officials are the sole enforcers.

• The penalty for violation is a fine or imprisonment or both, plus forfeiture of the office for the term of that office with respect to which the election was held. In cases where the person convicted was elected to either house of the state or federal legislature, the court does not declare him ineligible to hold office but sends a certificate setting forth the adjudication of guilt to the presiding officer of the body concerned. A candidate whose election has been annulled for violating the act may not be appointed or elected to fill a vacancy in the office occurring during that term of office.

• Corporate contributions are prohibited, and corporations may be penalized for making such contributions.

NEBRASKA

Open Meetings

The state legislature holds its deliberations and votes in open session. Committees of the state legislature may vote in private session, but the record of such vote is made public. The legislature may take voice votes on procedural motions and amendments. Votes conducted in legislative committees, while recorded and made public, are recorded only by aggregate, not by individual.

A separate legislative act requires open meetings of government bodies in the executive department and of independent boards, commissions, and bureaus that exercise legislative, executive, or administrative powers or are supported in whole or in part by public funds. Any of these groups must meet in a public building, and the meetings must be open to the public. Any of these groups may go into executive session, however, upon a majority vote of the body. Any vote to close the session must be held in open session. No formal action of any type, including the expenditure of funds, may be made in closed session.

LOBBYING DISCLOSURE

• Lobbying is defined as promoting or opposing legislation or promoting or opposing executive approval of legislation. A lobbyist is any person who engages in lobbying for hire.

• Both the lobbyist and his employer are required to register when the lobbying activities of an employed lobbyist begin. Registration is with the Clerk of the Legislature.

• It is mandatory that both the lobbyist and his employer file monthly statements showing expenditures, gifts, loans, etc. The legislature may require additional details at any time. The frequency of required reports and the requirement that both lobbyist and employer file reports make Nebraska's statute one of the most stringent in the country.

• The Attorney General of Nebraska is responsible for prosecuting violators of provisions of this statute, but the Legislative Committee may cancel the registration of any lobbyist after a hearing if it believes that the lobbyist has been involved in corrupt practices. Penalties for violating provisions of this statute are up to six months in prison or a fine of up to $500, or both.

• The employer of a lobbyist must sign a statement that no compensation will be paid contingent upon the outcome of any legislation.

CONFLICTS OF INTEREST

• The only comprehensive statewide provision dealing with conflicts of interest is found in the Constitution. No comprehensive statutory provisions exist. A mass of conflict of interest regulations can be found in specific legislation bearing on one subset of public officials or another. For instance, a prohibition of conflicts is found in regulations empowering zoning boards, school boards, and other local boards and commissions.

• Such constitutional provisions as exist prohibit the maintainance of conflicting employment by state legislators. No person holding office under the authority of the United States or holding any other position from which monetary income may be derived is eligible to take a seat in the state legislature until such conflicting employment is eliminated. Exempt from this provision are holders of township offices, justices of the peace, notary publics, and officers of the militia. Likewise, no member of the state legislature is eligible to receive any civil appointment to a state office while still holding his legislative position.

CAMPAIGN FINANCE

• This law applies to all statewide primary and general elections. It also applies to committees formed in support or of opposition to any measure submitted to the voters.
• Candidates are not required to have a treasurer and are responsible for their own expenditures. Every political committee is required to appoint a treasurer who is responsible for expenditures.
• Both candidates and committee treasurers must file a statement of contributions and expenditures. Individual contributions aggregating more than $100 must be indicated.
• Candidates must report within ten days after an election. Treasurers must file reports fifteen days before each election and within twenty days after each election. Statements are filed in the same office in which the nomination certificate or petition of the candidate is filed.
• There is a $1,000 limit on individual contributions.
• There are no spending limits.
• There is a specific provision allowing corporations to contribute to any candidate or committee (no limit). Within five days of making a contribution, the corporation must file a statement so indicating with the Secretary of State. No contributions may be made six days prior to or after the election. The penalty for a first-offense violation is a fine of $500 to $2,000 and cancelation of the corporation's charter or, if from another state, forfeiture of its right to do business in the state. The Attorney General is to prosecute violators.
• The filing of a statement is a prerequisite for certification of nomination or election. The penalty for failure to file is a fine.
• Any eligible voter may bring charges of violation or falsification in the filing of the statement against any public official (other

than a state legislator or U.S. Representative) by presenting the charges in writing to the Attorney General. It is the duty of the Attorney General to begin action within ten days. If the Attorney General does not take action within that time, the individual can bring the action at his own expense. If the public official is found guilty, he must vacate the office.
• For failure to submit a statement, a committee treasurer can be found guilty of a misdemeanor and fined.

NEVADA

Open Meetings

No provision—constitutional, statutory, or in the rules—requires that meetings of the Nevada State Legislature be open or that votes be taken in open session. As a matter of course, though, deliberations of both the legislature and its committees are open. This is not, however, a matter of law.

Meetings of all public agencies, commissions, bureaus, departments, and boards must be open to the public unless the matter discussed relates to personnel or to the disciplining of a public officer or employee. In those cases, executive sessions are permissible. This is the only specific exemption permitted from the standard open meetings provisions governing these bodies.

Separate sections of the Nevada State Statutes require open meetings of county governments, city governments, the Board of Regents of the University of Nevada, and local administrative organizations, such as school boards.

Lobbying Disclosure

No law.

Conflicts of Interest

No law.

Campaign Finance

No law.

NEW HAMPSHIRE

OPEN MEETINGS

State law requires that all meetings of state boards, commissions, and authorities and meetings of boards of subdivisions of the state be open as a general rule. However, executive sessions are permitted at the discretion of the committee, the only requirements being that a record be kept of proceedings of those sessions and be made available for public inspection, and that no ordinances, rules, resolutions, contracts, appointments, or official actions be finally approved in executive session. As in other states, this expansive exemption for executive sessions permits groups to make substantive decisions in private and then provides public exposure only to pro forma ratification of these decisions. Final votes are permitted in executive session only on personnel matters.

None of the provisions with respect to executive sessions applies to the state legislature. As a result, votes of committees are seldom conducted in the open. Such votes as are conducted in private are recorded by aggregate only, not by individual, and are available from the committee chairman or the secretary or clerk. Conference committee sessions are seldom announced in advance and are seldom open to the public.

LOBBYING DISCLOSURE

• A lobbyist, also called in this statute a legislative agent or counsel, is any person who shall be employed for consideration by any other person to promote or oppose legislation before the general court.
• Such lobbyist shall be required to register at the time of the commencement of his activities. No separate requirement is made with respect to the employers of lobbyists.
• Such registration is to be filed with the Secretary of State and maintained by him in open record.
• Registration shall include the following:

  1. the full name of employers and employed

2. their respective residences
3. the normal primary occupation of each individual listed
4. the date and character of employment, with duration of that employment, if known
5. the subjects of the legislation to which the employment relates.

Changes in the information provided at the time of registration must be indicated to the Secretary of State.

• Within thirty days after the prorogation of the legislature, each such legislative agent, counsel, or employee who has registered shall file with the Secretary of State a statement itemizing his fees and expenditures in connection with his legislative employment, and by whom, or to whom, those fees were paid or charged.

• Violators of this statute shall be fined not more than $1,000 and whoever shall make and file any statement under this statute that is to his knowledge false shall be deemed guilty of perjury and shall be punished by the laws of the State of New Hampshire. The Attorney General shall be responsible for enforcement of this statute.

CONFLICTS OF INTEREST

• Statute C.45 governs conflict of interest by public officials. This is one of the weakest conflict of interest laws on the books. It permits the promulgation of codes of ethics to govern executive officials and employees but does little more.

• No state statute prohibits the acquisition of conflicting interests, the maintenance of conflicting employment, the receipt of gifts, loans, or favors, or the receipt of extra or additional compensation from nonstate sources.

• No state law requires the disclosure of financial interests by any public official.

CAMPAIGN FINANCE

• This law applies to any general, special, or primary election except Presidential preference and delegate primaries and to any person seeking public office. It also applies to measures before the people.

• The political committee treasurer and the candidate's financial agent (who may be the candidate himself) are responsible for all expenditures.

• The state committee of a political party must file an itemized statement of receipts and expenditures. Major candidates (governor, Presidential elector, U.S. senator, representative) must file the same statements as state committees. Other candidates who spend in excess of $200 shall file a like statement.

• State party committees and major candidates file not later than 5:00 P.M. of the Wednesday preceding a biennial or special election and again not later than 5:00 P.M. the second Friday after the election. Filing is with the Secretary of State.

Other candidates file not later than 5:00 P.M. the second Friday after a primary or general election. Filing is with the Secretary of State and with the town or city clerk.

Political committees file no later than 5:00 P.M. the Wednesday preceding an election and again no later than 5:00 P.M. the second Friday after an election. Filing is with the Secretary of State.

• There is a limit of $5,000 on contributions per person (except a candidate in his own behalf).

• Spending limits are set as follows:

In a primary by or on behalf of a candidate:
  for governor, U.S. senator or representative, governor's counselor, county officer, or state senator—15 cents times the number of voters who were qualified to vote for the office the candidate seeks at the last preceding biennial election;
  for state representative (to the general court)—$500.
In general or special elections:
  by or on behalf a candidate—same amounts;
  by political party committees—not more than $1 times the number of voters in the state who were eligible to vote in the last biennial election.

• Groups prohibited from making campaign contributions include corporations, partnerships, labor unions, or any person employed in the classified service of the state.

• Any candidate or any person voting may file complaints with the Attorney General of suspected violations. The Attorney General must investigate and prosecute if a violation appears to have occurred.

No candidate is entiled to nomination or election until proper statements are filed.

Penalty for violation is fine and/or imprisonment.

NEW JERSEY

OPEN MEETINGS

While New Jersey has an open meetings statute, both the executive and legislative branches are exempt from its provisions, and sufficient exceptions exist by which executive sessions may be called as to render the statute virtually meaningless. Technically, the statute requires that all meetings of public bodies covered by the act at which an official action (that is, anything at which a determination is by vote) is taken must be held in open session. Executive sessions are permitted on such easy terms, however, that this is an ineffectual regulation.

Since the statute described above does not apply to the legislature, and since legislative rules in the area of open meetings are extremely weak, votes of legislative committees are never made public, nor are records kept of such votes either in the aggregate or by individual. The legislature as a whole votes in the open only on the final passage of bills as a matter of course. Procedural motions and amendments in the legislature may be recorded by roll call vote on request of five members of the legislature. The state Senate holds all of its deliberations and votes in closed session when considering gubernatorial nominations.

LOBBYING DISCLOSURE

• In lieu of the term "lobbyist," New Jersey statutes refer to a "legislative agent." He is defined as any person who receives compensation, including reimbursement for expenses, exceeding $100 in any three-month period to influence legislation by communication, personally or through any intermediary, to the legislature or the governor or his staff, or who holds himself out as engaging in the business of influencing legislation by such means, or who, incidental to his regular employment, engages in influencing legislation, unless his activities are isolated, exceptional, or infrequent.

The term "governor or his staff" includes the governor, secretary to the governor, counsel to the governor, and all other employees of the chief executive's office. The term "infrequent" is considered to mean fewer than twenty hours or less than 1 per cent of the time the individual spends working at his regular employment, whichever is less, during any calendar year. "Exceptional" refers to such activities as are not contemplated by his employment and are limited to less than three items of legislation in any two-year legislative term. "Isolated" means limited to one appearance before the legislature or the governor or his staff or to one item of legislation during any two-year legislative term. These definitions of terms are those commonly used by the Attorney General in the pursuance of his responsibilities to enforce this statute.

• Only the legislative agent is required to register. The employer of such an agent is not required to make any registration whatever.

• Registration is required within thirty days of the date of employment and should be filed with the Attorney General.

• If the legislative agent receives compensation from more than one person, he must file a separate notice of representation for each person.

• Every legislative agent is required to file with the Attorney General a quarterly report of his activities. That report is due between the first and tenth days of each calendar quarter. This is not, however, a statement of expenses. It includes, instead, a description of legislation on which the legislative agent has been active and an updating of any information required at the time of registration.

• Any person who is required to register with the Attorney General must keep and preserve for three years any records of financial transactions related to activities as a legislative agent. This does not apply to persons receiving less than $500 in compensation in any quarterly period.

• Failure to comply with any provision of this act is a misdemeanor. The Attorney General is the state official responsible for supervising and enforcing this statute.

• Additional responsibilities of the Attorney General with respect to this statute include:

1. to permit public inspection of statements filed under this act
2. to compile and summarize information filed and reported to the legislature and the governor
3. to give notice when statements are not filed on time
4. to investigate and prosecute violations
5. to report on the administration of this act and make suggestions and recommendations for its modification
6. to compile and publish at least once a month a list of all legislative agents registered.

CONFLICTS OF INTEREST

• The provisions of this statute apply to state officers and employees and members of the state legislature.

• No provision of this statute requires the public disclosure of financial holdings by any public official. The current governor of the State of New Jersey has required members of his cabinet to make voluntary financial statements available to the press, but this is a matter of custom, not a matter of law.

• No provision of this statute requires that any individual divest himself of any real or potential conflict of interest.

• No individual covered by the provisions of this statute may accept any gift or any other thing of value that he knows or has reason to believe is offered to him with the intent to influence him in the performance of his public duties and responsibilities.

• No member of the state legislature or state officer or employee may accept any additional compensation for work performed in the course of his official responsibility.

• Individuals covered by the provisions of this statute are prohibited from making certain representations before state regulatory agencies or participating in certain contract or agreement bidding with state agencies.

• This statute establishes a Joint Legislative Committee on Ethical Standards, which is responsible for supervising the provisions of the statute and making any advisory opinions that may be requested by any individual covered by any of the provisions of the statute. Additionally, the joint committee has the jurisdiction to initiate or review complaints regarding any violations of the provisions of this statute or of the code of ethics. In contrast to similar commissions in other states, the New Jersey Joint Legislative Committee on Ethical Standards does have the power to fine, or if necessary remove from office, or remove from employment of the state for a period of not more than one year, any individual whom they find to be in violation of the provisions of this statute.

• Also included in the statute is a code of ethics, which lists seven additional prohibitions with respect to officers or employees of state agencies. This code does not apply to state legislators. A state legislator is covered by the code of ethics included in the rules of his own chamber of the legislature.

CAMPAIGN FINANCE

• The law covers primary, general, municipal, or special elections but does not apply to special issues or questions. It includes federal, statewide, and local elections of any candidates allowed to spend more than $500 in campaign. Those candidates prohibited from spending more than $500 are not required to file or to have a campaign manager.

• The campaign manager (who may be candidate himself) must file financial statements. When the manager is someone other than the candidate, the candidate must file an affidavit of his statements. Every candidate allowed to spend more than $500 also must name a depository, which must file a statement after the election.

• Both expenditures and contributions are required in statements, including the names of *all* donors and amounts of *all* individual contributions.

• Statements are to be filed with the officer with whom the candidate is required to file his acceptance of nomination. The campaign managers' statements must be filed on the Friday or Saturday next preceding the primary or election and within twenty days after the primary or election. With each of these statements the candidate must file an affidavit, unless, of course, he is acting as his own manager. Additionally, the cashier or treasurer of the candidate's selected depository shall file, within twenty days after any primary, general, municipal, or special election, all of the deposit slips to and withdrawal vouchers from the campaign account, in chronological order.

• There is no limit on individual campaign contributions.

• All expenditure limits were repealed by laws 1969, ch. 192, Sec. 2.

• Corporations are prohibited from making campaign contributions. No similar prohibition exists for labor unions.

• Violation of this title is a misdemeanor. In addition to penalties for committing a misdemeanor, the offender may be subject to disenfranchisement and disqualification to hold any office of trust or profit for a length of time the court deems proper.

NEW MEXICO

OPEN MEETINGS

• The legislature always holds its deliberations and votes in open session. Roll call votes are published in the Journal of the Senate and House and appear separately in a voting record published at the end of each legislative session. Committees are generally open by custom, but no rule or law governs them. Voting is generally open but not recorded. There are no set requirements as to what conditions a committee must meet before it goes into executive session. Members of a committee meet privately and decide whether or not an executive session is justified. The record of New Mexico is that such closed sessions are rarely held. The full legislature votes on final passage of bills in open session, and the

votes are recorded. Votes on procedural motions and amendments are also open, and any one legislator may ask for a roll call vote.
• A separate New Mexico statute governs the open meeting of state bodies and bodies of its political subdivisions. Under this law administrative agencies, commissions, etc., may go into executive session, but no final action may be taken in such session. Votes must be open and recorded. Commissions are expected to keep minutes of all meetings and make them available to the public, but they are rarely published.

Lobbying Disclosure

• A lobbyist is defined as any person who, with compensation, promotes or opposes passage of any legislation, or any person whose duties as employee of another person include attempts to influence the passage of any legislation. All lobbyists are required to register annually. Employers of lobbyists are not required to file separate registrations. Registration is with the Secretary of State, who provides forms and maintains a file of registration forms returned for a period of four years. Bimonthly, while the Legislature and Senate are in session, he shall furnish copies of registration to the chief clerks of the House and the Senate and to the legislative counsel. Copies furnished shall be cumulative throughout the session. Registration forms shall require the name and address of the registering lobbyist, the name and address of the person employing this lobbyist, and a brief description of the legislation in reference to which the lobbyist's service is rendered.
• Neither the lobbyist nor his employer is required to make financial statements disclosing sources of income or expenditures related to lobbying activities.
• The statute has no provision whatever for enforcement, although any violation of the statute is considered a petty misdemeanor.
• Contingent payments are specifically prohibited.
• Anyone who, without compensation, seeks approval or veto of legislation by the governor and who performs no acts which would qualify him as a lobbyist, is exempt from the requirements of this statute.

CONFLICTS OF INTEREST

• The general statute applies to employees and officials of state agencies but specifically exempts legislators and judges.

• An employee who has a financial interest which he believes or has reason to believe may be affected by actions of the state agency by which he is employed must disclose the precise nature and dollar value of the financial interest to the Secretary of State of New Mexico in January of each year. A legislator who has a financial interest of $10,000 or more in a business regulated by official act of the State of New Mexico must make that business interest public in the manner required of employees.

• All information filed with the Secretary of State as required by these financial disclosure statements is a matter of public record except the dollar values included in the disclosures. Valuation is confidential except during official removal or impeachment proceedings. Compliance with this disclosure provision is a condition of entering upon and continuing in state employment.

• No state statute requires the divestment of real or potential conflicts of interest. An employee is prohibited, however, from acquiring new financial interests that are directly affected by the employee's official actions.

• No legislator or employee is permitted to use confidential information acquired in the course of his official responsibilities for personal gain. As a general rule, an employee of a state agency is required to disqualify himself from taking actions if he has a personal financial interest in the action being taken. This requirement may be waived by the governor, however, if the exception and the reasons for the exception are made clear in writing. This self-disqualification requirement does not apply to either legislators or judges.

• The Attorney General is responsible for overseeing enforcement of this statute. If he finds cause to file complaint against a legislator or any other employee removable by impeachment he refers the complaint to the House of Representatives of the state legislature. If nothing is done after he files the complaint, the Attorney General may make his charges public.

CAMPAIGN FINANCE

• This law applies to candidates in all primary, general, and special elections, including any proposal submitted to the voters.
• Candidates are responsible for their own expenditures. Only political committees are required to appoint treasurers.
• A candidate is required to file a statement of expenditures only. The treasurer of a political committee must file a statement of all receipts and disbursements.
• The statement of a candidate is due within ten days after an election and is filed, for primary elections, with the officer with whom the candidate's declaration of candidacy was filed. For general and special elections, the statement is filed with the Secretary of State, except in the case of a candidate for county office, who files with the county clerk. The statement of a political committee, filed by the treasurer, is due within thirty days after the relevant election and is filed with the Secretary of State, except in county elections, in which case the statement is filed with the county clerk.
• There is no individual contribution limit. There are no spending limits. There are no prohibitions on corporate or labor union contributions.
• Failure or refusal to file the required statements is a petty misdemeanor. No candidate is issued a certificate of nomination or election, nor is his name printed on the ballot nor is he allowed to take office, until all necessary statements are filed.

NEW YORK

OPEN MEETINGS

State statute requires that all public boards and commissions of any state agency or authority or of any agency or authority of a political subdivision of the state meet in open session and that no resolution, rule, regulation, or formal action shall be considered binding unless taken in open session. This statute does not apply to either the legislative branch of government or the executive branch, except as an executive branch may have commissions or state agencies. As a result, legislative committees rarely vote in open session. When votes are taken behind closed doors they are recorded by aggregate only, not by individual. Such voting records are available for the use of any legislator only and are not available to the public in any form. Conference committee sessions are seldom announced in advance and are never open to the public or the press. In addition, both the majority and minority parties of the state legislature regularly hold closed caucuses at which party policy is decided. These sessions are never open to the public.

LOBBYING DISCLOSURE

• In lieu of the word "lobbyist," New York statutes refer to "legislative counsels" and "legislative agents." These individuals are defined as being active in attempts to influence legislative action or executive action in regard to the passage or veto of legislative matters.
• The legislative counsels or legislative agents must file registration forms. No similar requirement is made with respect to the employers of agents or counsels. Forms must be filed with the Secretary of State at the commencement of lobbying activities and must include the names of any and all employers of the counsels or agents registering together with a brief description of legislation on which the agent or council will be lobbying.
• The employers of registered agents or counsels must file within two months after the date of adjournment of each legislative session a sworn, itemized statement that details all expenses paid, incurred, or directly or indirectly promised in connection with legislation pending as of the last session. This information must include the names of payees and the amount paid to each, including all disbursements paid, incurred, or promised to counsels or agents. It must specify the nature of the legislation toward which the expenditures were made and the interest of the employer in that legislation.
• Violation of these statutes is a misdemeanor punishable in the case of an individual by imprisonment of not more than one year or a fine of not more than $1,000 or both. In addition to these

penalties, any corporation or association failing to file the statements of legislative expenses within the time required shall forfeit to the state $100 per day for each day after the expiration
of two months within which the statement has not been filed.
The Attorney General of the State of New York is responsible
for enforcing these statutes.

CONFLICTS OF INTEREST

• The provisions of this statute, which call for prohibitions of
certain categories of activity, apply to members of the legislature,
legislative employees, and officers and employees of any state
agency.

• Only members of the legislature or legislative employees are
required to file a financial disclosure statement on or after December 15 and before the following January 15 of each year.
Members or employees of the Senate shall file these statements
with the Clerk of the Assembly. Statements should include the
following information:

1. each financial interest, direct or indirect, of himself or his
   immediate family, that is subject to the jurisdiction of a
   regulatory agency
2. every office and directorship held by him in any corporation,
   firm, or enterprise subject to the jurisdiction of a regulatory
   agency, including the name of the corporation, firm, or
   enterprise
3. any other interest or relationship that he determines in his
   discretion might reasonably be expected to be particularly
   affected by legislative action or should be disclosed in the
   public interest.

It is clear that substantial discretion is left with the individual
filing these annual statements. Whole categories of financial
holdings that may not be supervised by regulatory agencies are
exempted and would not appear on these statements. Also, the
general language of the third provision is so broad as to allow
total discretion on the part of the individual filing the statement.

• No requirement is made that any individual filing this state-

ment or any other individual covered by any other provision of
this statute divest himself of any real or potential conflicts of
interest.
• Certain outright prohibitions apply to all the individuals covered by any other provision of this statute.

  1. individuals covered may not receive additional compensation
     for work that is part of his official responsibilities
  2. no individual covered may accept any gift in value of more
     than $25 that he believes is intended to influence him in the
     course of this official decision-making
  3. no individual covered can enter into any agreement by
     which he will receive payment contingent upon the outcome
     of an official decision of the state.

• The New York statute also includes a general code of ethics,
setting nine standards, which all individuals covered by the provisions of the statute are expected to obey. Penalty provisions are
included, but no specific enforcing agent is listed. It may be
assumed that the state legislature is expected to perform a self-
policing function, since employees of that legislature, namely the
Clerk of the Assembly and the Secretary of the Senate, are the
individuals who receive the financial statements that are required
of both legislators and legislative employees.

CAMPAIGN FINANCE

• This law applies to any candidate for public office in any primary, general, or special election, including any proposition submitted to vote at a public election.
• Both the treasurer and the candidate are required to file sworn
financial statements of receipts, contributions, and expenditures.
Statements must be filed on the tenth day before the election
and within twenty days after the election. If debts are still out-
standing twenty days after the election, a final statement is required later. If the debt extends past the next January 2, the
filing of a statement each January 2 is required until the report is
complete.
• Candidates file as follows:

1. with the Secretary of State, if running for office in an area greater than a county or greater than the City of New York
2. with the New York City Board of Elections, if running for an office to be filled by vote of all or part of the voters of the City of New York
3. with the county board of elections, if running for an office to be voted for by all the voters of the candidate's county
4. if running for a city, town, or village office (other than in the City of New York), with the city, town, or village clerk, respectively.

Every candidate must file the required statements, except that the statements need not be filed by a candidate for party position at a primary if he expended nothing or if his only expenditures were for personal expenses in a sum not exceeding $10.

• Committee reports must be filed with the Secretary of State. Duplicate statements are also required to be filed in the office of the New York City Board of Elections if the committee aids or takes part solely in the election or defeat of a candidate voted for only within the City of New York.

• No limit is set on individual contributions.

• Limits are set on campaign spending as follows:

1. primary for party position—
   ten cents for each voter registered in the candidate's party in the political subdivision in which he is a candidate;
2. primary for nomination for public office—
   $2,500 if the total number of voters enrolled in the candidate's party in his potential constituency is 25,000 or fewer; if more voters are so enrolled, the candidate may spend an additional $10 for each 100 additional voters. If the primary is statewide, the limit is set at ten cents for each enrolled party member in the state;
3. general or special elections—
   If the total number of votes cast for governor from the potential constituency of the candidate was 50,000 or fewer, the candidate is permitted to spend $5,000. For each additional 100 votes cast the candidate may spend an additional $10.

• Violation of the provisions of this law is a misdemeanor.

NORTH CAROLINA

OPEN MEETINGS

• Separate statutes require that municipal governing bodies conduct their business in open session and that administrative boards of the state hold open meetings. Full and accurate journals of the proceedings of each of these groups shall be kept and shall be open to inspection by any qualified voter. Executive sessions may be called by any of the bodies specified above by a majority of the members present when considering the following: acquisition, lease, or alienation of property; negotiation between public employers and their employees; matters dealing with patients, employees, or medical staffs of hospitals or medical clinics, or any matter coming within a privileged relationship; and conferences with legal counsels relating to judicial actions in which a body is directly affected. Clearly, the conditions under which executive sessions may be called are sufficiently broad to permit bodies to circumvent the intent of the open meetings statute if they so desire.
• North Carolina legislative committees always meet in open session. Votes taken in an open committee session are available at the end of the session from the committee chairman.

LOBBYING DISCLOSURE

• In lieu of "lobbyists," "legislative agents" and "legislative counsels" are used. Counsels or agents are individuals who attempt to promote or oppose any legislation affecting any pecuniary interest.
• Every person, corporation, or association that employs any person to act as counsel or agent must within one week of such employment register the name of that person on the appropriate legislative docket. The legislative docket is maintained by the Secretary of State and is open to public inspection.
• Information required at the time of registration includes the names, occupation or business, and business address of the em-

ployer; the name, residence, and occupation of the person employed; the date of employment or agreement; the length of time employment is to continue; and the subjects of legislation to which the employment relates. Within ten days of entering his name on the docket, a legislative counsel or agent must file a written authorization signed by his employer authorizing him to act as counsel or agent in the employer's behalf.

• Each person, corporation, or association whose name appears on the docket of a given session must, within thirty days after final adjournment of that session, file a detailed statement of all expenses paid or incurred in connection with promoting or opposing legislation. Such statements are open to the public.

• Violation of this law is a misdemeanor punishable by fine of not less than $50 and not more than $1,000 and/or imprisonment not exceeding two years.

• Contingent payments are specifically prohibited.

• Provisions of this statute do not apply to any county, city, or municipality.

CONFLICTS OF INTEREST

No law.

CAMPAIGN FINANCE

• This law applies to primary, general, and special elections, including elections where measures are submitted to a vote of the people.

• Each candidate and the chairman and treasurer of any campaign committee are required to keep detailed and exact account of all contributions and expenditures (including name, address, amount, and date). Every person who receives contributions or makes expenditures on behalf of a candidate or committee must render the candidate or committee a detailed account within five days. An itemized statement (under oath) of all contributions and expenditures for that particular election must be filed by each committee chairman or treasurer. Statements are filed with the Secretary of State (or clerk of the superior court, if a county election) not more than fifteen days or less than ten days before the election and again not more than twenty days after the election. The law states that each candidate must file an itemized statement ten days before and twenty days after a primary election. (There is no mention of requiring a candidate to file a statement before and after general and special elections. Candidates are required to file in the same manner for all elections. This is apparently assumed in this law. North Carolina is in many respects a one-party state, so that after the primary the candidate has already won the election. This omission could present problems in the future and should be checked further.)

• There are no individual contribution limits. There are no spending limits. Contributions by corporations and labor unions are not prohibited.

• Failure to report is a misdemeanor, and a violator is subject to fine or imprisonment or both. The Secretary of State reports violators to the Attorney General, who notifies the proper prosecuting officer, who shall prosecute. There is no citizen's standing.

NORTH DAKOTA

OPEN MEETINGS

• A state statute requires that all meetings of public or governmental bodies, boards, bureaus, commissions, or agencies of the state or any political subdivisions of the state shall be open to the public. A separate constitutional provision, however, covers the state legislature and its committees. All meetings must be open, according to the state statute, except those in which a specific exemption is provided by separate law. These exemptions are numerous and, in the case of school boards, for example, executive sessions are permissible when any discussion is held with relation to a school employee.

• The Constitutional provision bearing on the state legislature is sufficiently vague to permit legislative committees to meet regularly in closed session. Votes that are closed are recorded by aggregate only, not by individual, and are available from the committee chairman, the Secretary or Clerk, or the legislative counsel. Conference committee sessions are seldom announced in advance and seldom open to the public. Meetings of the legislature as a whole are generally open, and votes are generally taken in open session except when the legislature is meeting to consider gubernatorial nominations. In such cases, both deliberations and votes are held in closed session. The committee chairmen of legislative committees are given substantial discretion with respect to both meetings and votes. Either the chairman or a majority of the committee members may request an executive session on either deliberations or votes.

LOBBYING DISCLOSURE

• In lieu of "lobbyists," the terms "legislative counsels" and "agents" are used, defined as any persons who attempt to promote or oppose in any manner the passage of legislation by the Legislative Assembly.

• Any person, corporation, or association that employs for any valuable consideration any person to act as counsel or agent shall within one week enter that person's name on a legislative docket. The person so employed must also enter his name on the docket. Either one can give notification of termination of employment. The Secretary of State prepares and maintains the legislative docket.

• Information required at the time of registration includes:

1. the names of all counsels or agents employed for consideration
2. the name and business address of the employer or employers of a given counsel or agent
3. the name, residence, and occupation of persons employed
4. the date of employment or agreement of employment
5. the length of time the employment is expected to continue
6. the special subject or subjects of legislation to which the employment relates.

As information required in registration changes, it is the responsibility of the employer to make such notification to the Secretary of State as may be necessary to update or correct the record.

- No requirement is made that either employee or employer file financial statements listing either expenditures or incomes derived from lobbying.
- The Attorney General is responsible for the enforcement of this statute. Any person, corporation, or association violating this statute can be fined not less than $200 or more than $500. Any legislative counsel or agent violating the statute shall be fined not less than $100 or more than $1,000 and shall be barred from such activities for three years.
- Contingent payments are specifically prohibited.

CONFLICTS OF INTEREST

No law.

CAMPAIGN FINANCE

- This law applies to all primary and general elections but does not apply to special questions.
- As of June, 1972, North Dakota had no state law requiring disclosures of either campaign contributions or expenditures.
- Expenditure limits are computed on the basis of 15 per cent of the annual salary of the office sought. Separate limits apply to primary and general elections. The limit applies only to expenditures by the candidate or on his behalf with his knowledge and consent.
- Corporations are specifically prohibited from making contributions to campaigns. No similar prohibition exists with respect to labor unions. No law sets a ceiling on individual contributions.

OHIO

OPEN MEETINGS

- All meetings of any board or commission of any state agency or authority and all meetings of any board, commission, or authority of any political subdivision of the state are to be open meetings. No resolution, rule, regulation, or formal action of any kind shall be adopted at any executive session of any such board, commission, agency, or authority. The minutes of a regular or special session or meeting of any of the above boards or agencies must be recorded and made available to the public promptly. No provision is made for calling executive sessions under any circumstances in this act. The act does not appear to apply to either the legislature or portions of the executive branch.

• A separate legislative rule deals with open meetings of the state legislature. All committee meetings are open with records of votes recorded in the journal. Only conference sessions are closed to the public. Votes taken in conference are usually unavailable to the public. Committee votes are recorded both by aggregate and by individual. The legislature itself votes and holds deliberations in open session.

LOBBYING DISCLOSURE

• Lobbyists are defined as individuals who, for compensation, attempt to influence the actions of either house of the General Assembly or the actions of any committee of the General Assembly.

• Only the employer of the lobbyist must register. The employee, that is, the lobbyist, is not required to make separate registration himself. Such registration as is required must be filed with the Secretary of State within one week of the commencement of lobbying activities. Registering employers must supply the name, address, and business of each individual, firm, corporation, or association that participated in or contributed to the hiring of the individual lobbyist. The employer must file separate registration forms for each lobbyist employed. Each form must include a description of the exact subject matter to be dealt with by the lobbyist involved.

• Within thirty days after final adjournment of any session of the General Assembly, any employer must file an itemized statement with the Secretary of State, including the names of the employees and the amounts paid to each and specifying the nature of the matter before the General Assembly on which the lobbyist was active and the interest of the employer in that matter.

• Every individual who receives money for the purpose of influencing legislation must file with the Secretary of State an itemized statement of money received and expended and liabilities incurred with respect to lobbying activities within thirty days after the final adjournment of the General Assembly. Note that this financial statement is required both of the employer and of the lobbyist, despite the fact that lobbying registration is required only of the employer, not of the lobbyist himself.

• The Attorney General is responsible for enforcing the provisions of this statute. Whoever violates this statute is subject to a fine and/or imprisonment.

• Contingent payments are specifically prohibited.

CONFLICTS OF INTEREST

No law.

CAMPAIGN FINANCE

• This law applies to candidates in all primary, general, and special elections. The following provisions apply also to persons, committees, and associations that support or oppose any proposition or issue submitted to the voters.

• There is a provision for the appointment of a treasurer for every committee, association, or group of persons. This apparently does *not* apply to candidates.

• Statements of contributions and expenditures are required from every candidate and campaign committee and every person, committee, association, or group of persons incorporated or unincorporated, including corporations and unions, who received or expended any money in connection with any election. When a candidate is up for nomination or election to a statewide office, the General Assembly or the U.S. Congress, campaign contributions made by registered lobbyists must be identified as such and listed separately. An individual need not file a statement of contributions, the receipt of which must be accounted for by others.

• Statements are due no later than the forty-fifth day after an election and are filed with the Secretary of State in statewide elections.

• Ohio campaign spending limits are as follows: governor, $5,000; U.S. Senate, $5,000; U.S. Representative, $4,000. These limits apply to candidates only. Expenditures by campaign committees or others are not explicitly included in the limit.

• Ohio law prohibits corporate campaign contributions but permits labor unions to contribute. No limit exists on individual contributions.

• The state will not certify the nomination or election of anyone failing to file a report. Such failure also results in the disqualification of the individual from seeking further elected office for a period of five to seven years. Penalty for excessive or illegal expenditure is forfeiture of nomination or election and fine and/or imprisonment. The Secretary of State, who receives all reports, notifies the Attorney General of violation, and he must prosecute. Citizens may present petitions to a court of common pleas, but the election law does not specifically provide for any special procedure for citizens' prosecution in this area.

OKLAHOMA

OPEN MEETINGS

• The only statewide open meetings statute in Oklahoma applies to governing boards of all municipalities located within the State of Oklahoma, the boards of county commissioners of the counties of the State of Oklahoma, the boards of public and higher education in the State of Oklahoma and all other boards, bureaus, and commissions in the state that disburse public funds. All the groups to which this law applies must meet in open session on all occasions except to discuss any individual for employment or appointment. In such cases the meetings may be closed, but votes and final action on such personnel matters must also be held in open session.

• The state legislature under legislative rules holds its deliberations and votes in open session. Legislative committees generally vote in open session. The House committees have no provision for closing legislative committee sessions, while Senate committee sessions may be closed by a majority voice vote. Votes taken in closed committees are recorded by aggregate only, not by individual, and are available from the Clerk or the Secretary.

LOBBYING DISCLOSURE

Oklahoma has no lobbying statute of the standard kind. Neither lobbyists nor employers are required to register in any systematic way, nor is either group required to file financial statements indicating expenditures or incomes related to lobbying. There are, moreover, no standard enforcement procedures in Oklahoma statutes with respect to lobbying activities. Oklahoma law does require the following:

1. If any person shall in any manner privately attempt to influence the act or vote of any member of the state legislature regarding a measure of legislation, he shall be deemed guilty of lobbying, which is a crime; except that any person not employed for valuable consideration is not prohibited from attempting to influence by arguments, briefs, or written statements any member of the state legislature;
2. any person employed as a legislative agent or counsel is prohibited from lobbying in any way other than by appearing before the regular committee when in session after having been granted permission by the presiding officer of that committee, or by newspaper publication, public address, printed or written statement, argument, or briefs delivered to the desk of each member of the House he wishes to reach thereby (this may be done only provided that before that person delivers such statements, arguments, or briefs he deposits at least twenty copies of such materials with the chief clerk of the house before which he wishes to appear);
3. no person in service or control of the government of the State of Oklahoma or the U.S. Government may lobby on any matter affecting his pecuniary interests.

CONFLICTS OF INTEREST

• The provisions of the conflict of interest statute apply to all officers, employees, or members of the executive, judicial, or legislative branch of the state government.
• The statute is limited to the establishment of a code of ethics, which sets out certain behavior to be followed and certain acts

that are prohibited. No requirement is made that any public official make financial disclosure of his personal holdings or that he divest himself of any real or potential conflicts of interest.
• The ethical conduct of public officials is governed by a state ethics commission established by provision of this statute. It is a three-man board empowered to promulgate rules and regulations and to hear complaints involving potential violations and to make recommendations to appropriate officials. It may issue subpoenas and call witnesses under oath. This commission is responsible for supervising all public officials except state legislators. Legislators are supervised by a similar commission called the Joint Legislative Ethics Commission. A public official or legislator who fails to comply with the provisions of this statute or with recommendations or guidelines established by either of the two commissions may be subject to dismissal or censure.

CAMPAIGN FINANCE

• This law applies to any candidate for any public office, at all levels, but "candidate" as defined in the law does not include any person who has withdrawn or any person whose candidacy is unopposed. Both primary and general elections are covered by the provisions of the law.
• Every candidate must designate a person to be his agent for the receipt and expenditure of contributions. The candidate may designate himself for the position. The agent, in turn, may designate as many subagents as he sees fit. The designations of agents and subagents must be made in writing and filed with the election board. Campaign committees are similarly required to designate such agents.
• Every candidate in Oklahoma running for state or federal office must report contributions or $500 or more. Campaign committees must report any individual contributions of $500 or more, or aggregates of $500 or more from one person. Every candidate for local office must report contributions of $250 or more. All other contributions are reported as one aggregate total. Reports of expenditures are also required.
• Candidates' reports of contributions and expenditures are filed with the state election board not more than fifteen days after

each general election and include information from the date the filing period opened or the date of his last report, whichever was more recent.

• No person or family can contribute more than $5,000 to a campaign committee or to a candidate for state or federal office. No person or family can contribute more than $1,000 to a candidate for local office. A state tax deduction is permitted for up to $100 in contributions each year. The law sets no campaign spending limits. No prohibition is made with respect to corporate or labor union contributions.

• Violation of this law is a misdemeanor. Punishment is a fine and/or imprisonment, and upon final conviction the person who violated the law shall forfeit the office to which he was elected. The election board is responsible for reviewing and evaluating financial reports filed.

OREGON

Open Meetings

• No statewide statute applies to open meetings. However, there are certain constitutional provisions (Section 14) and certain legislative rules that apply to open meetings of the state legislature. In addition, certain customs govern the actions of the state legislature. The legislature holds its deliberations and votes in open session as a matter of practice, not as a matter of law or rule. Legislative committees generally deliberate and vote in open sessions, although meetings of the Appropriations Committee to work on the state budget are sometimes held in closed session. Legislative rules permit a committee to hold sessions in secret if, in the judgment of that committee, the subject requires secrecy. Committee votes are recorded only on final passage of bills out of committee as a matter of course. Votes on all other procedural motions and amendments before vote on final passage may be recorded by roll call at the request of a committee member. The legislature as a whole records only final passage votes, although any member may request a roll call on any other motion voted.

• Conference committee sessions are never announced in advance but are always open to the public and the press. It is rare to have conference committees open in this manner. Votes of legislative committees that are recorded are available from the committee chairman, the Secretary, or the Clerk. After the session is over the Secretary of State maintains a complete list of all committee votes available for public inspection.

LOBBYING DISCLOSURE

• The term "lobbyist" is interpreted to mean any individual who for compensation seeks to influence the decisions of the legislature. Lobbyists are required to register with the legislative counsel. No separate registration is required of employers of lobbyists.
• While financial statements are not required of all lobbyists as matter of course, the Judicial Committee of the State Legislature must, on the complaint of five members of the Legislative Assembly, investigate and report on any alleged improper practice or wrongdoing by any lobbyist. It may as an incident of any such investigation require any additional information respecting the activities, compensation, and expenditures of the lobbyist that a majority of the committee may deem pertinent and necessary.
• A state code of ethics governs lobbyists' behavior and is considered in determining potential or suspected improper activities by lobbyists.
• Contingent payments are explicitly *permitted* by this statute. Oregon may well be the only state in the country that specifically permits payments of this kind.

CONFLICTS OF INTEREST

• Only the Oregon Constitution includes provisions dealing with conflict of interest of state legislators. The Oregon revised statutes establish a set of conflict of interest regulations covering other public officials and employees.
• Neither the Oregon Constitution nor the revised statutes require that any public official or state legislator make public disclosure of his personal financial holdings. Neither the Constitution nor the revised statutes call for the divestment of any real

or potential conflict of interest by any public official or state legislator.

• The Oregon Constitution prohibits legislators from holding any office created during their legislative terms. It also prohibits legislators from receiving a fee or from being engaged to prosecute a claim against the state. No commission is established to supervise or regulate or interpret these constitutional provisions, and enforcement is implicitly left to the state legislature itself. The Oregon revised statutes prohibit public officers and employees from having interests in contracts made in their official capacities. Again, there is no agency responsible for enforcing, supervising, or interpreting these limited provisions in the revised statutes.

• The provisions described above in no way constitute a comprehensive handling of the question of conflict of interest.

CAMPAIGN FINANCE

• This law covers primary, general, and special elections, including measures voted on by the people, and all candidates for any public office.

• Every candidate and committee must appoint a treasurer (a candidate can be his own treasurer). The treasurer is responsible for keeping accounts of all campaign contributions and expenditures. Statements of contributions and expenditures are required from both candidates and political campaign committees.

• Statements are due not more than ten or less than seven days before an election, and again not more than thirty days after the election. Supplemental statements of unexpended balances and deficits must be filed not more than thirty days after the last statement and every sixty days after that as long as necessary. If a candidate has received no contributions or made no expenditures, he must file a signed statement to that effect.

• Not more than thirty days after the date of each regular biennial general election, the political treasurer of the state central committee and the political treasurer of each county central committee of a political party shall file with the Secretary of State a statement of all contributions received and all expenditures made by or on behalf of the committee during the previous biennial period. The statement shall be signed and certified as

true and correct by the political treasurer of the committee.
• All individuals who contribute more than $50 in support of or opposition to one candidate, political committee, or measure must file a statement to that effect with the filing office.
• All candidates for statewide office, Congressional office, or office from any district covering more than the county must file required statements with the Secretary of State. Statements about money received or spent in connection with issue campaigns are similarly filed with the Secretary of State. Candidates for any office in one county and statements relating to county measures are filed with the county clerk. Statements on city or ward campaigns are filed with the city clerk, auditor, or recorder.
• No candidate can contribute or expend in support of his campaign more than an amount equal to 25 per cent on the annual salary of the public office he is seeking or $1,000, whichever is more.
• No limit is set on individual contributions. No prohibition is made on contributions by corporations or labor unions.
• Any registered elector may file with a filing officer a complaint that a statement filed with the filing officer does not conform to law or to the truth or that a person has failed to file a statement as required by law. Upon the petition of the Secretary of State, the Attorney General, or any registered elector, the circuit court for the county in which the filing officer has his office may compel filing by any political campaign treasurer or person who has failed to file any statement required. The candidate's name will not be printed on the ballot unless all required statements are filed. The name can be added if statements are late. Certificate of election is withheld unless statements are filed.

PENNSYLVANIA

OPEN MEETINGS

The only comprehensive Pennsylvania open meetings laws apply to county and state board and commission meetings, as well as various administrative state agencies such as the Pennsylvania Turnpike Commission. All groups covered by the provisions of this law must hold their meetings in open session and give the public advance notice of the convening of the meetings. No law, rule, or constitutional provision deals with meetings of the state legislature or the executive branch of Pennsylvania government. As a result, votes of legislative committees are never open to the public. Committee votes are recorded. This is solely for the benefit of state legislators; records of votes are not available to others either by individual or in the aggregate. Meetings of the conference committees are seldom announced and are never open to the public or the press.

LOBBYING DISCLOSURE

• A lobbyist is defined as any individual who, for compensation, attempts to influence legislative decisions or actions.
• Every lobbyist must file a registration form at the commencement of his lobbying activities. No similar requirement is made of the employer of a given lobbyist. The registration is to be submitted to the Chief Clerk of the House and the Secretary of the Senate in the form of a sworn statement. Registration information shall include the name and business address of the lobbyist, the name and business address of his employer or employers, and the expected duration of his employment.
• Neither the individual lobbyist nor his employer is required to file any financial statements listing either income or expenditures related to lobbying activities.
• No individual is given the specific responsibility of enforcing this statute. Technically, any person violating any provisions of the statute shall be guilty of a misdemeanor, punishable by a fine of not more than $500 or imprisonment of not more than one year, or both.

CONFLICTS OF INTEREST

• State law requires that state legislators disclose the amount, but they need not identify the source, of their financial interests. Legislators are required to disqualify themselves from official

actions in which they have an interest, but the nature of the interest is very poorly defined.
• No law prohibits the acquisition of conflicting interests. No law governs, regulates, or prohibits conflicts of interest among executive officials or executive employees. No law prohibits a lawyer-legislator from appearing before a state agency.

CAMPAIGN FINANCE

• This law applies to all candidates for public office in primary and general elections.
• Both candidate and treasurer are responsible for expenditures made in behalf of a candidate. Only they can collect or disburse money. Every political committee must have a treasurer.
• Statements of contributions and expenditures are required from both candidates and treasurers.
• If the aggregate receipts or disbursements and liabilities of a candidate or a political committee in connection with any primary or election do not exceed $150, the candidate or the treasurer of the committee, as the case may be, must, within thirty days after the primary or election, certify that fact under oath to the officer or board with which expense accounts are required to be filed.

If a candidate or political committee does not receive any contributions or make any disbursements or incur any liabilities, he or it is not required to file any account or to make any affidavit, but such candidate or political committee shall be deemed for all purposes of the act to have filed an expense account showing no receipts, disbursements, or liabilities for primary or election expenses.
• Statements are due within thirty days after the election. In statewide elections, they are filed with the Secretary of the Commonwealth. Others are filed with the appropriate county boards of elections.
• No limit is set on individual contributions. No limits are set on campaign spending. Contributions by corporations or unincorporated associations are prohibited.
• No enforcement provisions are included in the law.

RHODE ISLAND

Open Meetings

The only Rhode Island open meetings statute applies to such local bodies as school boards and requires that meetings of such groups be open. Votes taken in legislative committees are never open to the public. While they are recorded, the record is exclusively for the use of the legislature itself and is not available to the public either in the aggregate or by individual. Conference committee sessions are never announced in advance and are seldom open to the public and the press.

Lobbying Disclosure

• In lieu of the word "lobbyist," the terms "legislative counsel" and "legislative agent" are employed. Legislative counsels are those employed to appear at public hearings before committees for the purpose of making an argument, and also any legal counsel who acts or advises in relation to legislation. All other individuals who engage in attempts to influence any legislation affecting the pecuniary interest of any individual, association, or corporation, as distinct from the interests of the whole people of the state, are considered legislative agents.

• Both legislative counsels and legislative agents must place their names on the legislative docket. No similar requirement is made of employers of either counsels or agents. Registration must take place within one week after the date of employment. Information included on the docket at the time of registration includes the name and business address of the employer; the name, residence, and occupation of the person employed; the date of employment or agreement; the length of time the employment is to continue; and the special subject or subjects of legislation to which employment relates.

• Within thirty days of the final adjournment of the General Assembly, every person, corporation, or association having acted as legislative counsel or agent whose name appears on the docket must file a complete and detailed statement of expenses paid or incurred in connection with promoting or opposing legislation. Forms are prescribed by the Secretary of State, and the statements are open to public inspection. Note that here, as in the case of registration requirements, the employers of counsels or agents are not required to file separate statements or information.

• Any person, corporation, or association violating any provision of this statute is subject to fine of not less than $200 or more than $5,000. Any person employed as legislative counsel or agent or who shall act as such, contrary to the provisions of this statute, is subject to fine of not less than $100 or more than $1,000 and shall be barred from acting in that capacity for a period of three years from the date of conviction. The Attorney General, upon information received from the Secretary of State, is responsible for enforcing this statute.

• Contingent payments are specifically prohibited.

CONFLICTS OF INTEREST

No law.

CAMPAIGN FINANCE

No law.

SOUTH CAROLINA

OPEN MEETINGS

No statewide open meetings law exists in South Carolina. Legislative committees rarely vote in open session, and no voting records are kept of any committee votes, either in aggregate or by individual, for use by either the legislature itself or the public. Conference committee sessions are seldom announced in advance and are never open to either the public or the press.

LOBBYING DISCLOSURE

• In lieu of the word "lobbyist," the terms "legislative counsel" and "agent" are employed. Counsels and agents are persons employed to promote or oppose in any manner the passage by the General Assembly of any legislation affecting the pecuniary interest of any person.

• Both the legislative counsel or agent and his employer must enter their names on the legislative docket. Registration must be made within one week after the commencement of employment of a given legislative counsel or agent. The Secretary of State is responsible for registering legislative counsels and agents. Information required at the time of registration includes:

1. the name, occupation, business, and business address of the employer
2. the name, residence, and occupation of the person employed
3. the date of employment and length of time it is to continue
4. the subjects of legislation to which employment relates

This docket is open to public inspection. Any changes in the information provided at the time of registration require updating in the registration form maintained by the Secretary of State.

• Within thirty days after final adjournment of the General Assembly, every person whose name is on the legislative docket must file a statement to indicate all expenses incurred in connection with lobbying activities.

• Violation of this act is a misdemeanor punishable by a fine of not less than $24 or more than $100.

• Contingent payments are specifically prohibited.

• The provisions of this statute do not apply to any county or municipality. They shall apply to executive officers and legal staff regardless of whether they receive additional compensation for such services or not.

CONFLICTS OF INTEREST

No law.

CAMPAIGN FINANCE

• This law applies to candidates for public office in primary and general elections.

• State law requires only that each candidate file a statement itemizing disbursements both before and after each primary and general election. This statement is to be filed with the Secretary of State, but no specific deadlines for filing such statements are included in the law, and no forms are provided on which such statements are to be filed.

• No state law sets any expenditure limits with respect to any election. No state law regulates campaign contributions of any kind.

• If the winner of the election fails to file the required statements, the election is null and void. Failure to file is a misdemeanor punishable by fine and/or imprisonment.

SOUTH DAKOTA

OPEN MEETINGS

The official meetings of the state and its political subdivisions, including its related boards, commissions, and other agencies, and official meetings of boards, commissions, etc., created by statute and deriving their revenues from public funds are open to the public. Executive or closed sessions require a majority vote of the members present and voting. They can be called only to consider student, employee, or personnel matters. Any official action that results from either an open or a closed session must be made in an open official meeting. State agencies must keep detailed minutes. A certified copy of the minutes must be filed in the office of the Auditor General of the State Department of Audits and Accounts within fifteen days after the meeting. These files are open to the public.

Votes of legislative committees are held in open session on a regular basis. They are recorded and are available by aggregate and by individual.

LOBBYING DISCLOSURE

• The terms "legislative agent" and "legislative counsel" are used in lieu of the term "lobbyist" in South Dakota statutes.

Legislative counsels are individuals employed to appear at public hearings before committees. Legislative agents are all others who attempt to influence legislation affecting the pecuniary interest of any individual, association, or corporation, as distinct from the interest of the entire state.

• Both legislative counsels and legislative agents are required to register before commencing their lobbying activities. While the employers of legislative agents and counsels are not required to file separate registration statements, they are held equally responsible with their employees, the agents and counsels, for seeing that the agents and counsels themselves file.

• The Secretary of State maintains two separate legislative dockets, one for the legislative agents, the other for legislative counsels. Both dockets are open to public inspection. Information required of registrants at the time they place their names on the legislative docket includes:

1. the name and business address of the employer or employers of the agents and counsels
2. the name, residence, and occupation of persons employed for the purpose of influencing legislation as either counsel or agent
3. the date of employment and the expected duration of employment
4. the subjects of legislation to which the employment relates.

• Financial statements must be filed with the Secretary of State within thirty days after final adjournment of the legislature by every person, corporation, or association whose name appears on either of the two legislative dockets. These financial statements must be detailed and must include all expenses paid or incurred in connection with promoting or opposing any legislative action.

• The Attorney General is responsible for prosecuting suspected violators of any provision of this statute. The Secretary of State is responsible for supervising the filing of reports and financial statements. Any person violating any provision of this statute is subject to a fine of not less than $200 or more than $5,000.

• Contingent payments are specifically prohibited.

CONFLICTS OF INTEREST

• This statute applies to all public officers and employees of the State of South Dakota.

• An annual inventory of all personal property is required of public officers and employees. This report is to be made on December 31 or within ten days after the commencement of employment. School officers must file similar annual statements of financial holdings on July 1 or within ten days after the commencement of employment.

• No statutory requirement for the divestiture of conflicting interest exists in the South Dakota codes. It is neither required nor explicitly recommended that any public official or employee who has conflicting interest disqualify himself with respect to decision-making that relates to such interests.

• No contract awarded by the State of South Dakota involving any disbursement of state funds may be awarded to any officer or employee of the state. This regulation does not apply to notaries public or other state officials or employees who are not drawing a salary from the state.

• The penalty for violation of any of the provisions of this statute is a fine of not less than $200 or more than $1,000 or imprisonment of not less than thirty days or more than one year. It is not explicitly clear who is responsible for the enforcement of this statute.

CAMPAIGN FINANCE

• This law covers nominations and elections to office as well as questions submitted to the electors of the whole state or any political division thereof. The definition of "public office" is every office to which persons can be elected by vote of the people.

• Candidates are responsible for their own expenses, but political committees cannot receive or disburse money until a treasurer is chosen.

• Every candidate must file a statement of expenses. Treasurers of political committees must report all receipts and expenditures. Any person not a member of a political committee who collects or disburses funds exceeding $5 in the aggregate is required to file and verify a statement similar to that required of committee treasurers. Statements are due within thirty days after each election and are filed with the Secretary of State.

• There is no limit on individual campaign contributions.

• No candidate can spend more than the sum equal to 50 per cent of one year's salary of the office to which he aspires. This does not include expenses in connection with the printing or circulation of written or printed matter. Candidates for public office cannot spend any money directly to promote the passage or defeat of any constitutional amendment, initiated measure, or referred law.

• Campaign contributions by business or cooperative corporations are prohibited.

• Any violation for which no penalty is provided in this law is punishable by fine (up to $1,000) and/or imprisonment (not exceeding six months). It is the duty of the Attorney General to investigate and prosecute any violation. Any person nominated or elected to any office who has violated any provision of this law forfeits his office.

TENNESSEE

OPEN MEETINGS

No comprehensive general statute in Tennessee covers open meetings, but some city statutes require them. There is a provision in the state Constitution that requires the General Assembly to meet in public sessions unless the public interest requires executive session. This provision, which in itself is ambiguous and weak, does not apply to committees of the General Assembly. General Assembly votes are recorded, however, whether in the aggregate or by individual. Conference committee sessions are usually announced in advance and are always open to the public and the press. Few states have open conference committee sessions.

LOBBYING DISCLOSURE

• A lobbyist is defined as any individual who for compensation attempts to influence a decision of the legislature.

• The lobbyist himself, but not his employer, is required to register. Each registrant must file within one week of the commencement of his employment upon the docket maintained by the Secretary of State for that purpose. The information required at the time of registration includes the name, occupation or business, and business address of the employer of the lobbyist; the name, residence, and occupation of the lobbyist; the date of his employment; the duration of employment if it can be determined; and all subjects of legislation to which the employment relates.

• Neither the lobbyist nor his employer is required to file any financial statement listing either income or expenditures related to lobbying activities.

• The Secretary of State is responsible for publishing information about registrants and making the information available to the members of each house of the General Assembly.

• Violation of any provision of this statute is a misdemeanor punishable by a fine of from $100 to $1,000 for each such offense.

• If a lobbyist makes a statement at the time of his registration disclosing the terms of his employment and the terms of his compensation, he may then accept employment on a contingent basis.

• It is unlawful for any person to solicit employment as a lobbyist, and each person registering as a lobbyist must file a statement with the Secretary of State swearing that he did not solicit such employment.

CONFLICTS OF INTEREST

• A new Tennessee statute requires that all members of the General Assembly, constitutional officers, officers of the governor's Cabinet, the governor, the judges and counselors of the State of Tennessee, and all candidates for or appointees to those offices must make full financial disclosure of personal holdings and the holdings of their spouses and minor children. For elective officers, the disclosure statements must be filed no later than ten days following the last day provided for qualifying as a candidate. In the case of appointed officers, disclosure statements must be filed within twenty days after the date of employment. Such statements are filed with the Secretary of State and must be updated annually.

• Information required at the time of financial disclosure is a list of any investments made and offices and directorships maintained.

• No individual is specifically charged with the responsibility for enforcing the provisions of this statute.

CAMPAIGN FINANCE

• This law applies to candidates for public office in primary and general elections.

• Candidates and their campaign managers are required to file statements itemizing their expenditures thirty days after primary and general elections. No law requires that the candidate, or any group working in his behalf, file such statements prior to elections.

• Campaign expenditure limits were repealed by laws 1970, ch. 4, sec. 1.

• Corporations are specifically prohibited from contributing to any political campaign. No similar prohibition exists with respect to labor union contributions. No Tennessee law limits individual contributions.

• No certificate of nomination or election will be issued if required statements are not filed. Violators are also subject to fine and/or imprisonment.

TEXAS

OPEN MEETINGS

• A statewide provision applies to boards, commissions, departments, or agencies within the executive branch of the state, as well as city councils and other boards and departments of political subdivisions of the state. All the groups to which the law applies must hold meetings in open session except when considering questions of the appointment, employment, or dismissal of a public officer or employee, the acquisition of additional real estate, or matters affecting the security of the state. These exceptions are sufficiently broad to permit any meeting to be held in private and rationalized in terms of the exemptions. The law does not apply to the legislature or to legislative committees.

• Votes taken in legislative committees are by legislative rule open to the public and the press. Vote totals are available in aggregate from the committee chairman, the Secretary, or the Clerk. Conference committee sessions are usually open. The Senate may operate in closed session when considering gubernatorial nominations. Either house of the legislature or committees of the legislature may meet in closed session for organizational purposes. The term "organizational" is not sufficiently defined. Votes taken in the state legislature as a whole, both on final passage of bills and on procedural motions and amendments, are to be open and recorded.

LOBBYING DISCLOSURE

• A lobbyist is considered to be any person who (1) for compensation undertakes any direct communication to promote or oppose the passage of any legislation by the legislature or the approval or veto thereof by the governor; (2) without compensation but acting for the benefit of another person undertakes by direct communication to promote or oppose the passage of any legislation by the legislature or the approval or veto thereof by the governor; or (3) acting on his own behalf and without compensation makes an expenditure or expenditures totaling in excess of $50 during a session of the legislature for direct communication with the legislature.

• Each individual thus described as a lobbyist must register within five days after the commencement of lobbying activities with the Chief Clerk of the House of Representatives. The registration must include the name, occupation, and address of the registrant; the name, occupation, and address of the person or persons employing or retaining the registrant to perform lobbying services; and a brief description of the legislation in which the registrant is interested.

• Each registered lobbyist must file, between the first and fifteenth day of each calendar month succeeding the month during which the legislature was in session for as much as one day, a written statement giving the total expenditures made by him during the preceding month in connection with lobbying activities. The statements do not have to list personal, sustenance, and office expenses, clerical help, lodging, and travel. Entertainment expenses incurred for purposes of direct communication with a_ member of the legislature must be reported. These financial statements must be filed each month under the provisions described above until the individual ceases to be a lobbyist.

• The law includes both monetary and prison penalties for violation of any of its provisions, but no enforcing authority is specified.

• Contingent payments are specifically prohibited.

CONFLICTS OF INTEREST

No law.

CAMPAIGN FINANCE

• This law applies to each opposed candidate whose name and whose opponent's name are printed on the ballot at a first primary, general, or special election. Candidates are required to file statements which include reports from their committees. Contributors of more than $100 are responsible for reporting those contributions if not reported by the candidate.

• Contribution and expenditure statements must be filed not less than seven or more than ten days before any first or second primary, general, or special election, and within ten days after such election. Statements for county office are to be filed with the county clerk; for a district or state office, with the Secretary of State; for a municipal office, with the city clerk or secretary;

and for an office of a political subdivision, with the secretary of the governing board of the political subdivision.

• There are no limits on individual contributions and no limits on campaign expenditures in the law. Corporations are prohibited from making campaign contributions, but labor unions are not so prohibited.

• Candidates in violation of the law forfeit their places on primary or official ballots, except that "no candidate in the general election shall forfeit the right to have his name printed on the ballot for such election if the Constitution of the state prescribes the qualifications of the holder of the office sought by the candidate. Any person found in violation of the law may be fined or imprisoned, or both. Any citizen who is entitled to vote for a candidate may institute suit and all such proceedings shall be heard and disposed of by both the trial and appellate courts."

UTAH

OPEN MEETINGS

• All meetings of legislative bodies or state and local agencies, including school boards and boards of control of state universities and colleges, must be open to the public. Meetings are defined in such a way, however, as to permit executive sessions to discuss any subject of the group's choosing. All final resolutions, rules, regulations, contracts, or appointments must be approved, however, in open session. As in other states, the requirement that final votes be held in open session in no way inhibits secrecy, as such open sessions may involve little more than pro forma ratification of decisions reached in closed session. No provision of this state law requires that votes be recorded or that minutes be kept.

• State legislative rules, as well as the law described above, require that the legislature itself deliberate and vote in open session. Votes are recorded in the Senate and House journals. Legislative committees seldom vote in open session, and no record of any votes is kept in any form for use either by the public or by the legislature itself. A committee may move to record votes taken, but if the motion passes the votes are recorded in minutes available only to members of the committee and to the legislature, never to the public. The legislature votes openly, and the votes are recorded not only on final passage of bills but on procedural motions and amendments as well. Conference committee sessions are seldom announced in advance and seldom open to the public.

Lobbying Disclosure

No law.

Conflicts of Interest

No law.

Campaign Finance

• This law applies to candidates for public office in primary and general elections.
• Candidates and political committees are required to file contribution and expenditure statements with the Secretary of State. The candidate, the candidate's personal committees, state committees, and all other political committees must file fourteen days prior to any primary or general election and on the second Friday following any primary or general election.
• Campaign expenditure limits were repealed by laws 1961, ch. 42, sec. 1.
• Corporations are specifically prohibited from making campaign contributions. No similar prohibition exists for labor unions. No limit is set on individual contributions.
• Failure to file the required statements means that the candidate's name will not appear on the ballot and that he will be disqualified from holding office until statements are filed. Excessive or illegal expenditure is a misdemeanor and, in cases where the violator won, the election is voided and the person ousted and excluded from office. The county attorney is responsible for prosecuting violators. Candidates or voters may petition a district judge, the Attorney General, or the Governor to investigate alleged violations.

VERMONT

OPEN MEETINGS

Vermont has no statewide regulation, constitutional provision, or legislative rule dealing with open meetings. By custom, however, both legislative committees and the legislature as a whole vote and meet in open session, and votes are recorded in the aggregate.

LOBBYING DISCLOSURE

• In lieu of the term "lobbyist," the statute refers to "legislative counsel" and "legislative agent." As is customary, legislative counsels are individuals who appear at public hearings before committees, and legislative agents are individuals who use other means of attempting to influence legislative action on specific legislation that either is before the legislature or may come before the legislature.

• If legislative counsels or legislative agents receive compensation for their efforts, they must register. Registration is with the Secretary of State and must be completed before the commencement of lobbying activities, either as a legislative counsel or as a legislative agent. In addition to the requirement that agents and counsels register, the employers of either of these categories of lobbyists are also required to file separate lobbying registration reports.

• Information required from each registrant, either employee or employer, includes the names of the legislative counsel or agent and of his employer, the address of each, the date and basis of employment, and the subject on which the individual agent or counsel will lobby. The legislative docket is arranged so that under the name of each employer shall appear the names of all employed by him for the purpose of lobbying, and under the name of each counsel or agent appear the names of all employers he represents.

• No financial statements are required either from legislative agents or legislative counsels or from their employers.

• The Attorney General is responsible for enforcing the provisions of this statute. Violators shall be fined not less than $100 or more than $500.
• Contingent payments are specifically prohibited.

CONFLICTS OF INTEREST

No law.

CAMPAIGN FINANCE

• This law applies only to candidates in primary elections.
• Each candidate is required to file a statement of contributions and expenditures with the Secretary of State ten days after the primary election.
• An expenditure limit of $7,500 is placed on candidates for governor in the primary.
• No state law regulates campaign contributions of any kind.
• There is a penalty of fine and/or imprisonment for failure to file the required statement or for excessive expenditures. No one is specifically charged with the responsibility for enforcing the law.

VIRGINIA

OPEN MEETINGS

• Committee votes are usually held in open session. Votes held in either open or closed session are recorded both by individual and in aggregate and are available in those forms from the Clerk or the Secretary or from the committee reports themselves. Conference committee sessions are never announced in advance and are never open to the public or the press.
• The 1968 Virginia Freedom of Information Act required that meetings of the executive and administrative branches be open to the public. Exceptions are made in cases where personnel matters are being discussed.

LOBBYING DISCLOSURE

• Lobbying means promoting, advocating, or opposing any matter that may come or is pending before either house of the General Assembly or any committee thereof by an individual who is an employee of a person, whether his employment is for the purpose of lobbying or otherwise, or who is employed or retained for such purpose in whole or in part, and who appears either on behalf of or for any other person for such purpose.

• Lobbyists must file registration forms, but no separate registration requirement applies to employers of lobbyists. Registration must be made before an individual may commence lobbying and must be filed with the Secretary of the Commonwealth, who maintains a docket for this purpose.

• Information required at the time of registration includes the following:

1. the full name, residence, and business address of the registrant and a description of the matters and purposes for which he expects to be lobbying
2. the name, address, and principal occupation of each person by whom the lobbyist is employed or retained and the lobbyist's position with that firm or person
3. the name and address of the person maintaining the financial records, which would include income and expenditures stemming from lobbying activities
4. the amount of money paid or to be paid or the value of any other consideration given, including expenses, whether or not the lobbyist is on periodic retainer
5. if the lobbyist is on retainer only, the amount of the retainer allocated
6. if the lobbyist is on a basic retainer with the option of additional compensation available, the amount of that compensation received, including expenses
7. if an applicant is on annual salary, an estimate of the amount to be spent on lobbying as compared with time spent on nonlobbying activities.

• Each lobbyist whose name appears on the docket must file a statement of expenses within thirty days of adjournment of any session of the General Assembly. This is to include a complete and detailed statement signed by the employer showing all expenses, retainers, and annual salaries paid or incurred in connection with lobbying by the person for whom the lobbyist is registered and showing the matters and purposes for which the person lobbied, and a complete and detailed statement signed by the lobbyist showing expenses and salaries received or paid out by him in connection with lobbying. These statements are open to public inspection.

• Violation of any provision of this statute is a misdemeanor with a penalty of a fine of not less than $5 or more than $500 or possible confinement in jail not exceeding twelve months, or both.

CONFLICTS OF INTEREST

• The provisions of this statute apply to all governmental officers or employees of the Commonwealth of Virginia.

• Any officer or employee who has a material financial interest that he believes or has reason to believe may be substantially affected by his actions in a governmental or advisory agency of which he is an officer or employee must disclose in writing the existence of that interest. This disclosure is to be filed with the Attorney General of the Commonwealth of Virginia. All individuals who have thus filed are required to continue to file each succeeding January after the initial disclosure is made. Note, however, that this is not a requirement that all officers or employees make public financial disclosures. Only those who themselves deem their financial interests to represent possible conflicts are required to do so. This gives scope to substantial discretion and makes evasion possible. While the Attorney General is empowered to deliver advisory opinions at the request of any employee or officer with respect to the desirability of filing a financial statement, the individual requesting an advisory opinion is not obliged to follow the recommendations of the Attorney General.

• No requirement is made that any officer or employee who is covered by the provisions of this statute divest himself of any real or potential conflicts of interest.

• Certain kinds of activities are specifically prohibited by this statute, and the prohibitions apply to all individuals covered by any provision of the statute. For example:

1. No individual so covered may be a contractor or subcontractor with the government agency of which he is an officer or employee, other than in his contract of employment.
2. No individual covered by the statute may solicit or accept any money or any other thing of value in addition to his official compensation for the services that he renders in the course of his official duties.

• The Attorney General and the commonwealth's attorneys are specifically charged with the responsibility of enforcing the provisions of this statute. The Attorney General shall supervise all officers or employees serving at the state level of government, and each attorney for the commonwealth is responsible for prosecuting violations by employees serving at the local level of government in or for the jurisdiction served by the attorney for the commonwealth.
• Note that there is no specific reference to the state legislature or state legislators in any provision of the statute. It is therefore not explicitly clear whether state legislators are covered by the provisions of this law, the only comprehensive conflict of interest statute in Virginia.

CAMPAIGN FINANCE

• This law applies to all elections held within the commonwealth and to candidates for offices at all levels.
• Each candidate must have a treasurer. Any political party committee that receives or disburses any money, in lieu of reporting to a candidate's treasurer, can designate its own treasurer. Reports of contributions and expenditures are required from candidates' treasurers and political party committee treasurers. Any person receiving or disbursing any money or thing of value not paid, delivered or reported to a candidate, his treasurer, or a political party committee must file a report with the State Board of Elections. Contributions in excess of $51 are listed by the contributor.
• Contribution and expenditure statements are due:

1. no later than noon on the seventh day preceding any election (this report shall include all contributions received or reported and expenditures made, reported, or contracted for relative to the candidate's nomination or election, since the date of the last preceding election to fill the office for which he is a candidate)
2. no later than noon on the thirtieth day after the election or prior to taking office, whichever occurs first
3. if any unpaid bills or deficits remain to be paid at the time the report or statement is filed, sixty days after the election
4. if any unpaid bills or deficits remain to be paid at the time the report or statement in paragraph 3 above is filed, six months after the election
5. if any unpaid bills or deficits remain to be paid at the time the report or statement in paragraph 4 above is filed, one year after the election.

It is the joint responsibility of the candidate and treasurer to file the statement of a candidate, and they shall file the report or statement in full and accurate detail. Statements are filed with the electoral board where the candidate resides and with the State Board of Election.

• There are no individual contribution limits and no campaign spending limits in the law. No prohibition against contributions by corporations or labor unions exists.

• No person failing to file the required reports will be allowed to take office, nor will that person receive a certificate of election.

WASHINGTON

OPEN MEETINGS

• The legislature holds its deliberations and votes in open session. Legislative committees generally vote in open session. Votes of the legislature on procedural motions and amendments, as well as on final passage of bills, are recorded and open.

• While Washington has no single comprehensive open meetings statute, a series of more specific, narrow statutes generally provides for meetings of the executive branch, state administrative agencies, and departments and for meetings of boards of subdivisions of the state to be open and public.

LOBBYING DISCLOSURE

• A lobbyist is any person employed for compensation to influence legislation.
• All lobbyists must register before they begin their lobbying activities. No similar requirement is made of employers of lobbyists. Registration is with the Secretary of State. Information required at the time of registration includes:

1. the name and business address of the lobbyist
2. the name and address of the lobbyist's employer
3. the duration of employment
4. the method of payment for the lobbyist
5. written authorization from each employer
6. the areas of legislative interest on which the lobbying will take place.

• Persons required to register must also file a statement of contributions and expenditures within sixty days after adjournment of any regular or extraordinary legislative session. Note that in the case of financial statements, as in the case of registration, lobbyists but not their employers are required to file.
• Anyone who fails to comply with provisions of this act or who gives false information is guilty of a gross misdemeanor punishable by a fine of not more than $5,000 or imprisonment for not more than twelve months, or both. Any person filing false statements is guilty of a felony. Any person convicted is prohibited from registering as a lobbyist for ten years and is liable for any damages. The Attorney General is responsible for enforcement of and prosecution under this statute.
• Contingent payments are specifically prohibited.
• This statute does not apply to persons acting in their own behalf, providing professional services related to drafting legislation, appearing or testifying before a committee in support of or opposition to any legislation, or giving testimony on request, nor

does it apply to working members of the news media pursuing their professional duties.

CONFLICTS OF INTEREST

• All public officials and most public employees are required to make public financial disclosure of their personal holdings on or before January 31 of each year. Every candidate for any public office must make similar financial disclosure at the date when he files the declaration of candidacy. Such statements are filed with the Secretary of State.
• Statements must include the following:

1. the name of any corporation, firm, or enterprise subject to the jurisdiction of the regulatory agency in which the individual who is filing has a direct financial interest of a value in excess of $1,500 (the possession of insurance policies or accounts in banks, savings and loan associations, or credit union is not considered a financial interest.
2. every office or directorship held by him or his spouse in any corporation, firm, or enterprise is subject to the jurisdiction of a regulatory agency
3. the name of any person, corporation, firm, partnership, or other business association from which he received compensation in excess of $1,500 during the preceding twelve-month period by virtue of being an officer, director, employee, partner, or member of any such person, corporation, firm, partnership, or other business association
4. if the individual is an attorney, all dealings between the firm of which he is a member and any agency of the state
5. the legal descriptions of all real property in the State of Washington in which he has any interest whatever.

• There is no requirement that any public official, employee, or candidate divest himself of any real or potential conflict of interest.
• The Secretary of State is responsible for receiving and reviewing these disclosure statements and making them public on a regular basis.
• Separate statutory provisions prohibit any state employee from

participating in any transaction involving the state in which he or any member of his family may derive special personal financial gain. Also prohibited is the receipt of any gift, gratuity, favor, or any other thing of economic value from any individual if the recipient believes the donor is attempting to influence official public decisions by means of the gift.

CAMPAIGN FINANCE

• The law covers primary elections only.
• The candidate is held responsible for all expenditures made in his behalf. A statement of contributions and expenditures is required of him within ten days after a primary election. The candidate, within thirty days after filing a declaration of candidacy, must file a personal financial disclosure report, which is to be available to the public. Contribution and expenditure statements, giving aggregate totals only, must be filed with the officer with whom the nomination papers are filed. Personal financial disclosure reports are filed with the Secretary of State.
• No limit is set on individual contributions or on campaign expenditures. Neither corporations nor labor unions, nor any other groups, are prohibited from making campaign contributions.
• Violation of this law is a misdemeanor.
• *Note:* A new campaign finance law has been passed by the legislature and will be subject to the approval of the people in November, 1972. Important additions in the new law would include:

1. designation of treasurers for candidates and campaign committees
2. reports on contributions of $100 or more and all expenditures by both candidates and committees for all elections
3. campaign expenditure limitations.

WEST VIRGINIA

OPEN MEETINGS

• West Virginia has no comprehensive open meetings statute. Legislative rules, however, bear on open meetings of the state legislature specifically. The legislature, according to the rules, holds deliberations and votes in open session. It is permitted to hold closed meetings of the Committee of the Whole and to hold closed party caucuses. By permitting these two types of closed meetings the rules effectively countenance the conduct of much significant business in closed session. Legislative committees never vote in open session. Votes are recorded only in aggregate, not by individual, and are available in aggregated form from the committee chairman, the Secretary, or the Clerk. Hearings of legislative committees are generally held in closed session, although upon request of a committee member they may be held in open session. Conference committee sessions are never announced in advance and never open to the public. The legislature takes only voice votes on procedural motions, amendments, and final passage of bills, unless one member of the legislature requests that the votes be recorded.

• A few limited specific statutes bear on open meetings of the executive branch, administrative agencies, and political subdivisions of the state. In general these statutes are weak and permit closed meetings at the discretion of the body meeting.

LOBBYING DISCLOSURE

No law.

CONFLICTS OF INTEREST

• The provisions of this statute apply to members of the state legislature; officers, agents, servants, or employees in the executive branch of state government; and judges or their employees.
• Each of the individuals covered by this statute is required to file a financial statement between January 1 and January 15 of each year. Members of the State Senate must file with the Clerk of the Senate; members of the House of Delegates file with the Clerk of the House; members of the executive branch file with the Secretary of State; and employees or judges of the judicial branch file with the Clerk of the Supreme Court.
• The information required on the financial disclosure form includes:

1. the name of every corporation, firm, association, partnership, or sole proprietorship then furnishing or having within the previous calendar year furnished to the state any commodities, if the individual filing that report or a member of his immediate family has a substantial interest in that firm, corporation, etc.
2. the names of any business establishments in which the individual filing the report or his immediate family has a professional business relationship that to the actual knowledge of the individual filing the report has furnished the state with any commodities during the previous year
3. any other interest or relationship that might reasonably be expected to be particularly affected by legislative action or in the public interest.

Note that substantial discretion as to what should or should not be included in the financial statement is left to the individual filing the statement. It is not required to be a comprehensive listing of all financial holdings. Decisions about potential conflicts of interest are left to the individual filing the form, not to the enforcing agents or the public.

• No requirement is made that any individual who has a real or potential conflict of interest divest himself of the financial holding that is the basis of the conflict. This is particularly notable with respect to state legislators, as no state law requires legislators who are members of law firms to remove their names from those law firms if they serve on legislative committees that have a bearing on the activities of those firms.

• The individuals who are responsible for receiving such financial statements as required are responsible for overseeing and enforcing the provisions of this statute as they apply to the people from whom they receive statements.

CAMPAIGN FINANCE

• This law applies to all political campaign contributions, receipts, and expenditures incident to primary, special, and general elections. It also applies to measures voted on by the people.

• Any candidate, his political agent, his representative, or any person acting for him and on his behalf and the treasurer of each political party committee are responsible for receipts and expenditures. A statement of contributions and expenditures is required from each treasurer of a candidate or committee. All contributions are listed by contributor. Statements are required not less than seven or more than fifteen days before each election, and again within thirty days after each election. They are filed with the Secretary of State by candidates for state and other offices elected by voters of a political division greater than a county. All others file with the county clerk.

• A limit of $5,000 is placed on individual contributions.

• Campaign spending limits are:

1. candidates for U.S. Senate or any state office, the sum of $75 for each county in the state, for the primary, and a like amount for the general election

2. candidates for members of the legislature, the sum of $125 for each county in which the candidate is voted for, for the primary, and a like amount for the general election

3. candidates for U.S. House of Representatives, the sum of $75 for each county in the district for the primary and a like amount for the general election.

4. for any county office, a sum not to exceed $200 in each county, for each election

5. for all others, a sum not to exceed $50 in the political division in which a person is a candidate, for each election.

The candidate can delegate any amount of this limit to his agent or any committee acting in his behalf.

• Corporate political contributions are prohibited. No similar prohibition exists with respect to labor union contributions.

• Failure to file the required statements is a misdemeanor punishable by fine and/or imprisonment. In addition, a candidate nominated who fails to file will not have his name printed on the ballot. A candidate who is elected and fails to file will not be allowed to take office. Violation of any other provisions of this act is a misdemeanor punishable by fine and/or imprisonment.

WISCONSIN

Open Meetings

• Antisecrecy laws apply to administrative agencies and commissions and require them to deliberate and vote in open sessions. Votes are recorded by roll call. Agencies hold executive sessions only when personnel matters are discussed.
• The state legislature has limited rules dealing with open meetings. The legislature's deliberations and votes are held in open session, but roll call votes are taken only on fiscal matters, on constitutional amendments, or at such other times as the presiding officer may order. Legislative committees hold public hearings but deliberate and vote in executive session. Roll call votes are recorded by the committee chairman and then printed in the history of the bill when that becomes available to the public from the Secretary of State's office.

Lobbying Disclosure

• A lobbyist is defined as any person lobbying for hire whose activities are not restricted to the following:

   1. appearances before legislative committees when in session
   2. newspaper publications
   3. public addresses to persons other than legislators
   4. preparation and delivery of briefs to legislators.

Lobbying for hire shall be interpreted to include the activities of any officer, agent, employee, or attorney of any principal who is paid a regular salary or retainer fee for the purposes of attempting to influence legislation.
• Lobbyists must file registration forms before commencing their lobbying activities. No similar registration requirement is made of employers of lobbyists. Wisconsin law makes a distinction between licensed and unlicensed lobbyists, licensed lobbyists being those who have filed registration forms and complied with the law and are therefore permitted to attempt to influence legislative action. Unlicensed lobbyists are those who have not complied

with the requirements and are therefore limited in their activities and relationships with the legislature to those guaranteed by the constitutional right to petition governments.

• A legislative docket on which registrations are recorded is maintained by the Secretary of State.

• Information required at the time of registration includes the lobbyist's name and business address, the name and business address of the lobbyist's employer or employers, and the subjects of legislation to which employment relates. Additions or corrections to the information on the docket must be made as changes in that information occur. The lobbyist must also file an authorization statement from each employer within ten days of the date of registration.

• Each lobbyist must file with the Secretary of State a sworn statement of expenses met or obligations incurred by himself or any agent operating in his behalf, with the exception of expenses related to personal living or travel, within ten days after the end of each calendar month. Lobbyists are exempted from this requirement if they incurred no expenses during that calendar month.

• The employer of a licensed lobbyist must file, within thirty days after the adjournment of the legislature, a sworn statement of expenses paid or incurred with respect to lobbying. He is also equally responsible, along with the lobbyist, for seeing that the lobbyist meets the registration requirements included in this statute.

• Employers of unlicensed lobbyists are to file within thirty days of adjournment a sworn statement of expenses paid or incurred related to lobbying activities.

• The Attorney General is responsible for enforcing the provisions of this statute. Any employer who violates any provision of this statute may be fined from $200 to $5,000. Any lobbyist who fails to submit the required statement may be fined up to $500 or imprisoned for six months or both. Any lobbyist who files a false statement may be fined not less than $500 or more than $1,000 or imprisoned in county jail for not less than thirty days or more than one year, and any lobbyist who fails to comply with any other provision or who is not duly licensed may be fined not less

than $100 or more than $1,000 and shall be barred from acting as a lobbyist for three years.
• Contingent payments are specifically prohibited.

CONFLICTS OF INTEREST
No law.

CAMPAIGN FINANCE
• This law applies to all primary, general, and special elections, including measures voted on by the people. Presidential and Vice-Presidential candidates are included in the definition of candidate for this law.
• Any candidate may select a single personal campaign committee to consist of one or more persons. A campaign committee does not have to appoint a treasurer. The secretary of a campaign committee is responsible for filing the necessary statements.
• Statements of contributions and expenditures are required from each candidate and each campaign committee. Any contribution over $5 in value must be listed by the contributor, and any expenditure over $5 must be indicated. In the event there are no receipts, disbursements, or obligations, a statement to that effect must be filed.
• Statements are due on the Tuesday preceding any primary or general election and on the Tuesday following any primary or general election. The statement of every candidate and the statement of his personal campaign committee are filed with the filing officer of the candidate. The statement of every state central committee and of every Congressional campaign committee is filed with the Secretary of State. All others are filed with the appropriate county clerk.
• There are no limits on individual contributions. The following expenditure limits apply, separately, to each primary and general election and do not include media expenses:

U.S. senator	$10,000
U.S. representative in Congress	2,500
Governor	10,000
Judge of the Supreme Court or state superintendent of public instruction	10,000

Other state offices	10,000
State senator	1,000
Member of Assembly	400
Presidential elector at large	1,000
Presidential elector for any Congressional district	300

For any candidate for a county, city, village, or town office, judgeship, or other office not heretofore mentioned who, if nominated and elected, would receive a salary, the limit is a sum not exceeding one-third of the salary to which he would be entitled during the first year of his incumbency of such office. If the candidate would not receive a salary, it is a sum not exceeding one-third of the compensation his predecessor received during the first year of the predecessor's incumbency. If the candidate would not receive a salary and has had no predecessor (and in all other cases not specifically provided for) he may spend no more than $25. Each candidate is also allowed to buy a total of one-fourth page of political advertising in newspapers for each election.

Any candidate may delegate any portion of his expenditure limit to a committee.

The state central committee of any political party entitled by law to have names placed on the ballot may make additional disbursements not exceeding in the aggregate the sum of $10,000.

• Political contributions by corporations are prohibited.

• The Attorney General will prosecute any person who fails to file the required statements.

The name of a candidate chosen in the primary will not be printed on the ballot if he has not filed the required statements, nor will he be certified if elected in a general election.

Any person violating this chapter will be subject to fine and/or imprisonment and will not be permitted to take or hold the office to which he was elected.

WYOMING

Open Meetings

There are no statewide constitutional provisions, statutes, or legislative rules dealing with open meetings. The legislature as a whole holds its deliberations and votes in open session and holds roll call votes upon request. The standing legislative committees are not open as a matter of course. By legislative rule, a standing eleven-member management council sets policy for open meetings. Most committee votes are taken by informal voice vote and are not recorded. Committees do not keep records of such votes. There is no procedure by which a committee member may force a recorded vote.

LOBBYING DISCLOSURE

• While the term "lobbyist" is not specifically defined, it may be inferred from the statute that a lobbyist is any person who on behalf of any association, corporation, labor union, or any interest other than himself attempts to influence legislative action and who is reimbursed for that attempt.
• Each such lobbyist is required to register. No separate registration requirement applies to the employers of such lobbyists. Registration must be filed before the commencement of any lobbying activities on a docket maintained by the state legislature. The only information required at the time of registration is the name and business address of the lobbyist. A copy of the registration is given to each member of the legislature.
• Neither the individual registering lobbyist nor his employer is required to make any financial statement reflecting the incomes or expenditures of the lobbyist with respect to lobbying activities.
• While no specific authority is designated as responsible for enforcing this statute, anyone failing to file a registration form, who should legally do so, is guilty of a misdemeanor and subject to a fine of not more than $200.
• The provisions of this statute are not applicable to any public official acting in his official capacity.

CONFLICTS OF INTEREST

• The Wyoming Constitution provides that legislators shall not vote on a measure in which they have a personal interest (Article 3, Section 46). This is the only conflict of interest provision relative to legislators in either the constitutional or the statutory law of Wyoming.

• There are various statutes prohibiting public officials from having any interest in a contract with the state or other public entity. Still other statutes require public officials to devote full time to their offices and not to maintain secondary employment elsewhere. No statute deals specifically with conflicts of interest.

CAMPAIGN FINANCE

• This law applies to candidates for any office to be voted for at any primary, municipal, or general election.
• Candidates, party central committee chairmen, and political committee treasurers are responsible for expenditures.
• Every candidate for office in primary, municipal, or general elections must file a detailed statement of all sums of money disbursed, expended, or promised directly or indirectly by him or on his behalf. The chairman of each party central committee for the state, district, or county must file a statement of receipts and expenditures.
• Every person receiving or expending money by authority or in behalf of, or to promote the success or defeat of, any candidate or other person or political party or any organization must within twenty days after such receipt or expenditure give the candidate or party on whose behalf it was incurred a detailed account. This account then becomes part of the files of the person to whom given. This includes all payments of more than $5 in aggregate. If the amount of value received or expended by any person is greater than $50, that person must file an itemized account.
• All statements are due within twenty days after the election and are filed with the county clerk in local elections and with the Secretary of State in all others.
• There is no individual contribution limit. Contributions by corporations are specifically prohibited.
• Expenditures by a candidate are limited to 50 per cent of one year's salary for the office he is seeking. This applies to his campaign for nomination and his campaign for election (50 per cent for each). Any traveling expenses incurred need not be included.
• The statements are to be inspected within ten days after they are filed. If someone fails to file or if the statement does not con-

form to law, the delinquent person is notified in writing. If the person is still delinquent after ten days, the prosecuting attorney of the county where the violation occurred shall institute proceedings. The name of a candidate nominated in a primary election will not be printed on the ballot in the general election until expenditure statements are filed. No person shall receive a certificate of election until a statement of expenditures is filed. Citizens as well as prosecuting attorneys can bring action for violation in filing statements. Original jurisdiction is granted to the district court of the county where the statement is filed. The court can declare the selection or election of such a candidate void.

• Penalty for violation is a misdemeanor punishable by a fine of up to $1,000 and/or imprisonment for not more than one year.

IV · Enforcement:

There Ought To Be a Lawyer

*I think I can and do say with pride that
we have legislatures that bring higher prices
than anywhere in the world.*
MARK TWAIN

It is self-evident that no law is useful if it goes unenforced. Yet citizens who cry out for reform legislation and applaud when it is passed often show little concern for its enforcement. The results are predictable.

The Kentucky conflict of interest laws prohibit legislators from participating in decision-making from which they may derive personal financial gain. Kentucky is less likely, then, to be plagued with legislative decisions distorted by special-interest pressures than are states without such a law. Or so one would think. But the make-up of the Kentucky House Banking and Insurance Committee suggests the contrary. The committee membership includes bank managers, insurance executives, and even the executive secretary of the Kentucky Bankers Association. These committee members must feel pressure to favor their past or present employers and associates. How can that happen? Why hasn't the law prevented it?

The answer is that enforcement is the most neglected part of government reform. The Kentucky law, and nearly all others like it around the country, is in part unenforced, in part unenforceable. Indeed, this law has no specific enforcement provisions at all. Many reformers tend to operate on the assumption that the way to solve the problem is to seek new laws. Yet the fact is that no law is any better than the enforcement it receives. Illinois has a reasonable conflict of interest law, but recent scandals show that the law is ignored. Until their repeal early in 1972, the federal Hatch Act amendments of 1940 set a $5,000 ceiling on individual campaign contributions to a single candidate or committee, but the stories of individual gifts over $10,000 filled the press.

It is a standard practice for legislators to enact apparently comprehensive reform statutes but to include no mandate for vigorous enforcement. The laws either omit enforcement procedures altogether or are so vague that no court would uphold a prosecution brought under their provisions. As a result, the public must blindly depend on voluntary compliance and the goodwill of public officials. The reformer must be alert to such maneuvering at the time the legislative language is being worked out. (The model bills at the end of this book include language that would make strong enforcement possible. Following each model statute are annotations, which explain how some seemingly innocuous changes could weaken the law and render it unenforceable.)

Vague language is a problem in federal as well as state laws. Special Assistant Attorney General Irving Kaufman attempted to enforce the federal lobbying law from 1947 to 1953. He even went so far as to investigate the apparent lack of compliance of the National Association of Manufacturers. In 1953, however, Kaufman indicated that the investigation was being dropped because Justice Department officials found that the law's vagueness made enforcement impossible. By then, at least one federal judge had called the law unconstitutionally vague.

The nonenforcement of reform legislation is not simply a matter of poor or devious drafting. Most enforcing agents are not inclined to enforce reform laws even to the extent that the language allows. There are five basic reasons for this.

First, in most cases the enforcement of laws in the four reform fields is left to the clerk of the lower house of Congress or a legislature or the secretary of the upper house. At both state and federal levels, the clerk and secretary are employees of the bodies they are expected to police. They do not have a natural impulse to bring legal action against their employers.

Second, responsibility for enforcing a given law is often divided between the individual who receives required financial campaign or lobbying statements, such as a clerk or secretary, and the supposed prosecutor, usually the Attorney General. In such situations, the clerk or secretary (with whom statements are usually filed) does not have the power to prosecute violations, and the Attorney General may well lack the data to determine that a violation has occurred. In most cases the clerk or secretary is expected to inform the Attorney General of any apparent violations, but the mechanism for doing this is usually either nonexistant or informal. This means that a clerk or secretary who is inclined toward nonenforcement can effectively prevent enforcement by failing to inform the prosecutor. In Massachusetts, for example, lobbyists must register with the Secretary of State, who in turn is responsible for informing the Attorney General of suspected violations. Because these two key officials are not specifically required by law to seek out, investigate, and prosecute possible violators, the law goes largely unenforced. Last year the man reputed to be the highest paid lobbyist in Boston failed to file, yet the Attorney General took no action until this fact was disclosed months after the filing deadline by the *Boston Globe*. The absence of clear linkage and mandated responsibilities resulted in a "failure to communicate" between the Secretary of State and the Attorney General. The public was the loser.

Third, the law may designate an enforcing agent who lacks the facilities, time, staff, expertise, or funding necessary for actively enforcing the law. The designated offices of the Congress and of most state legislatures are understaffed, and many are underpaid. When asked to take on major new supervisory responsibilities, such staffs usually can make only token efforts.

The 1971 Federal Election Campaign Act requires all candidates for Congress to file contribution and expenditure statements with the Clerk of the House (for House candidates) and the Secretary of the Senate (for Senate candidates). The clerk and secretary were already responsible for enforcing the federal lobbying law, among other regular responsibilities. Under these circumstances, about the best the supervisory official can do is to file the reports as they come in. Indeed, at one point the Clerk of the House had only one of his assistants assigned to receive and record all the lobbying statements that came into his office. Although the clerk is supposed to evaluate the statements received and report violators to the Attorney General, that evaluation must be superficial indeed.

The fourth reason for nonenforcement flows naturally from the third. If the enforcing agent is stretched to the limit merely by filing the reports, he surely will not have the ability to deal with large numbers of violators. In testimony before the House Committee on Standards of Official Conduct on the subject of his attempts to enforce the lobbying law, House Clerk Pat Jennings gave a clue to the magnitude of the problem. He said that more than a quarter of the 1,331 reports he received for the second quarter of 1970 were improper or incomplete even after he had requested that revisions be made. "I'm convinced," he told the committee, "that some of those we're sending forms back to are saying to heck with it and throwing them in the wastebasket." The number of violations rendered an already overextended supervisor incapable of enforcement.

The fifth factor leading to nonenforcement is the absence of public scrutiny. Few prods can be as effectively applied to public officials as a simple look over the shoulder. Many violations of law in the fields of open meetings, lobbying disclosure, conflict of interest, and campaign finance are sufficiently flagrant that they may be uncovered by active, alert citizens and media reporters. These violations make news. The enforcing agents know this, of course, so when the public expresses no outrage at nonenforcement and the press fails to editorialize against flagrant abuses, the enforcers rightly assume the public is not concerned, or at least not informed, and feel no pressure to enforce the law.

ENFORCEMENT OF FEDERAL LAWS

It is easy to trace the nonenforcement of the federal laws to these factors. In the thirty-two years from 1940 to early 1972, during which federal law prohibited contributions of more than $5,000 to political candidates, not a single person was charged with violating the law. This provision was repeatedly violated, yet the Attorney General never filed charges against anyone. Other sections of that law and its predecessors were scarcely better enforced. In the sixty-two years from 1907 to 1969, the Justice Department prosecuted only three corporations for violating the ban on corporate political giving. More vigorous enforcement in 1969 and 1970 led to indictments of fourteen companies, mostly California based. Thirteen of the fourteen were found guilty and fined.

In the field of conflict of interest, the Congress has virtually assured itself that the law will go unenforced by making enforcement an intramural matter. Each house has created an ethics committee. The Senate's is the Select Committee on Standards and Conduct. The House has the Committee on Standards of Official Conduct. Those committees are responsible for setting guidelines for legislative conduct, investigating complaints, and recommending appropriate action to the full house. The most likely action a house would take against one of its members is a vote of censure. In the history of the Congress this has been done only four times in the Senate and sixteen times in the House of Representatives.

Only in the few instances that have received national publicity has the Congress acted. Indeed, many observers believe that even in the well-publicized case of Senator Thomas Dodd the Senate would never have voted for censure had not Dodd asked the Select Committee to meet and "clear his name."

In 1972, at least fifty-nine House and Senate members were actively associated with law firms or otherwise engaged in the practice of law. As of mid-1972, 101 members were still associated with banks and other financial institutions (thirty-four of them on the boards of banks). It is unlikely that the ethics committees or the Congress as a whole will take any action on these persistent conflicts.

Enforcement of conflict of interest regulations within the federal executive branch is an internal matter and not publicly reported. Still, the absence of any evidence of prosecutions suggests that the inability of the public or the press to monitor the enforcement process has led to nonenforcement. Not since two members of President Warren G. Harding's Cabinet were prosecuted for their roles in the Teapot Dome Scandal has there been any evidence of real enforcement of federal conflict of interest regulations in the executive branch. One hopes that another scandal of the same magnitude will not be needed to jog the executive branch into enforcing and observing its own regulations. It is not only the blatant scandals that are at issue. Equally damaging is the insidious corruption of officials that results when laws are chronically unenforced and public officials habitually retain possible conflicting interests while considering themselves above scrutiny.

In the field of open meetings the record is mixed. Rules requiring the full House of Representatives and Senate to meet in open session and record votes have been observed largely because the public has come to expect and demand that they be followed.

Since no comparable rules exist with respect to Congressional committees, few meet or vote in open session.

The public has been either unable or unwilling to demand that executive and administrative meetings be open or that records of such meetings be available, as required by the Freedom of Information Act. The primary enforcing agent of this law is the public, which is granted access to the courts for redress of grievances. Yet, as the *Columbia Journalism Review* reported in 1967, "ironically, the court-enforcement provision of the law adds to the possibilities of blockage of government information. . . . Court action is not a good news-gathering tool." The enforcement procedure is sufficiently cumbersome, time-consuming, and expensive to discourage most citizens. Indeed, since most of the information sought or the access to meetings desired must be timely to be useful, ultimate success in court may well be too late for the purposes of the citizen. In a 1972 article, the *Congressional Quarterly* reported: "It can take months to get information. . . . The agency may take weeks to answer the initial request. An appeal to the department head takes more time. If the requester decided to sue, the government has sixty days to reply, and it can appeal an unfavorable decision at the district court level." This is enough to discourage any citizen. This law, too, goes unenforced.

ENFORCEMENT OF STATE LAWS

The record of enforcement at the state level is difficult to construct, but it is probably just as meager as enforcement at the federal level. Most states do not keep accurate records of the court cases brought under a given statute. The recollections of current attorneys general are not complete enough to indicate the degree to which a law is enforced.

The best available source of information is the annotated codes of each state. These codes are organized in such a way that appellate decisions of legal interest that result from cases brought under a given statute are listed after the law itself. Normally, the first appellate decision of a case brought under a given statute would be important enough to be listed. By checking through the annotated codes for each state in each of the four fields (and under related code sections as well), it is possible to make a close estimate of the number of court cases brought on which appellate decisions were rendered. Obviously, cases in which the defendant is acquitted or pleads guilty are not recorded, because no appeal takes place. Because there are constitutional implications in each of the four issues, however, it is likely that most guilty verdicts would have been appealed and would appear in the codes.

A comprehensive search through the annotated codes of all fifty states has yielded results that are both predictable and regrettable. The record of known enforcements in nearly all of the fifty states in each of the four fields is sparse indeed. Most states' codes indicate that not a single case was brought under the existing laws in at least three of the four fields.

No appellate decisions were rendered with respect to comprehensive open meetings statutes in any of the fifty states. A few references do appear with respect to more limited statutes, but these cases are, in every instance, challenges to closed school board meetings, zoning commission meetings, and the like. It appears that, as of 1971, the date of the most recent codes in most cases, no cases had been brought under any of the laws that apply to state legislatures or major executive or administrative boards, commissions, or agencies. This record may change slightly, since a few aggressive attorneys general, notably Robert Shevin of Florida, are taking special interest in the subject. Shevin has begun to enforce the comprehensive Florida open meetings law vigorously. Known as the "Sunshine Law," the Florida statute has been the model for other state laws and may serve as the basis for a federal bill as well.

In the area of lobbying, the record is nearly as poor. State lobbying laws are more common than are laws in any of the other three fields, yet in only three states' codes are any appellate cases found, for a total of eight appellate decisions: four in Louisiana, three in Wisconsin, and one in Kentucky. That means forty-seven states have either no law or no evident enforcement. Of the four cases in Louisiana, one occurred in 1875 and one in 1895. The 1875 case, *Durbridge v. Slaughter-House Co.*, dealt with a fund created for the apparent purpose of corrupting members of the legislature. The case was later heard by the U.S. Supreme Court, and the decision, which interprets the Fourteenth Amendment, is one of the most signifiant in American Constitutional law. Apart from this later significance, it should be noted that this case is one of the few examples of enforcement of a state lobbying statute. It is lamentable that so few cases have since been brought against similar attempts to corrupt public officials.

In Wisconsin, the opinion in *State v. Hoebel* (1950), reaffirmed the validity of the state lobbying statute in the face of due process arguments. In *State v. Decker* (1951), the opinion redefined the terms "lobbyist" and "principal" as used in the statute. *State ex. rel. Arthur v. Superior Court of Dane County* (1950) tested the legislature's intent that violations of the statute be prosecuted by the Attorney General. Each of these questions, and others, could legitimately be raised as a basis for appealing adverse decisions rendered under the lobby laws of any other state. The fact that references to similar opinions do not appear in the annotated codes of other states strongly suggests that the record of enforcement of state lobby laws is in fact woefully inadequate.

An additional indication suggests an even more pervasive lack of interest in lobbying disclosure laws. The codes list any opinion of attorneys general or legislative counsels requested for purposes of clarifying the laws. Requesting such a clarification is one way of exhibiting an interest in and concern for the statute. Opinions of this type are not given in the course of court cases; they are merely for clarification. References to only sixty-nine such opinions appear in the codes. These opinions are divided among only eight states: forty-one in California, ten in Wisconsin, seven in Michigan, and the rest divided among Massachusetts, New York, Ohio, Oregon, and South Dakota. No references to opinions appear in the codes of forty-two states.

Various state and local officials have been convicted of making private financial gain from their public offices. Yet the indictments were almost always under state or federal bribery or tax evasion laws. These laws, plus jury tampering, were the provisions under which former West Virginia Governor William Wallace Barron was charged in 1968. Similar laws were the basis of charges against former Texas Speaker Gus Mutscher. A check of the state codes with respect to conflict of interest statutes turned up only one relevant appellate decision and one opinion. *Anderson v. Lewis,* brought under a 1948 Idaho law regulating contract bidding by public officials, is the only case brought under any law regulating the personal financial activities of statewide public officials in any of the fifty states. (Some minor cases brought against members of realty boards, zoning boards, and the like appear under laws of limited jurisdiction in various states.) The one opinion that appeared in the codes was rendered in Maine, and that in 1912. With such a record of nonenforcement, small wonder that laws are ignored, the public is disillusioned, and "business as usual" too often means business for private gain, not the public good.

A search of the codes for decisions rendered with respect to state campaign finance codes showed that laws in this area have been more regularly enforced than in the other three fields. Whether or not this is because candidates carefully scrutinize the practices of their opponents is unclear. At any rate, evidence of some enforcement appears in most states. Many of the decisions were rendered on relatively minor procedural questions, but some —in Arkansas, Kentucky, Ohio, and elsewhere—suggest serious enforcement.

Because the evidence of nonenforcement at the state and federal levels is so conclusive, we would be fools indeed to devote ourselves to seeking new legislation without taking on the companion task of working for enforcement of both the new laws and laws already on the books. For too long, special-interest corporations, labor unions, and individuals have simply stood by as reform legislation was enacted, knowing it would go unenforced. One of the tragic results of this special-interest cynicism is that it has led to an increasing public cynicism. Let us not try to con the public into believing the government is working. Let us work for the kind of government that will work for us. The public should see more in its government but repeated evidence of official disregard for the law.

V · Citizen Action:

How To Take Back Your Government

> *Your every voter, as surely as your chief magistrate, exercises a public trust.*
> GROVER CLEVELAND

Earlier chapters have set out the problems and provided the data needed to work intelligently for government reform. Now it is time to pick up hammer and saw and get to work. Yet, as with most major tasks, the question for citizen reformers must be, "Where do I begin?" Targets must be carefully selected, and strategy must be designed to maximize the citizen's impact.

This chapter suggests some methods of reform and how these methods might best be employed at the federal level and state by state.

SEEKING ENFORCEMENT

Most reformers focus their efforts on securing new, more progressive legislation. Such legislation is often needed, but by concentrating on that point reformers have neglected one of their most powerful strategies: seeking enforcement of existing statutes. While reformers must depend on sometimes recalcitrant legislators to enact new laws, they have allies in the courts and the press when seeking the enforcement of existing laws. A variety of strategies are available for cultivating those allies and seeking enforcement.

The method that makes best use of a potentially sympathetic press is to *attempt to uncover violations of the law that have gone unprosecuted and to publicize them through the media*. Such publicity will serve to put pressure on both the violator and the delinquent enforcer. In many instances, the investigative research will not be difficult. The press regularly reports stories about large campaign contributions, secret meetings, or, to a lesser extent, the passage of special-interest bills or the efforts of a powerful lobby. What is required is to connect these stories with the relevant state or federal law on the subject.

The summaries of existing state and federal laws in the four reform fields should provide anyone with the tools he needs to uncover the story behind the story. If, for example, news stories regularly refer to the name of a lobbyist for a labor union or steel company and you wonder whether he is obeying the law, it is easy enough to go to the office of the individual with whom lobbyists are to register and see if the lobbyist has met the law. If you wish to check in a more enterprising way, find a sympathetic legislator and ask him to help you compile a list of active lobbyists. Check to see whether all of them have met the law. Clearly, the more examples you can find of nonenforcement and delinquent lobbyists, the stronger your case against the supposed enforcer and the more newsworthy your findings will be.

This strategy assumes that some violators and some enforcers will take the law more seriously if they know people are watching. Undoubtedly, not all will do so, and more serious action will be necessary. Two approaches are available: *Sue the violator* or *sue the enforcer*.

In many instances the law assigns specific responsibilities to the enforcing agent. He may be required to notify those who fail to file required statements, to inform the Attorney General when violations have occurred, to recommend action to the appropriate legislative committee, or to take some other action that bears on enforcement. Since you as a citizen are the loser if the law is not enforced, it is frequently possible to get standing in court and sue the enforcer for nonenforcement.

Such suits have two beneficial effects. First, they will likely generate heightened press coverage of your attempt to seek enforcement and will help demonstrate your willingness to see the matter to its conclusion. In these ways, you may apply the additional pressure on the enforcer necessary to get him to perform his duties voluntarily. Second, you may win the suit and the court may instruct the enforcer to take action. Even if neither voluntary nor forced compliance results from the lawsuit, the groundwork will have been laid with the press, the public, and the legislature if and when the time comes to seek a new law.

Under certain circumstances, it may be possible to *sue the violator directly*. Some state laws, mainly in the area of campaign finance, include citizen complaint or citizen suit provisions. These procedures generally permit an opposing candidate (and sometimes any registered voter) to file a complaint in court or with a supervisory body charging that a violation has occurred. Where such laws exist they should be used in preference to suing the enforcing agent. The citizen suit provisions eliminate the sometimes difficult legal problem of getting standing in court, that is, of demonstrating that you are an injured party and therefore have a right to sue the suspected violator.

Suits against violators themselves should not automatically be ruled out, however, merely because no citizen suit provision is in a law. Increasingly, courts are recognizing the right of an individual or a group of citizens to claim standing in cases where a large class of persons suffers, in the aggregate, a substantial injury as a result of an illegal act.

The change in the courts' attitude toward citizen suits began with the environmental suits, where citizens sought to sue polluters on behalf of themselves and society. The precedent was reinforced in an important case in 1971 in which Common Cause sued the National Republican Party, the National Democratic Party, and the Conservative Party of New York for encouraging individuals to contribute in excess of the $5,000 individual contribution limit set in the Corrupt Practices Act. Refusing a defense motion that the case be dismissed, the judge indicated that Common Cause, a citizen's group, could sue on behalf of its own members and society. Such suits will, no doubt, be increasingly used by citizens seeking better enforcement of the laws.

Another technique for seeking enforcement flows naturally from the last two suggestions. Where no citizen suit procedure is in the law and where citizens have not been granted standing in court, it may be necessary to seek *legislative* remedy. Citizens should *work for a separate legislative act granting citizen standing* in a broad range of specified situations, including the failure of responsible enforcing authorities to act. Failing the passage of such a comprehensive act, citizens should work for the passage of an amendment to the particular unenforced law granting citizens standing in cases specifically related to the act.

All of these attempts at achieving standing in either a specific or general way are cumbersome and time-consuming. For that reason, when seeking new legislation in any of the four fields it is important to fight for the inclusion of citizen standing provisions. Each of the four model bills included in this book contains such citizen standing provisions.

CHANGING THE LAWS

When it appears that existing laws will be unenforced or are unenforceable, or where they do not deal with the subject in a sufficiently comprehensive and vigorous manner, it is necessary to seek new and stronger laws. A series of alternatives exists when seeking new laws: statutory change, executive order and initiative, and constitutional amendment. Various advantages and disadvantages are associated with each of these alternatives.

The most widely used and most efficient way to change laws is through statutory change; that is, by act of the legislature. Such a method has several advantages: (1) Citizens are in a comparatively good position to influence legislators; (2) the new law can usually be enacted in a reasonable length of time; and (3) the legislature can enact laws governing all citizens and public officials in all branches of government. The major problem with the use of the statutory change is that in many cases it is the behavior of the legislature itself that is the citizens' target for reform, and some legislators may have a vested interest in seeing that strong reform legislation is not enacted.

When beginning to seek enactment of reform legislation, *take a preliminary sounding of legislators' views on the reform topic.* A simple, straightforward inquiry to the offices of each legislator, asking for a preliminary reaction to certain key parts of a strong law, should be sufficient. This will serve three purposes: It makes legislators aware of your intentions; it will help you identify potential sponsors and cosponsors of your legislation; and it will help you to develop a strategy for lobbying legislators as the bill proceeds through committee and onto the floor.

Make an active effort to seek bipartisan cosponsorship for the legislation. This is important not only to keep yourself from being branded as partisan, but also because it will help remove suspicion that the legislation will benefit one political persuasion at the expense of another. Any attempt at enacting legislation should be a good-government effort, not a partisan effort. Bipartisan sponsorship is particularly important when seeking new campaign finance legislation. Politicians are wary of any real or potential threat to their power base. In Illinois, for example, a proposed state campaign finance law was threatened because the Democrats viewed it as anti-union and therefore, by extension, anti-Democratic Party.

It is equally important to *have the bill introduced in both houses of the legislature at or near the same time and in the same form*. This will speed the process of passage, since each house knows the other is considering a companion bill and because any expression of public or press support of the legislation can be focused on both houses. This eliminates the need to duplicate your publicity efforts.

An additional benefit is derived from having identical or similar bills introduced in each house. If the language of bills passed in the two houses is different, a conference is convened to work out compromise language acceptable to both houses. In many cases, these are the most secretive committees in the state legislatures. Conference committees tend to be difficult to lobby. It is difficult to follow the progress of their deliberations. They are, however, permitted to draft new language only in those areas where the two versions of the bill differ. By minimizing the opportunities for conference committee drafting, you decrease the power of a frequently unresponsive body.

Special effort should be made to *ensure that the bill is considered at open public hearings*. This is important to provide an opportunity for reform groups to testify. It is also consistent with the basic reform position that a government must be open to be accountable.

In many states the legislators lack adequate professional staff. As a result, legislative drafting offices exist to which legislators may turn when they wish to introduce legislation but lack the expertise or staff to draft the bill themselves. These legislative drafting offices are themselves overworked and, quite naturally, cannot be expert on every legislative issue. It is sometimes productive, therefore, to *offer to assist such offices in the drafting of legislation* on the four reform issues. At a minimum, they should be provided with copies of the model legislation contained in this book.

In a more general way, it should be the goal of the reformer to attempt to establish himself as an information source and as a source of expertise with the public, the press, and the legislature on the issue in which he is interested. While it is extremely difficult for average citizens to establish themselves as experts on such complex issues as the reform of education, it is quite possible to do so on the issues of government reform. There are few "professional experts" in the four reform fields. The issues do not have a technical complexity. A citizen's effectiveness will be immeasurably increased if he becomes a resource person for the press by keeping up with the issue and, at the same time, a resource for the legislature by knowing the facts of a given position. Any attempt at seeking enforcement of old laws or enactment of new ones can be made if the reformer will *actively seek to cultivate relationships and alliances* with other individuals, with like-minded groups, with the press, and with sympathetic legislators.

Even if all of the above strategies are employed, some legislatures may be intractable. A fallback alternative exists. The President and most governors have the right to issue executive orders. These orders, which do not require legislative approval, have the force of law but are limited in scope. They may govern the actions of members of the executive branch only. Still, it may be profitable to *urge a governor or the President to issue an executive order* in an area where the legislature has failed to act. This strategy has historical precedent. In 1965 President Lyndon Johnson issued an executive order requiring all officials of the executive branch with salaries over a certain level or in sensitive positions to make full disclosure of their financial holdings. In 1972, Governor John Gilligan of Ohio issued a similar order requiring financial disclosure by officials of the executive branch of the state, an action Gilligan himself had voluntarily taken for the previous few years. Similarly, Governor Sargent of Massachusetts issued an executive order in 1972 dealing with lobbyists' attempts to influence many executive branch decisions. While limited in scope and not covering attempts to influence the governor's office itself, this attempt is better than no law at all.

The task of seeking the issuance of such orders is different from seeking the enactment of legislation. Since it is an executive decision, lobbying effort is naturally focused on the governor's office alone. The effort may be generally more informational than coercive. The executive may not have thought of issuing such an order. He himself may have been stymied in attempts to get the legislature to act in the reform field and may be a natural ally in reform efforts. The executive may be interested in the favorable publicity that such a reform would bring him.

In cases where the executive is not naturally sympathetic, the same alliance of press and public interest groups available in working for legislative action may be used to move the executive to action. At the national level, the size of the executive bureaucracy and the degree to which the President is insulated from individual public interest "lobbyists" makes it unlikely that citizens will themselves be able to influence decisions. Efforts at the national level should be focused on attempts to generate media interest in the issue in hopes of making it a national issue that the President will have to face.

If attempts to influence the legislature and the executive fail, the next recourse available in most states is the *initiative*. This procedure, by which measures become law by direct vote of the people, is generally more time-consuming than is direct legislative action. As long as campaign finance laws are unreformed, special interests may spend massive sums to urge the electorate to defeat initiatives. In California, it is not unusual for opposing sides to spend millions of dollars on an initiative proposition. The initiative does have the advantage that whatever language is drafted will be voted on. It may not be amended and thereby weakened to accommodate special interests.

A quick check of the legislative articles of a state's constitution will tell whether the initiative is an option and what procedures must be followed in getting an initiative on the ballot. The organization necessary to mount a successful campaign suggests a different kind of citizen effort from that required to lobby either the legislature or the executive. The key to such an effort is to build coalitions with other groups interested in the issue. The organizational problems associated with circulating petitions can best be dealt with by seeking alliances with existing membership organizations.

Here, too, as in all national efforts, the role of the media may be critical. It is important to urge the print and broadcast media to editorialize in support of the initiative and to report on it as they would on any other statewide election vote. Media interest should be easily generated in an initiative for an open meetings law in which the press has a vested interest. Media support for initiatives in the other three fields may require more research.

The constitutional amendment is the last resort for citizens seeking to change the law. Working for passage of amendments is an even more time-consuming, complicated, and expensive proposition than is the passage of initiatives. Furthermore, since only fundamental matters should be included in a constitution, an amendment should deal only with the basic reforms insofar as they are the rights of all citizens. The specifics should be left for statutory law. The Constitution of the United States is a brief, clean document—it sets out basic principles, which are supported by more specific, particular statutory law. In contrast, most state constitutions are cluttered with details and specifics better suited to statutes. Thus, too many revisions of state laws require constitutional amendments. Too few problems can be resolved by the legislatures in order to avoid further exacerbating this problem. Constitutional amendments in the four reform fields should be written to assure basic citizen rights. Specifics such as exact dollar limits on campaign contributions are better left for statutory law, where they may be changed as conditions change.

Whether the goal is new legislation, an executive order, news media assistance, or more vigorous enforcement, citizens should not be trapped into evaluating potential allies on the basis of their liberal or conservative credentials. Honest men of all political persuasions are movable on government reform issues. Just because an individual may have opposed your efforts on some other issue, do not overlook him as a potential ally on government reform.

WHERE TO BEGIN

Obviously, no one can take on all needed reforms at once. What follows is a series of specific suggestions about the most important points of departure for federal and state reformers.

Separate recommendations are given for the federal government and for each state. Each of the state suggestions is preceded by an estimate of the relative quality of each of the four laws when compared with the model legislation and with the laws of the other states. A summary of the comparison precedes state recommendations. No attempt has been made to assign numerical values to these rankings, as the difference between the twenty-fifth and twenty-sixth best law would certainly be indistinguishable. The intent is merely to suggest that some laws are better than others and therefore that, while all laws can be improved, some more urgently need attention than others. Again, these are comparative evaluations. While a given law may be listed as adequate, this merely means it is better than one listed as partly effective, which, in turn, is better than one listed as ineffective.

FEDERAL RECOMMENDATIONS

Since no federal law deals comprehensively with both legislative and executive meetings and votes, the first priority in the open meetings field should be to seek a widely applicable federal open meetings law. It should allow citizen access to all meetings at which public policy is deliberated or decided in the legislative, executive, and administrative branches of government. All votes taken should be recorded by individual member and, along with all minutes taken, should be available to the public, except where subjects discussed deal with national security or personal privacy.

Short of such a comprehensive law, Congressional rules should be changed to require that all floor, committee, and caucus votes be taken in public and recorded by individual if so requested by a specified minority of voting members. Additionally, the exemptions in the Freedom of Information Act should be narrowed or eliminated, and active legislative oversight of government adherence to the regulations of the act should be increased. The latter may be accomplished by requiring that each agency file complete annual reports to Congress explaining each instance in which the exemptions in the act were invoked as a justification for refusing requested information.

In the area of lobbying disclosure, the current law should be strengthened in several ways. The definition of lobbying should be written to eliminate the "principal purpose" clause, which provides the loophole through which special interest groups avoid registration. The definition should be further strengthened by defining lobbying to include "grass-roots" lobbying efforts and attempts to influence the executive branch. To increase the prospects for enforcement, supervision should be made the responsibility of an independent agency empowered to subpoena witnesses and issue cease and desist orders against violators of the law. This independent agency should be required to make public and to disseminate lobbying reports quickly enough to make them useful to interested citizens or legislators. A citizen standing provision should be added as a further guarantee that the law will be enforced.

No comprehensive act currently deals with federal conflicts of interest. Such an act should be the primary objective of federal reformers in this field. By this act, public officials should be required to make full public disclosure of their financial holdings and to divest themselves of all holdings that create a real or potential conflict of interest with their official responsibilities. Thus, congressmen on the Banking and Currency Committee could not retain their directorships in banks, and senators on the Judiciary Committee could not be partners in law firms. Legislators should meet the same rigorous divestment requirements the Congress has imposed on executive officials. Members of the Federal Communication Commission cannot own stock in television stations; officials in the Defense Department must give up interests in corporations receiving or bidding on defense contracts.

The new law should be enforced by an independent commission, which, like the lobbying commission, could subpoena witnesses and issue cease and desist orders. The same commission could perhaps oversee and enforce both laws. As in the case of lobbying reforms, citizens must be granted standing in courts to sue both enforcing agents and suspected violators of the law.

In the field of campaign finance, the most attractive goal is public financing of campaigns, which could substantially reduce the corrupting influence of money on politics. It would be possible to supervise more effectively the amounts and manner of spending by candidates for federal office. While public financing of campaigns presents some problems, such as the difficulty of giving every candidate an equal chance without requiring the government to finance a limitless number of campaigns, these questions can eventually be resolved. Short of total public financing, some form of partial subsidy should be sought. One such approach would be to couple limits on the size of individual contributions with incentives to small givers, such as tax credits and tax check-offs, in hopes of broadening the base of political contributions. Such an approach has been enacted and will take effect for the 1974 elections. Obviously, each of these techniques would have to be linked to an over-all ceiling on campaign spending by a candidate.

In the absence of such substantial reform, some specific modification of the newly enacted Federal Election Campaign Act must be encouraged.

The new law repealed the limit on individual contributions, which had been a part of the Corrupt Practices Act. Such a limit must be put back into the law if the law is to effectively control the degree to which candidates become indebted to sources of wealth at election time. Although a limit is now set on the amount of money a candidate may spend on the media, unlimited spending is still permitted in all other areas, including travel expenses and mailing costs. As the costs in these areas rise, so will candidate spending, until, again, only those with personal wealth or access to wealth will be able to seek office. The campaign spending law should include limits on nonmedia expenditures of kinds that can be practically monitored.

The law should be supervised by an independent commission with subpoena and cease-and-desist powers. Citizens should be guaranteed the right to file complaints with the commission and use the courts to seek enforcement where the commission fails.

STATE-BY-STATE RECOMMENDATIONS

The table on the following pages presents a comparative evaluation of existing state laws on the four reform topics, as measured against the model legislation and the laws of other states. While a given law may be listed as adequate, this means merely that it is better than one listed as partly effective, which, in turn, is better than one listed as ineffective.

Existing State Laws as Compared with Common Cause Model Bills

State	Open Meetings	Lobbying Disclosure	Conflicts of Interest	Campaign Finance
Alabama	ineffective	ineffective	no law	partly effective
Alaska	partly effective	partly effective	no law	no law
Arizona	partly effective	ineffective	no law	partly effective
Arkansas	adequate	ineffective	adequate	ineffective
California	adequate	adequate	adequate	ineffective
Colorado	partly effective	ineffective	ineffective	ineffective
Connecticut	partly effective	partly effective	ineffective	ineffective
Delaware	ineffective	ineffective	no law	no law
Florida	adequate	partly effective	partly effective	adequate
Georgia	partly effective	ineffective	ineffective	no law
Hawaii	partly effective	no law	ineffective	ineffective
Idaho	ineffective	no law	no law	no law
Illinois	adequate	adequate	adequate	no law
Indiana	ineffective	partly effective	no law	partly effective
Iowa	adequate	ineffective	ineffective	ineffective
Kansas	partly effective	partly effective	adequate	partly effective
Kentucky	ineffective	partly effective	ineffective	partly effective
Louisiana	ineffective	no law	ineffective	no law
Maine	ineffective	ineffective	ineffective	ineffective
Maryland	ineffective	partly effective	ineffective	adequate
Massachusetts	ineffective	adequate	ineffective	partly effective
Michigan	ineffective	ineffective	ineffective	partly effective
Minnesota	adequate	partly effective	ineffective	adequate
Mississippi	ineffective	partly effective	ineffective	ineffective
Missouri	ineffective	partly effective	ineffective	partly effective
Montana	ineffective	partly effective	no law	partly effective

State				
Nebraska	partly effective	adequate	ineffective	partly effective
Nevada	partly effective	no law	no law	no law
New Hampshire	ineffective	partly effective	ineffective	adequate
New Jersey	ineffective	adequate	ineffective	ineffective
New Mexico	ineffective	ineffective	ineffective	ineffective
New York	ineffective	partly effective	adequate	adequate
North Carolina	partly effective	partly effective	no law	partly effective
North Dakota	ineffective	ineffective	no law	ineffective
Ohio	adequate	partly effective	ineffective	partly effective
Oklahoma	partly effective	ineffective	ineffective	ineffective
Oregon	ineffective	ineffective	ineffective	adequate
Pennsylvania	ineffective	ineffective	no law	ineffective
Rhode Island	ineffective	partly effective	no law	no law
South Carolina	ineffective	partly effective	partly effective	ineffective
South Dakota	partly effective	partly effective	adequate	partly effective
Tennessee	ineffective	ineffective	no law	ineffective
Texas	ineffective	adequate	no law	partly effective
Utah	ineffective	no law	no law	partly effective
Vermont	no law	ineffective	ineffective	ineffective
Virginia	adequate	partly effective	adequate	partly effective
Washington	partly effective	partly effective	adequate	ineffective
West Virginia	ineffective	no law	no law	adequate
Wisconsin	ineffective	adequate	ineffective	adequate
Wyoming	no law	ineffective	ineffective	partly effective

SUMMARY OF THE COMPARISON

8 adequate	7 adequate	8 adequate	8 adequate
13 partly effective	20 partly effective	2 partly effective	17 partly effective
27 ineffective	17 ineffective	23 ineffective	17 ineffective
2 no law	6 no law	17 no law	8 no law

CRITERIA FOR COMPARING EXISTING LAWS

Open Meetings

Adequate
Laws include:
1. Coverage beyond legislative to executive branch;
2. executive sessions either prohibited or permissible in extremely limited circumstances;
3. provisions that void actions taken at illegally closed sessions;
4. requirements that legislative votes be taken in public and recorded.

Partly effective
Laws include:
1. Coverage more limited than in "adequate" law;
2. the permissibility of executive sessions in certain circumstances by vote of the meeting body;
3. less stringent rules for the opening and recording of legislative votes.

Ineffective
Laws include:
1. Some law on the books with coverage excluding either legislative or executive branch meetings;
2. rules regulating the closing of meetings either lax or ambiguous, with meetings easily held in private;
3. no provision that legislative votes be held in open session or recorded.

No law.

Lobbying Disclosure

Adequate
Laws include:
1. Requirements that both lobbyists and their employers register;
2. provisions that lobbyists and employers file financial statements both during and after legislative sessions;
3. The assigning of enforcing responsibility to a specific agent (preferably such agent would be independent of legislative pressure).

Partly effective
Laws include:
1. Requirements that both lobbyists and their employers register;
2. provisions that lobbyists and/or employers file financial statements, 'with such statements not due until after the end of the legislative session;

3. enforcement left to a committee or agent of the legislature.

Ineffective
Laws include:

1. Some law on the books, with the registration requirements offering opportunities for circumvention;
2. no requirements that either employers or lobbyists file financial statements.

No law.

Conflicts of Interest

Adequate
Laws include:

1. Coverage to legislators, legislative employees, and executive officials and employees;
2. requirements that public officials make full public disclosure of personal financial holdings;
3. ideally, requirements that officials divest themselves of real or potential conflicts (at a minimum, to disqualify themselves from voting on decisions in which they may have an interest);
4. enforcement responsibility clearly mandated to a specific agent.

Partly effective
Laws include:

1. Coverage more limited than in "adequate" laws but still applicable to legislators;
2. provisions that financial disclosure be required —but such disclosure either not made public or required only when the official himself believes a conflict may exist;
3. no divestment requirement (however, legislators are at least urged to disqualify themselves from decisions in which they have a financial interest);
4. enforcement responsibility left to an internal committee or employee of the legislature.

Ineffective
Laws include:

1. Some law on the books, but limited to either a code of ethics or weak or general guidelines for official behavior;
2. no disclosure requirements.

No law.

Campaign Finance

Adequate
Laws include:

1. Coverage extending to candidates and political committees;
2. a particular person or persons responsible for campaign expenditures for each candidate or committee;
3. requirements that statements listing both contributions and expenditures be filed with a supervisory officer and made publicly available, both before and after all elections;
4. the setting of a limit on individual contributions;
5. the setting of a limit on campaign expenditures;
6. requirements that a specific agent has responsibility for supervising and enforcing the law.

Partly effective
Laws include:

1. Coverage extending to candidates and committees;
2. naming of a person (or persons) responsible for a candidate or committee's campaign expenditures;
3. requirements that statements listing both contributions and expenditures be filed with a supervisory officer—with reports not due until after election;
4. the setting of a limit on campaign expenditures (with the limit either unrealistically low or excessively high);
5. no limit being set on individual contributions;
6. the responsibility for enforcement authority clearly assigned.

Ineffective
Laws include:

1. Some law on the books but not covering all candidates or committees;
2. weak, ambiguous or nonexistent requirements that candidates disclose contributions received and expenditures made;
3. no limit set on individual contributions;
4. no limit set on campaign expenditures;
5. responsibility for enforcing the law either left to a committee or employee or the legislature or left unassigned.

No law.

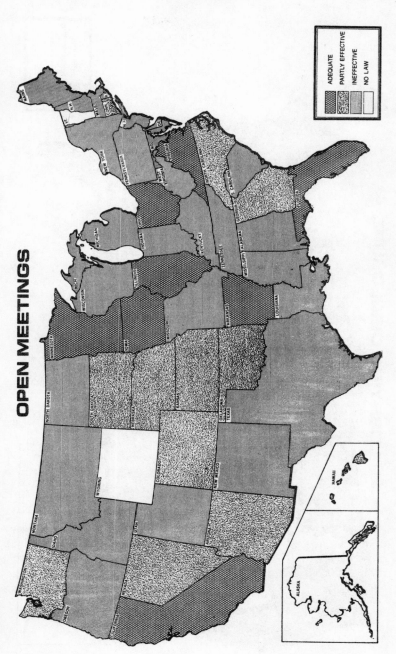

OPEN MEETINGS

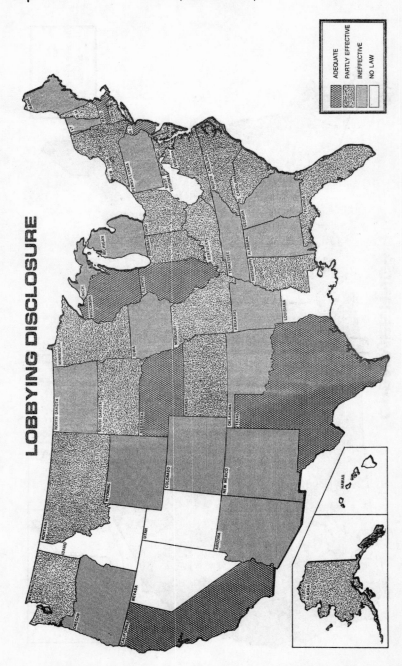

LOBBYING DISCLOSURE

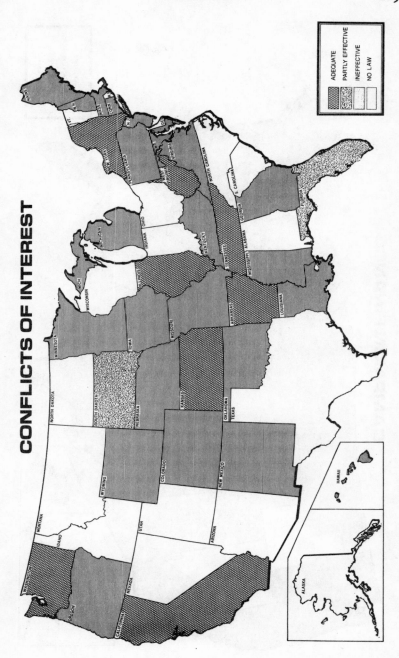

CONFLICTS OF INTEREST

ADEQUATE
PARTLY EFFECTIVE
INEFFECTIVE
NO LAW

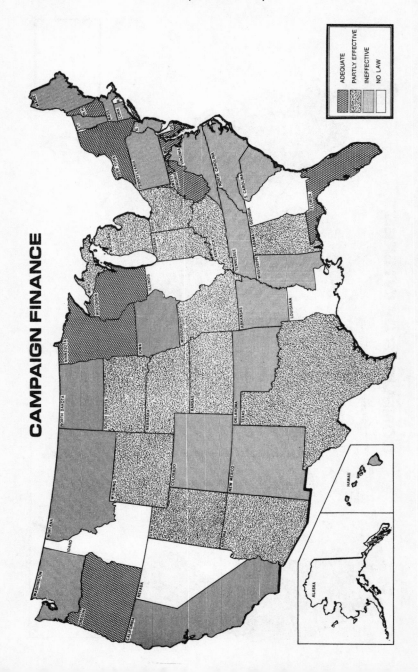

CAMPAIGN FINANCE

ADEQUATE
PARTLY EFFECTIVE
INEFFECTIVE
NO LAW

Alabama

OPEN MEETINGS—*ineffective*
LOBBYING DISCLOSURE—*ineffective*
CONFLICTS OF INTEREST—*no law*
CAMPAIGN FINANCE—*partly effective*

Alabama statutes in government reform fields are generally poor. While citizen action is called for in all four fields, the absence of any state conflict of interest statute and the total inadequacy of existing open meetings laws should receive primary attention. The media share an interest with the citizen in improving open meetings practices, since they, too, are thwarted in getting the information they need when statutes and rules are nonfunctional. For this reason the media should be potential allies on this issue. Any attempt to reform or strengthen existing lobbying statutes should focus on the need for reporting requirements for both lobbyists and their employers. Under the current law, neither category is required to make any financial statements listing either income or expenditures. The campaign finance law could be most significantly strengthened by requiring that financial statements be filed prior to, as well as after, elections and by setting a limit on individual contributions.

Alaska

OPEN MEETINGS—*partly effective*
LOBBYING DISCLOSURE—*partly effective*
CONFLICTS OF INTEREST—*no law*
CAMPAIGN FINANCE—*no law*

Work should begin to seek the enactment of laws in conflicts of interest and campaign finance, where no law currently is on the books. The lobbying law should be strengthened by including a clear definition of the term "lobbyist" and by requiring that financial statements currently due thirty days after adjournment would be filed on a more regular basis throughout and following the legislative session. The open meetings law could be strengthened by limiting the number of legitimate topics that can be discussed in closed session.

Arizona

> OPEN MEETINGS—*partly effective*
> LOBBYING DISCLOSURE—*ineffective*
> CONFLICTS OF INTEREST—*no law*
> CAMPAIGN FINANCE—*partly effective*

The open meetings law should be improved by making it more difficult to go into executive session, by more clearly limiting the types of activities permitted in such sessions, and by redefining the term "official meeting" so that the law may not be circumvented by holding "unofficial meetings." The lobbying law should be strengthened by requiring that both lobbyists and their employers file financial statements listing both expenditures and incomes derived from lobbying. To be operational, the enforcement provisions of the law must also be changed, taking supervision out of the hands of the Rules Committee of the House of Representatives. No rules whatever exist with regard to attempts to lobby the state Senate. An entirely new statute must be enacted to cover this inadequacy. The primary target for citizen action should be the enactment of comprehensive conflict of interest laws. The campaign finance law should be strengthened by setting limits on individual contributions, by extending the expenditures limits to cover general and special elections, and by requiring that the financial statements now due thirty days after general elections be filed at reasonable intervals before as well as after elections.

Arkansas

> OPEN MEETINGS—*adequate*
> LOBBYING DSCLOSURE—*ineffective*
> CONFLICTS OF INTEREST—*adequate*
> CAMPAIGN FINANCE—*ineffective*

Citizen attention should focus on needed requirements in the areas of lobbying and campaign finance. Employers of lobbyists should be required to register separately from their employees. Supervision of the law should be taken out of the hands of officers of the state legislature. Financial statements listing both income and expenditures derived from lobbying should be required of both lobbyists and their employers and should be filed at regular intervals throughout and after legislative sessions. Enforcement and penalty provisions should be enacted in the statute. Needed campaign finance requirements include the setting of individual contribution limits and spending limits, prohibition of corporate and labor union contributions, and requirements that comprehensive financial statements be filed with state officials and made publicly available both prior to and after primary and general elections. Additionally, the scope of the law should be expanded to cover campaign activities and expenditures of political committees as well as candidates.

California

OPEN MEETING—*adequate*
LOBBYING DISCLOSURE—*adequate*
CONFLICTS OF INTEREST—*adequate*
CAMPAIGN FINANCE—*ineffective*

The most needed reform in California is in the area of campaign finance. The law should be amended by requiring candidates and political committees to file contribution and expenditure statements before as well as after elections. Further amendments should set limits on individual contributions and campaign expenditures. Strong enforcement provisions should be included in the law. The open meetings law, while good, could be improved by the inclusion of strong enforcement provisions. Better still, a comprehensive new law that would apply uniformly to all branches of government should be urged. The lobbying law should be strengthened by requiring employers of lobbyists, as well as lobbyists themselves, to register and file financial statements. The conflict of interest law could be strengthened by

requiring public officials to divest themselves of personal holdings
that represent real or potential conflicts of interest.

Colorado

OPEN MEETINGS—*partly effective*
LOBBYING DISCLOSURE—*ineffective*
CONFLICTS OF INTEREST—*ineffective*
CAMPAIGN FINANCE—*ineffective*

The absence of any statutory lobbying regulations must be
remedied by the passage of a new, comprehensive state lobbying
law. Such a law must take supervision of the regulation of
lobbying out of the hands of the state legislature itself. The
conflict of interest law should be strengthened by requiring that
the financial disclosure statements filed by state legislators become
a matter of public record and that any holdings that represent
real or potential conflicts of interest be divested. As with the
lobbying law, responsibility for supervision and enforcement must
be taken from the legislature itself and granted to an independent
commission more capable of objective, rigorous scrutiny. Such
scrutiny should be further promoted by the inclusion of citizen
standing provisions in each of these two laws. The most needed
reforms of the campaign finance law include the setting of
limits on individual contributions and campaign expenditures
and a ban on corporate and labor union political contributions.
Open meetings laws should be modified to make it more difficult
for boards, commissions, and committees to go into executive
session.

Connecticut

OPEN MEETINGS—*partly effective*
LOBBYING DISCLOSURE—*partly effective*
CONFLICTS OF INTEREST—*ineffective*
CAMPAIGN FINANCE—*ineffective*

The most needed reform is in the conflict of interest field.
The law must be strengthened by requiring that public officials
make public disclosure of personal financial holdings and that

they divest themselves of any holdings that represent real or potential conflicts of interest. Enforcement of the statute must be taken from the hands of the legislature itself and given to a more independent, responsible enforcing agent. Despite the fact that the conflict of interest law referred to here was just recently enacted, and indeed will not take effect until January 3, 1973, this area remains the one most critically in need of reform in Connecticut. The campaign finance law should be strengthened by setting limits on individual contributions and campaign expeditures and by requiring that financial statements be filed before as well as after primary and general elections. The comprehensive open meetings law, which applies to administrative and executive boards, should be expanded to include the legislature and its committees as well. This would effectively deal with the current permissible practice of calling executive sessions without sufficient justification. The lobbying law should be improved by requiring that the financial statements now due sixty days after adjournment of the legislature be filed periodically throughout the session as well. Employers of lobbyists should be required not only to meet these more regular financial statement deadlines but also to register at the beginning of each legislative session.

Delaware

OPEN MEETINGS—*ineffective*
LOBBYING DISCLOSURE—*ineffective*
CONFLICT OF INTEREST—*no law*
CAMPAIGN FINANCE—*no law*

Most urgently needed is the passage of new comprehensive statutes covering conflicts of interest and campaign finance. Nearly as important, however, is the strengthening of the lobbying statute by the inclusion of requirements that both lobbyists and their employers file comprehensive financial statements both during and after legislative sessions. The open meetings law now permits executive sessions of a vast array of subjects. The law should be tightened to permit executive sessions only in the most limited of circumstances.

Florida

OPEN MEETINGS—*adequate*
LOBBYING DISCLOSURE—*partly effective*
CONFLICTS OF INTEREST—*partly effective*
CAMPAIGN FINANCE—*adequate*

The most needed reform is in the area of conflicts of interest, where financial disclosure requirements should be strengthened so that all public officials must make such disclosure, not merely those who themselves believe they have a conflict. Additionally, the law should be modified to require public officials who have holdings that may be real or potential conflicts of interest to divest themselves of such holdings. Despite the fact that the campaign finance law is one of the better laws in the country, it could be strengthened by setting lower campaign expenditure limits. Similarly, a good state lobbying law could be improved by requiring that financial statements be filed during, as well as after, legislative sessions.

Aside from these improvements in existing law, and because the laws in three of the fields are generally strong, citizen efforts should focus on enforcement of existing laws.

Georgia

OPEN MEETINGS—*partly effective*
LOBBYING DISCLOSURE—*ineffective*
CONFLICTS OF INTEREST—*ineffective*
CAMPAIGN FINANCE—*no law*

Entirely new conflict of interest and campaign finance laws should be enacted, since current legislation in conflicts of interest is limited to a code of ethics, and since no state campaign finance statute exists. The lobbying law must be strengthened by requiring that employers of lobbyists, as well a lobbyists themselves, register and that both lobbyists and employers file financial statements listing lobbying-related income and expenditures both during and after legislative sessions. Enforcement of the law, now in the hands of the legislature itself, must be given to a more independent body. To promote enforcement, a citizens standing provision should also be written into the law. An odd provision in the Georgia Constitution, which makes lobbying illegal, should be constitutionally amended, thereby eliminating one of the most substantial ambiguities and contradictions in the laws of any state. The recently passed state open meetings law should be substantially strengthened by making it more difficult for legislative, executive and independent agencies to go into execution session. The specific exemptions to that law, particularly those which apply to certain state senate and house committees, should be removed.

Hawaii

OPEN MEETINGS—*partly effective*
LOBBYING DISCLOSURE—*no law*
CONFLICTS OF INTEREST—*ineffective*
CAMPAIGN FINANCE—*ineffective*

Of primary concern for citizens is the enactment of a comprehensive lobbying disclosure act. The provision of the current conflicts of interest law that exempts legislators and judges from coverage should be stricken. Public disclosure of financial interests should be required of all public officials, not only in instances where a conflict exists, but on a regular basis whether or not the official believes the conflict exists. A requirement should also be made that public officials divest themselves of any holdings that represent either real or potential conflicts of interest. Similarly, legislators should be required to disqualify themselves in official dealings if a conflict exists. The Ethics Commission, which is responsible for enforcing the law, should be encouraged to do so by including a citizens standing provision in the statute. The campaign finance law should be strengthened by setting limits on individual contributions and on campaign expenditures. The financial statements currently required after elections should be required both during and after elections, and enforcement and penalty provisions should be included in the law. Open meetings legislation should be strengthened by strictly limiting the topics that may be discussed in executive session.

Idaho

> OPEN MEETINGS—*ineffective*
> LOBBYING DISCLOSURE—*no law*
> CONFLICTS OF INTEREST—*no law*
> CAMPAIGN FINANCE—*no law*

Obviously, the place to begin is to seek the enactment of new, comprehensive legislation in each of the four fields. While some law exists with respect to open meetings, it is so inadequate that an effort should be made to seek enactment of a completely new law.

Illinois

> OPEN MEETINGS—*adequate*
> LOBBYING DISCLOSURE—*adequate*
> CONFLICTS OF INTEREST—*adequate*
> CAMPAIGN FINANCE—*no law*

Clearly, the area of government reform needing most citizen attention is campaign finance. A rigorous effort should be made to enact a new, comprehensive campaign finance statute. In addition, while Illinois has some of the best existing statutes in the other three fields, there is some evidence that the laws are unenforced. Citizens should actively seek rigorous enforcement of existing statutes and urge the legislature to add citizen standing provisions to the laws in each of the fields to help ensure that needed enforcement will occur.

Indiana

> OPEN MEETINGS—*ineffective*
> LOBBYING DISCLOSURE—*partly effective*

CONFLICTS OF INTEREST—*no law*
CAMPAIGN FINANCE—*partly effective*

Most needed is the enactment of a comprehensive new conflicts of interest statute. Currently no such statewide statute exists. Next in importance is a substantial overhaul of the state open meetings law. Currently the language of the law is sufficiently broad to permit closed meetings in great numbers of cases. Requirements for closed meetings should be tightened. In addition, rules dealing specifically with the state legislature should be amended to require that all committee votes be taken in open session and recorded by individual. Currently, deliberations of legislative committees—and, indeed, of the legislature as a whole—are not as a matter of course included in the Journal. They should be. The lobbying law should be amended to require that employers and lobbyists file financial statements not only after the adjournment of the General Assembly but throughout the legislative session as well. The campaign finance law should be strengthened by the inclusion of limits on individual contributions and by requiring that financial reports listing contributions and expenditures be filed before as well as after each election.

Iowa

OPEN MEETINGS—*adequate*
LOBBYING DISCLOSURE—*ineffective*
CONFLICTS OF INTEREST—*ineffective*
CAMPAIGN FINANCE—*ineffective*

Citizen efforts should focus on passage of a comprehensive new conflicts of interest law. The lobbying law should be strengthened by requiring both the lobbyist and his employer to register and file statements periodically throughout the legislative session, listing income and expenditures related to lobbying activities. Changes in the campaign finance law should require candidates and political committees to file contribution and expenditure statements before and after all elections. A limit should be set for individual contributions. To ensure their effectiveness, all four laws need strong enforcement provisions.

Kansas

> OPEN MEETINGS—*partly effective*
> LOBBYING DISCLOSURE—*partly effective*
> CONFLICTS OF INTEREST—*adequate*
> CAMPAIGN FINANCE—*partly effective*

The open meetings law, which currently applies only to the executive branch and state administrative agencies and departments, should be expanded in coverage to apply to the legislative branch as well. The law should be amended to require that votes in committee and in the legislature be recorded and available by individual and that conference committee sessions, as well as all other committee meetings, be open to the public. The lobbying law should be amended to require that financial statements now due only once each year be filed more regularly throughout the year. Currently, only those lobbyists who receive compensation of $1,000 or more or expend $1,000 or more are required to file. This dollar figure should be removed in favor of more general filing. The campaign finance law should be expanded to apply to candidates for federal office from Kansas as well as state office. Additionally, limits should be set on individual contributions, and corporations and labor unions should be prohibited from making political campaign contributions. The conflicts of interest law could be strengthened by requiring public officials to divest themselves of any financial holdings that represent real or potential conflicts of interest.

Kentucky

> OPEN MEETINGS—*ineffective*
> LOBBYING DISCLOSURE—*partly effective*
> CONFLICTS OF INTEREST—*ineffective*
> CAMPAIGN FINANCE—*partly effective*

While Kentucky has some open meetings legislation, it is so

inadequate as to justify an effort at enacting an entirely new open meetings law. The conflict of interest law, while broad in coverage, requires neither the public disclosure of financial holdings nor the divestment of any real or potential conflicts. Nor does it include any penalty or enforcement provisions. All of these absences should be corrected. It may be simpler to seek a new comprehensive law than to amend a law that has so many gaps. The lobbying law should be strengthened by requiring that employers and lobbyists file financial statements during, as well as after, the adjournment of the General Assembly. The reporting requirements of the campaign finance law are excellent, but limits must be set on individual contributions and campaign expenditures. Additionally, a prohibition against contributions by corporations or labor unions should be enacted. The provision of the law that exempts candidates who run unopposed from reporting contributions and expenditures should be repealed, as unopposed candidates may still incur expenses in the course of a campaign.

Louisiana

OPEN MEETINGS—*ineffective*
LOBBYING DISCLOSURE—*no law*
CONFLICTS OF INTEREST—*ineffective*
CAMPAIGN FINANCE—*no law*

The total inadequacy of the existing open Meetings and conflict of interest laws and the absence of any statewide statutes regulating lobbying or campaign finance suggest that the best approach for citizen action is to seek the enactment of new, comprehensive statutes in each of the four fields.

Maine

OPEN MEETINGS—*ineffective*
LOBBYING DISCLOSURE—*ineffective*
CONFLICTS OF INTEREST—*ineffective*
CAMPAIGN FINANCE—*ineffective*

Citizen action on conflicts of interest should focus on passage of a comprehensive new law requiring regular and public disclosure of financial holdings by public officials. The campaign finance law should be expanded to require that candidates and committees file contribution and expenditure statements before and after all elections. Limits should be set on individual contributions and on campaign expenditures. Changes in the lobbying law should require that lobbyists and their employers file statements throughout the legislative session listing income and expenditures related to lobbying activities. The open meetings law is quite comprehensive in its coverage but should be improved by limiting the circumstances permitting executive sessions. Stronger enforcement provisions are needed in open meetings and conflicts of interest.

Maryland

> OPEN MEETINGS—*ineffective*
> LOBBYING DISCLOSURE—*partly effective*
> CONFLICTS OF INTEREST—*ineffective*
> CAMPAIGN FINANCE—*adequate*

Citizen action should focus on passage of new, comprehensive laws in the areas of open meetings and conflicts of interest. The lobbying law should be improved by requiring the employer as well as the lobbyist to register and file a statement of incomes and expenditures.

Massachusetts

> OPEN MEETINGS—*ineffective*
> LOBBYING—*adequate*
> CONFLICTS OF INTEREST—*ineffective*
> CAMPAIGN FINANCE—*partly effective*

Efforts should be made to pass a comprehensive new open meetings law and a new conflict of interest law requiring disclosure of financial holdings by public officials. The campaign finance law should be improved by requiring candidates and committees to file statements of contributions and expenditures before as well as after all elections. Limits should be set for campaign expenditures.

Michigan

OPEN MEETINGS—*ineffective*
LOBBYING DISCLOSURE—*ineffective*
CONFLICTS OF INTEREST—*ineffective*
CAMPAIGN FINANCE—*partly effective*

Citizen action should focus on the passage of new, comprehensive laws on open meetings and conflicts of interest. As it now stands, the lobbying law requires no financial statements. It should be strengthened by requiring both lobbyists and their employers to file statements throughout the legislative session listing incomes and expenditures related to lobbying activities. Employers of lobbyists should also be required to register. Improvements in the campaign finance law should be made by requiring the filing of expenditure and contribution statements before as well as after all elections. A limit should be set for individual contributions.

Minnesota

OPEN MEETINGS—*adequate*
LOBBYING DISCLOSURE—*partly effective*
CONFLICTS OF INTEREST—*ineffective*
CAMPAIGN FINANCE—*adequate*

Citizen activities should focus on passage of a new, comprehensive conflict of interest law requiring regular disclosure of financial holdings by public officials. This is clearly the area most in need of improvement. The lobbying law should be improved by taking enforcement responsibility out of the hands of employees of the legislature and placing it in the hands of a more objective party. It should also be improved by requiring employers as well as lobbyists to register and file statements of incomes and expenditures. A comprehensive law would be preferable to the separate rules now governing the House and the Senate.

Mississippi

OPEN MEETINGS—*ineffective*
LOBBYING DISCLOSURE—*partly effective*
CONFLICTS OF INTEREST—*ineffective*
CAMPAIGN FINANCE—*ineffective*

The only current Mississippi laws regulating open meetings appear in legislative rules. A new, comprehensive, statewide open meetings statute should be enacted as a matter of high priority. The only existing conflict of interest regulations are a series of prohibitions in the Constitution. It is therefore necessary to seek enactment of a new, comprehensive conflict of interest statute. The Mississippi campaign finance law includes excellent requirements with respect to the filing of campaign finance reports. The law is weak, however, in most of its other provisions. It should be amended to require that the representatives of political committees, as well as candidates, file statements. Limits should be set on individual contributions and on campaign expenditures. Enforcement and penalty provisions must be added to the law. The lobbying law should be amended to require that the lobbyist as well as his employer file forms and to require that both lobbyist and employer file financial statements during each legislative session as well as after adjournment.

Missouri

OPEN MEETINGS—*ineffective*
LOBBYING DISCLOSURE—*partly effective*
CONFLICTS OF INTEREST—*ineffective*
CAMPAIGN FINANCE—*partly effective*

The absence of any comprehensive statewide open meetings statute makes it necessary to seek enactment of an entirely new state law. The conflict of interest law should be amended so that all public officials are required, as a matter of course, to make public disclosure of personal financial holdings. The current law is inadequate in that it leaves discretion as to the extent of a possible conflict of interest to the public official himself. A specific enforcing agent must be appointed to supervise the conflict of interest law. Additionally, state legislators should be required to disqualify themselves from votes or decisions in which they have a personal financial interest. No such prohibition currently exists in the law. The lobbying law should be strengthened by requiring that employers of lobbyists register and by requiring that financial reports be filed periodically throughout the legislative session, as well as at the end of that session. Enforcement of the lobbying law should be taken from the hands of the employees of the legislature and given to an independent agency or commission. The campaign finance law should be strengthened by requiring financial statements before, as well as after, each election and by setting limits on individual campaign contributions.

Montana

OPEN MEETINGS—*ineffective*
LOBBYING DISCLOSURE—*partly effective*
CONFLICT OF INTEREST—*no law*
CAMPAIGN FINANCE—*partly effective*

Principal goals for citizen involvement should be the enactment of new, comprehensive legislation in the fields of open meetings and conflicts of interest. No comprehensive conflict of interest law is currently on the books. The open meetings law in no way prevents closed meetings of the legislature and includes too many exemptions with respect to state agencies and executive departments. The lobbying law could be strengthened by requiring that employers of lobbyists register separately from their employees and file separate financial statements. Enforcement responsibility should be more clearly articulated. The campaign finance law could be improved by setting limits on individual contributions.

Nebraska

OPEN MEETINGS—*partly effective*
LOBBYING DISCLOSURE—*adequate*
CONFLICTS OF INTEREST—*ineffective*
CAMPAIGN FINANCE—*partly effective*

The absence of any comprehensive statewide conflict of interest law suggests that the appropriate first effort is to seek a new comprehensive statute in this field. Open meetings statutes should be amended to require that votes in legislative committees be re,corded and available by individual, not merely by aggregate. Further, the current requirement that meetings may be closed by majority vote should be amended to permit closed meetings only under more limited circumstances. The campaign finance law should be strengthened by requiring that candidates as well as treasurers file financial statements prior to, as well as after, elections. Limits should be set on campaign spending, and corporations should be prohibited from making campaign contributions.

Nevada

OPEN MEETINGS—*partly effective*
LOBBYING DISCLOSURE—*no law*
CONFLICTS OF INTEREST—*no law*
CAMPAIGN FINANCE—*no law*

Since Nevada has no statewide statutes in three of the four fields, efforts should be made to seek enactment of new, comprehensive statutes. The strong open meetings provision applicable to public agencies, commissions, bureaus, departments, and boards should be applied to the legislature as well.

New Hampshire

OPEN MEETINGS—*partly effective*
LOBBYING DISCLOSURE—*ineffective*
CONFLICTS OF INTEREST—*ineffective*
CAMPAIGN FINANCE—*adequate*

Citizen action should focus on passage of comprehensive new open meetings and conflict of interest laws. The lobbying law should be improved by requiring the employer as well as the lobbyist to register and to file statements throughout the legislative session, listing incomes and expenditures related to lobbying activities.

New Jersey

OPEN MEETINGS—*ineffective*
LOBBYING DISCLOSURE—*adequate*
CONFLICTS OF INTEREST—*ineffective*
CAMPAIGN FINANCE—*ineffective*

The current open meetings law must be amended to include executive and legislative branch meetings. Specific provisions must be included to require that legislative committees meet in open session and that votes in committees and in the legislature be recorded by individual and be publicly available. Recorded votes should also be taken on procedural motions and amendments. The conflict of interest law should be strengthened by requiring that public officials make full public disclosure of financial holdings and that they divest themselves of any real or potential conflicts of interest. The law would be improved by moving the enforcement and oversight responsibilities from a joint legislative committee to an independent commission. The New Jersey legislative committee does, however, have reasonable power, and if it operated efficiently and objectively it could be an effective oversight authority. While the deadlines included in the campaign finance law for filing campaign expenditure and contribution statements are acceptable, the law must be improved by setting individual contribution limits and campaign expenditure limits. A specific enforcing authority must be created to supervise and enforce provisions of the campaign finance law.

New Mexico

OPEN MEETINGS—*ineffective*
LOBBYING DISCLOSURE—*ineffective*

CONFLICTS OF INTEREST—*ineffective*
CAMPAIGN FINANCE—*ineffective*

The open meetings law must be strengthened so that executive sessions are permissible only in the most limited circumstances, and then by recorded vote of the body going into such closed session. The lobbying law should be amended to require that lobbyists and employers file financial statements disclosing sources of income and expenditures related to lobbying periodically throughout the legislative session and at the conclusion of such sessions. Responsibility for overseeing and enforcing the provisions of the lobbying law should be placed in the hands of an independent enforcing agent. Currently, no specific enforcing agent, independent or otherwise, is named in the law. The conflict of interest law must be strengthened by requiring that all public officials make full public disclosure of their personal financial holdings. Currently, statements are required only from those legislators who have financial interests of $10,000 or more in businesses regulated by the state. Such a formula is unacceptable. The law should be further strengthened by requiring that public officials divest themselves of real or potential conflicts of interest. The campaign finance law must be strengthened by requiring candidates and representatives of political committees to file campaign expenditure and contribution statements prior to, as well as after, all elections. Additionally, limits must be set on individual campaign contributions and on campaign expenditures. Corporate and labor union contributions should be prohibited.

New York

OPEN MEETINGS—*ineffective*
LOBBYING DISCLOSURE—*partly effective*
CONFLICTS OF INTEREST—*adequate*
CAMPAIGN FINANCE—*adequate*

No comprehensive statewide open meetings statute applies to the executive or legislative branch. The appropriate citizen strategy, therefore, would be to seek enactment of such a comprehensive new statute. This statute should include, among general provisions, a requirement that the legislature and its committees deliberate and vote in open session and that votes be recorded by individual. The lobbying law should be strengthened by requiring that employers and lobbyists register. Even more important, lobbyists and employers should be required to file statements listing expenditures and income related to lobbying on a regular basis throughout the legislative session, as well as at the end of each session. The personal financial disclosure requirements made in the current New York conflict of interest law are excellent but could be further strengthened by requiring additional categories of information in such statements. Public officials should also be required to divest themselves of any personal financial holdings that represent real or potential conflicts of interest. Enforcement responsibility should be removed from employees of the legislature and given to an independent commission. While the campaign finance law is acceptable, it should be strengthened by setting a limit on individual contributions, by prohibiting corporate and labor union contributions, and by establishing specific enforcement responsibilities for the provisions of the law.

North Carolina

> OPEN MEETINGS—*partly effective*
> LOBBYING DISCLOSURE—*partly effective*
> CONFLICTS OF INTEREST—*no law*
> CAMPAIGN FINANCE—*partly effective*

Citizens should work for the adoption of a comprehensive new conflicts of interest statute. The open meetings law should be strengthened by setting more rigorous requirements for convening executive sessions. A percentage greater than a simple majority should be required to close meetings. The circumstances under which closed meetings are permissible should be more precisely defined. The lobbying law should be amended to require that lobbyists, as well as their employers, register. Financial reports should be made at regular intervals throughout, as well as after, the legislative session. Specific responsibility to enforce the lobbying law should be included in the law. While the topics covered in the campaign finance law are well conceived, the law fails to set limits on individual contributions or campaign spending. It also fails to prohibit corporation and labor union political contributions. Such failures should be corrected.

North Dakota

OPEN MEETINGS—*ineffective*
LOBBYING DISCLOSURE—*ineffective*
CONFLICTS OF INTEREST—*no law*
CAMPAIGN FINANCE—*ineffective*

Since no statewide conflict of interest law exists, citizens should work for the adoption of a new, comprehensive statute. Despite the existence of various statutory and constitutional open meetings regulations, the most reasonable strategy is for citizens to urge the passage of a new, comprehensive law. The lobbying law should be substantially strengthened by requiring both lobbyists and their employers to file regular reports itemizing their expenditures and income related to lobbying. The existing campaign finance law is sufficiently weak to justify a citizen effort aimed at adoption of a new law in this field as well.

Ohio

OPEN MEETINGS—*adequate*
LOBBYING DISCLOSURE—*partly effective*
CONFLICTS OF INTEREST—*no law*
CAMPAIGN FINANCE—*partly effective*

Citizens should work most vigorously for the adoption of a comprehensive statewide conflict of interest law. Secondary goals should include the revision of the lobbying law to require itemized financial statements periodically throughout as well as after legislative sessions and the expansion of the campaign finance law to set limits on individual contributions and to require that campaign financial statements be filed before as well as after elections.

Oklahoma

OPEN MEETINGS—*partly* effective
LOBBYING DISCLOSURE—*ineffective*
CONFLICTS OF INTEREST—*ineffective*
CAMPAIGN FINANCE—*ineffective*

Although a law exists with respect to lobbying activities, citizen efforts in this area should focus on passage of a new law requiring lobbyists and their employers to register and file statements of expenditures and incomes related to lobbying. The existing law does not require such statements or registration. Current conflict of interest legislation is limited to a code of ethics. A new law is needed requiring public officials to disclose financial interests and to divest themselves of real or potential conflicts. The campaign finance law should be strengthened by requiring the reporting of all contributions, not just those of $500 or more; by requiring statements of contributions and expenditures before as well as after elections; by setting campaign spending limits; and by prohibiting corporate and labor union contributions. The open meetings statute is quite comprehensive in regard to state agencies, but efforts should be made to improve it by including the legislature and its committees.

Oregon

OPEN MEETINGS—*ineffective*
LOBBYING DISCLOSURE—*ineffective*
CONFLICTS OF INTEREST—*ineffective*
CAMPAIGN FINANCE—*adequate*

Citizens should work for a comprehensive statewide open meetings law. Current disparate constitutional provisions, rules, and customs are not sufficient to keep executive and legislative sessions open. The new law should specifically require the legislature and its committees to meet and vote in open session with all votes recorded by individual. A new, comprehensive conflicts of interest law should be adopted to supplement the weak constitutional provisions. The lobbying law should be strengthened by requiring that all lobbyists and their employers file financial statements regularly throughout the legislative session as well as after such sessions. An independent agent should be given explicit responsibility for enforcing the law. While the campaign finance law is good, it could be strengthened by setting limits on individual contributions and by prohibiting corporate and labor union political contributions.

Pennsylvania

> OPEN MEETINGS—*ineffective*
> LOBBYING DISCLOSURE—*ineffective*
> CONFLICTS OF INTEREST—*ineffective*
> CAMPAIGN FINANCE—*ineffective*

Reform efforts in the areas of open meetings and conflicts of interest should focus on passage of comprehensive new laws. Changes in the lobbying law should require that employers of lobbyists as well as lobbyists register and file statements periodically throughout the legislative session listing incomes and expenditures related to lobbying activities. The campaign finance law should be improved by requiring that candidates and committees file statements of contributions and expenditures before and after all elections. Limits should be set for individual contributions and campaign expenditures. To ensure their effectiveness, the campaign finance law and the lobbying law need stronger enforcement provisions.

Rhode Island

> OPEN MEETINGS—*ineffective*
> LOBBYING DISCLOSURE—*partly effective*
> CONFLICTS OF INTEREST—*no law*
> CAMPAIGN FINANCE—*no law*

Highest priority for citizen action is the enactment of new, comprehensive laws in the fields of open meetings, conflicts of interest, and campaign finance. At somewhat less priority, the lobbying law should be improved by requiring that lobbyists and their employers file financial statements at regular intervals during as well as after legislative sessions.

South Carolina

> OPEN MEETINGS—*ineffective*
> LOBBYING DISCLOSURE—*partly effective*
> CONFLICTS OF INTEREST—*no law*
> CAMPAIGN FINANCE—*ineffective*

Current practices regarding open meetings amount to virtually no law. A new law is needed. Citizen efforts should center on passage of new laws in the area of conflicts of interest, where no law currently exists, as well as the area of open meetings. Improvements in the campaign finance law should focus on setting specific deadlines for filing contribution and expenditure statements. Limits should be set on individual contributions and campaign expenditures. Corporation and labor union contributions should be prohibited. While the lobbying law is a good one, it should be improved by requiring that expenditure statements be filed throughout the legislative session as well as after final adjournment and by including provisions for enforcement of the law.

South Dakota

> OPEN MEETINGS—*partly effective*
> LOBBYING DISCLOSURE—*partly effective*
> CONFLICTS OF INTEREST—*partly effective*
> CAMPAIGN FINANCE—*partly effective*

The open meetings law should be strengthened so that more than a simple majority is required to close official meetings. The lobbying law should contain a requirement that both lobbyists and employers file financial statements at regular intervals during, as well as after, legislative sessions. While the conflict of interest statute includes good financial disclosure requirements, it should be strengthened by requiring that public officials divest themselves of holdings that represent real or potential conflicts of interest. The law would be further improved by requiring legislators to disqualify themselves from decisions from which they may derive personal gain. The campaign finance law should be amended to require candidates and committees to file financial statements before, as well as after, elections. Additionally, limits should be set on individual contributions. With these improvements, an already good campaign finance law could be distinctly improved.

Tennessee

OPEN MEETINGS—*ineffective*
LOBBYING DISCLOSURE—*ineffective*
CONFLICTS OF INTEREST—*adequate*
CAMPAIGN FINANCE—*ineffective*

Citizen action in the area of open meetings should focus on passage of a new comprehensive law covering the General Assembly, its committees and agencies and boards in the executive branch. The lobbying law should be strengthened by requiring the employer as well as the lobbyist to register and also by requiring each of them to file a financial statement listing both income and expenditures related to lobbying activities. Contingent employment should not be allowed. Improvements should be made in the campaign finance law by requiring both candidates and campaign committees to file statements of expenditures and contributions before, as well as after, elections. Limits should be set on campaign expenditures and on individual contributions. The conflict of interest law is good, but efforts should be directed toward enacting strong enforcement provisions to ensure its effectiveness.

Texas

OPEN MEETINGS—*ineffective*
LOBBYING DISCLOSURE—*adequate*
CONFLICTS OF INTEREST—*no law*
CAMPAIGN FINANCE—*partly effective*

Since Texas has no comprehensive statewide conflict of interest law, the enactment of such a statute should be the first order of business for citizens seeking legislated reform. The open meetings law, which applies to executive branch meetings, should be expanded to cover legislative meetings as well. The law should be strengthened by eliminating the "security of the state" rationale for closing the meetings. Work in the area of campaign finance should be amended to set limits on individual contributions and campaign expenditures. In other respects, the Texas campaign finance law is excellent, and citizens should actively work to see that it is enforced. The good lobbying law should be strengthened further by establishing more specific enforcement responsibility.

Utah

OPEN MEETINGS—*ineffective*
LOBBYING DISCLOSURE—*no law*
CONFLICTS OF INTEREST—*no law*
CAMPAIGN FINANCE—*partly effective*

The most glaring need in Utah is the passage of new, comprehensive statutes dealing with lobbying and conflicts of interest, since no comprehensive law is currently on the books in either field. Nearly as important are amendments of the existing open meeting laws and rules. The preconditions to be met before an executive meeting is held should be tightened. Under current law, meetings can be easily closed. Further legislative rules should be amended to require that all legislative committees meet and vote in open session and that votes in the legislature and its committees be recorded by individual and publicly available. The campaign finance law should be strengthened by setting limits on individual contributions and campaign expenditures.

Vermont

OPEN MEETINGS—*no law*
LOBBYING DISCLOSURE—*ineffective*
CONFLICTS OF INTEREST—*no law*
CAMPAIGN FINANCE—*ineffective*

Highest priority should be assigned to efforts to seek new, comprehensive statewide statutes in the fields of open meetings, conflicts of interest, and campaign finance. No such law is currently on the books in either open meetings or conflicts of interest, and the present campaign finance law is extremely weak and ineffectual. The lobbying law should be improved by requiring both lobbyists and their employers to file financial statements at regular intervals throughout and after legislative sessions.

Virginia

> OPEN MEETINGS—*adequate*
> LOBBYING DISCLOSURE—*partly effective*
> CONFLICTS OF INTEREST—*ineffective*
> CAMPAIGN FINANCE—*partly effective*

The conflict of interest law deserves particular citizen scrutiny. It should be strengthened by requiring that all public officials make public disclosure of their financial holdings, not just those who themselves believe a conflict may exist. The law should be further strengthened by requiring that officials divest themselves of any personal holdings that represent real or potential conflicts of interest. It is unclear whether the existing conflict of interest law applies to state legislators. If it does not, it should be amended to include them. The lobbying law should be amended to require that financial statements be filed by lobbyists and their employers at regular intervals during, as well as after, legislative sessions. The campaign finance law has excellent reporting requirements but should be strengthened by the inclusion of limits on individual contributions and campaign expenditures. Further, corporations and labor unions should be prohibited from making campaign contributions.

Washington

> OPEN MEETINGS—*partly effective*
> LOBBYING DISCLOSURE—*partly effective*
> CONFLICTS OF INTEREST—*adequate*
> CAMPAIGN FINANCE—*ineffective*

The area most in need of reform in Washington is campaign finance. The current law sets no limits on individual contributions or campaign expenditures. It requires statements listing campaign contributions and expenditures only after the election. No provision prohibits corporate or labor union political contributions. No agent is clearly responsible for enforcing the law. Even if a new campaign finance law passed by the legislature and subject to popular ratification in November is adopted, there will be no limit on individual contributions. These areas should be the primary targets for citizen reform efforts in the field of campaign finance. While various limited open meetings statutes and rules result in a good record in this field for Washington, the legislation could be simplified and strengthened by the adoption of a single comprehensive open meetings law. The lobbying law could be improved by requiring employers of lobbyists to register and by requiring both lobbyists and their employers to file financial statements at regular intervals during, as well as after, legislative sessions. An excellent conflict of interest law could be further improved by requiring that public officials divest themselves of any financial holdings that represent real or potential conflicts of interest.

West Virginia

OPEN MEETINGS—*ineffective*
LOBBYING DISCLOSURE—*no law*
CONFLICTS OF INTEREST—*adequate*
CAMPAIGN FINANCE—*adequate*

The most-needed reforms are in the fields of lobbying and open meetings. The absence of any state lobbying law makes the enactment of a new comprehensive law in that field a particularly important goal. While various legislative rules and limited state statutes deal with open meetings, none is sufficiently comprehensive or strong to require that legislative or executive meetings be open as a matter of course or that legislative votes be open and recorded by individual. A new comprehensive, state-wide open meetings law should be the goal of reformers in West Virginia. The existing conflict of interest law is good but should be improved by requiring that public officials divest themselves of financial holdings that represent real or potential conflicts of interest.

Wisconsin

OPEN MEETINGS—*ineffective*
LOBBYING DISCLOSURE—*adequate*
CONFLICTS OF INTEREST—*no law*
CAMPAIGN FINANCE—*adequate*

Highest priority for reformist citizens should be the enactment of new comprehensive, statewide open meetings and conflict of interest laws. The existing open meetings laws are weak and not comprehensive. They allow excessive closed meetings and closed unrecorded votes. No comprehensive conflict of interest law is currently on the books. A good campaign finance law should be improved by setting limits on individual contributions.

Wyoming

OPEN MEETINGS—*no law*
LOBBYING DISCLOSURE—*ineffective*
CONFLICTS OF INTEREST—*ineffective*
CAMPAIGN FINANCE—*partly effective*

New statewide comprehensive legislation is needed in the areas of open meetings, lobbying, and conflicts of interest. No statewide law currently regulates government practices with respect to open meetings or votes. While the current lobbying law requires that lobbyists register, the information required at the time of registration is inadequate, and neither lobbyist nor employer is required to file financial statements listing either expenditures or income related to lobbying activity. The only conflict of interest regulations are a constitutional prohibition against legislators' participation in decisions in which they may derive personal gain and various limited statutory regulations bearing tangentially on conflicts of interest. The campaign finance law should be strengthened by requiring that candidates and political committees file expenditure and contribution statements before, as well as after, elections. The law should be further amended to set limits on individual contributions and to designate a specific enforcing agent.

Appendixes

Appendix A: GLOSSARY

ASSEMBLY: The name given to the lower house of the legislature in some states.

CITIZEN STANDING PROVISION: A guarantee that a citizen has access to the courts or to regulatory or supervisory bodies to file complaints of violation of the law.

CLERK: The clerk of the lower house of a state legislature or the Clerk of the U.S. House of Representatives.

CONFERENCE COMMITTEE: A committee composed of members of both houses of the legislature, convened to reconcile differences in versions of a bill passed by the two houses.

CONTINGENT PAYMENT: The practice of paying lobbyists so that the amount of remuneration is dependent on the passage or defeat of certain legislation.

DOCKET: As used in this book, either the official list of all registered lobbyists, legislative agents, or legislative counsels, or a calendar of business to be acted upon by the legislature.

EXECUTIVE SESSION: A meeting of a legislative committee, government agency, or any policy-making body that only members of that body may attend.

HOUSE: The lower (more numerous) house of a state legislature or the U.S. Congress.

INITIATIVE: A procedure enabling voters by petition to propose a law and secure its submission to the electorate or to the legislature for approval.

JOURNAL: The official record of proceedings of a legislature. The term does not include the verbatim report of speeches.

LAWYER-LEGISLATOR: A member of the legislature who is also actively engaged in the practice of law.

LEGISLATIVE AGENT: An individual or firm that, for hire, does anything to promote or oppose legislation except to appear as legislative counsel.

LEGISLATIVE COUNSEL: An individual or firm that is employed to appear before legislative committees to give testimony on proposed legislation but that is engaged in no other lobbying activities.

MEASURE: Any proposal submitted to the people for their approval or rejection at an election.

OFFICIAL MEETING: Any meeting of an agency, board, commission, or other policy-making body.

POLITICAL COMMITTEE: Two or more individuals whose primary or incidental purpose is to support or oppose any candidate or measure.

PRINCIPAL: As used in this book, the employer of a lobbyist, legislative counsel, or legislative agent.

PROROGATION: Termination of a regular or special session of the legislature.

PUBLIC OFFICIAL: Any elected or appointed official or employee of the state, including the executive agencies and the judicial branch; any official or employee of a county, municipality, or other political subdivision; any legislator; or any legislative employee.

RECALL: The procedure by which, on petition, an official may be removed from office by vote of the people.

REFERENDUM: The procedure of submitting to popular vote a measure passed upon or proposed by a legislative body or by popular initiative.

ROLL CALL VOTE: Balloting in which each member states his vote when his name is called.

SECRETARY: As used in this book, the Secretary of the Senate of a state legislature or of the U.S. Senate.

SENATE: The upper house of the state legislature or the U.S. Congress.

SPECIAL ELECTION: An election other than a primary or general election called to fill a vacancy in the unexpired portion of an elective office. In some states, the term also refers to iniatives, referendums, and recalls.

THIRD READING OF LEGISLATION: The reading of a bill after action has been completed on amendments. It is the last step before the bill is brought to a vote.

VOTES RECORDED BY INDIVIDUAL: The recording of the way each individual voted.

VOTES RECORDED IN AGGREGATE: The recording of the total number of yeas and nays only.

Appendix B: MODEL OPEN MEETINGS BILL

AN ACT PROHIBITING SECRET MEETINGS OF PUBLIC BODIES

Section 1. The laws of _____ are amended by adding a new section as follows:

It is hereby declared to be the policy of this state that the formation of public policy is public business and may not be conducted in secret.

(a) All meetings of two or more members of any board, committee, commission, or other policy-making body of any state agency or authority or any agency or authority of any county, municipality, or any political subdivision or of the legislature, at which any public business is discussed, or at which any formal action is taken by such board, committee, commission, or other policy-making body, are declared to be public meetings open to the public at all times, except as otherwise provided in the Constitution.

(b) Any such meetings at which the discussion or adoption of any proposed resolution, rule, regulation, or formal action occurs, or at which a majority or quorum of the body is in attendance, shall be held only after full and timely notice to the public.

(c) The secretary or clerk of each such board, committee, commission, or other policy-making body shall maintain a list of persons who request notification of all meetings, or of meetings when certain specified policies will be discussed, and shall provide such reasonable advance notification.

(d) No resolution, rule, regulation, ordinance, or formal action of a board, committee, commission, or other policy-making body shall be valid unless taken or made at a meeting that meets the requirements of subsections (a) and (b).

(e) The minutes of a meeting of any such board, committee, commission, or other policy-making body shall be promptly recorded, and such records shall be open to public inspection.

(f) The circuit courts of this state shall have jurisdiction to issue injunctions to enforce the purposes of this section upon application by any citizen of this state.

(g) In addition to the public notice required by subsections (b) and (c), the secretary or clerk of each such board, committee, commission, or other policy-making body of a state agency or authority or of the legislature shall submit, prior to December 31 of each year, a schedule of the regular meetings of such body to be held during the succeeding year to the Secretary of State, and the secretary or clerk of each such board, committee, commission, or other policy-making body of a county, municipality, or political subdivision shall submit, prior to December 31 of each year, such a schedule to the clerk of the county within which the body is located. Such schedules shall be open to public inspection and copies thereof shall be printed for distribution to citizens.

(h) Any person who attends a meeting of a board, committee, commission, or other policy-making body of which he is a member, not held in accordance with the provisions of this section, is guilty of a misdemeanor and upon conviction thereof shall be fined not more than $500 or be imprisoned not more than six months, or be both fined and imprisoned.

Section 2. If any provision of this act, or the application thereof, to any person or circumstance is held invalid, the validity of the remainder of such act and the application of such provision to other persons and circumstances shall not be affected thereby.

Section 3. This act shall take effect one month from passage into law.

Annotations to Model Open Meetings Bill

Section 1(a). Any modification of this section, either by increasing the number of people who must assemble before the meeting must be public or by narrowing the coverage of the bill, would substantially weaken the bill. Clearly, public policy is often merely a matter of two powerful men arriving at a mutually acceptable compromise.

Section 1(b). The key here is to fight for the inclusion of the word "discussion." If it is omitted, meetings can be held in private with public sessions being little more than pro forma ratification of secretly arrived at decisions.

Section 1 (d). This subsection provides a built-in enforcement mechanism.

Section 1(f). This subsection grants citizens recourse to the courts to ensure enforcement. Deletion of the subsection would substantially weaken the bill. Make your stand on this issue.

Appendix C: MODEL LOBBYING DISCLOSURE BILL

Section 1. The legislature hereby declares that the operation of responsible democratic government requires that the fullest opportunity be afforded to the people to petition their government for the redress of grievances and to express freely to individual members of the legislature, to committees of the legislature, and to officials of the executive branch their opinions on legislation, on pending executive actions, and on current issues; and that, to preserve and maintain the integrity of the legislative and administrative processes, it is necessary that the identity, expenditures, and activities of certain persons who engage in efforts to persuade members of the legislature or the executive branch to take specific actions, either by direct communication to such officials, or by solicitation of others to engage in such efforts, be publicly and regularly disclosed.

Section 2. As used in this Act, unless the context requires otherwise:

(a) "Administrative action" means the making of any recommendation, report, or decision or the taking of any official action by one or more officials in the executive branch or by a state regulatory commission, agency, or other body in the executive branch, and includes a decision to postpone a decision or action;

(b) "Legislative action" means introduction, sponsorship, debate, voting, and any other official action on any bill, resolution, amendment, nomination, appointment, report, and any other matter pending or proposed in a legislative committee or in either house of the legislature, or any matter which may be the subject of action by the legislature;

(c) "Official in the executive branch" means any member or employee of a state regulatory commission, agency, or other body in the executive branch, and any official or employee of the state who takes any administrative action;

(d) "Official in the legislative branch" means any candidate for the legislature in a primary, special, or general election, any member or member-elect of the legislature, any member of a commission established by and responsible to the legislature or either house thereof, and any staff person, assistant, or employee of same, whether or not they receive compensation from the state;

(e) "Person" means an individual, corporation, association, firm, partnership, committee, club, or other organization or group of persons;

(f) "Lobbyist" means any person, whether or not compensated or reimbursed for expenses, who:

(1) communicates directly with any official in the Legislative branch or in the executive branch with the purpose of influencing any legislative action or administrative action (A) on behalf of another person, or (B) if a person other than an individual, on behalf of or for the specific benefit of its members; or

(2) makes or receives a payment for the conduct of such communication; or

(3) makes an expenditure (not including payment of membership dues) to solicit others, either directly or by an advertising campaign, to communicate directly with any official in the legislative branch or in the executive branch with the purpose of influencing any legislative action or administrative action, provided that an individual acting solely on his own behalf who does not spend an amount in excess of $10 for personal postage and telephone for such solicitation shall not be deemed to have made an expenditure under this subsection; or

(4) represents himself as engaging in such communication or such solicitation as a business.

Section 3.(a) Each lobbyist who engages in activity described in subsection 2(f) shall, not later than two days after the beginning of such activity, file a registration form with the state Ethics Commission. Registration or reports by a lobbyist in no way exempt that lobbyist's employer and/or the person whom the lobbyist represents from registering or filing reports.

(b) Such registration form shall be prescribed by the state Ethics Commission and shall include the registrant's full name and complete address; place of business; the full name and complete address of each person, whether or not an employee, who will lobby on behalf of the registrant; the full name and complete address of each person, if any, by whom the registrant is retained or employed or on whose behalf the registrant appeals; the date on which the registrant expects his lobbying to end; a description of any contingency fee arrangements; and a description of the matters on which the registrant expects to lobby (including, if known and relevant, bill numbers and whether the registrant supports or opposes each bill listed). If the registrant lobbies or purports to lobby on behalf of members, such registration form shall include a statement of the number of members, and a full description of the methods by which the registrant develops and makes decisions about positions on policy.

(c) Each registrant under this section shall file with the state Ethics Commission a report concerning his activities during the preceding calendar quarter by January 10, March 10, June 10, and September 10 of each year as long as such registrant continues to engage in any activity listed in subsection 2(f) of this section. Such report shall be on a form prescribed by the state Ethics Commission, and shall include a complete and up-to-date statement of the information required to be supplied under subsection (b) of this section, plus the following information for the preceding calendar quarter:

(1) the registrant's total expenditures on lobbying and a breakdown of such expenditures into the following categories: original and derivative research done to support an argument or presentation; the cost for publication and distribution of each publication used in lobbying; other printing; media; advertising, including production costs; postage; travel; salaries and fees, including allowances, rewards, and contingency fees; entertainment; telephone and telegraph;

(2) a list of every contribution and membership fee of $500 or more paid to the registrant regardless of whether it

was paid solely for the purpose of lobbying, with the full name and complete address of each payer and the issue area, if any, for which such contribution was earmarked;

(3) a list of every honorarium, gift, loan, or political contribution, including a service or anything of value, paid to an official in the legislative or executive branch, or to support or oppose a candidate for elective public office, by the registrant, any employee of the registrant, any lobbyist who received compensation or reimbursement for expenses from the registrant, or, if the registrant is a person other than an individual, any officer or official of the registrant;

(4) a list of every legislative action and every administrative action supported or opposed by the registrant, by any employee of the registrant, or by any person retained or employed by the registrant or appearing on his behalf, together with a statement of the registrant's position for or against such action.

(d) Each person about whose activities a registrant is required to report by subsection (c) of this section shall provide a full account of such activities to the registrant at least five days before such registrant's report is due to be filed.

(e) Each person shall file a supplementary registration form with the state Ethics Commission no later than five days after any change in the information supplied in his last registration form under subsection (b) of this section. Such supplementary registration form shall include a complete description of the information that has changed.

Section 4. Each registration form and report required to be filed under this Act shall be signed and certified as true and correct by the registrant, or, if the registrant is a person other than an individual, by an appropriate officer of such registrant.

Section 5. Each person required to file a registration form or report under this Act shall file a registration form or report that conforms to law and to the truth.

Section 6. No person shall knowingly or willfully make any

false statement or misrepresentation of the facts to any official in the legislative branch or in the executive branch, or knowing a document to contain a false statement, cause a copy of such document to be received by an official in the legislative branch or in the executive branch without notifying such official in writing of the truth.

Section 7. For the purposes of computing state or local income tax, lobbying expenditures shall not be claimed as a business expense or otherwise deducted from taxable income.

Section 8. (a) There is hereby created a state Ethics Commission, which shall be composed of five members, not more than three of whom shall be members of the same political party and who shall be appointed by the Governor with the consent of the state Senate. No official meeting the definition of either Sec. 2(c) or Sec. 2(d) shall be appointed to membership on the commission. One of the original members shall be appointed for a term of one year, one for a term of three years, one for a term of five years, one for a term of seven years, and one for a term of nine years, beginning from the date of enactment of this Act, but their successors shall be appointed for terms of nine years each, except that any individual chosen to fill a vacancy shall be appointed only for the unexpired term of the member whom he shall succeed. The commission shall elect one member to serve as chairman of the commission and one member to serve as vice-chairman. The vice-chairman shall act as chairman in the absence or disability of the chairman or in the event of a vacancy in that office.

(b) A vacancy in the commission shall not impair the right of the remaining members to exercise all the powers of the commission, and three members thereof shall constitute a quorum.

(c) The commission shall at the close of each fiscal year report to the legislature and the governor concerning the action it has taken; the names, salaries, and duties of all individuals in its employ and the money it has disbursed; and shall make such further reports on the matters within its jurisdiction and such recommendations for further legislation as may appear desirable.

(d) Members of the commission shall while serving on the

business of the commission be entitled to receive compensation at a rate of $50 per day.

(e) The office of the commission shall be in or near the state capital, but it may meet or exercise any or all of its powers at any other place in the state.

(f) All members, officers, agents, attorneys, and employees of the commission shall be subject to the provisions of law prohibiting political activity of state employees.

(g) The commission shall appoint an executive director to serve at the pleasure of the commission. The executive director shall be responsible for the administrative operations of the commission and shall perform such other duties as may be delegated or assigned to him from time to time by regulations or orders of the commission. However, the commission shall not delegate the making of regulations to the executive director.

Section 9. In addition to other duties prescribed by law, it shall be the duty of the state Ethics Commission:

(a) to prescribe forms for statements and reports required to be filed by this Act, and to furnish such forms to persons required to file such statements and reports;

(b) to prepare and publish a manual setting forth recommended uniform methods of accounting and reporting for use by persons required to file statements and reports by this Act;

(c) to accept and file any information voluntarily supplied that exceeds the requirements of this Act;

(d) to develop a filing, coding, and cross-indexing system consonant with the purposes of this Act;

(e) to make statements and reports filed with it available for public inspection and copying during regular office hours, and to make copying facilities available free of charge or at a charge not to exceed actual cost;

(f) to preserve such statements and reports for a period of five years from date of receipt;

(g) to prepare and publish monthly, quarterly, and annual summaries of the statements and reports received—these summaries shall list separately individual lobbyists and other persons;

(h) to prepare and publish such other reports as it may deem appropriate;

(i) to provide for wide public dissemination of its summaries and reports;

(j) to make investigations with respect to statements and reports filed under the provisions of this Act, and with respect to alleged failures to file any statements or reports required under the provisions of this Act, and, upon complaint by any individual, with respect to alleged violation of any part of this Act;

(k) to report suspected violations of law to the appropriate law enforcement authorities;

(l) to issue, upon request, and publish advisory opinions on the requirements of this Act, based on a real or hypothetical set of circumstances;

(m) to prescribe and publish rules and regulations to carry out the provisions of this Act.

Section 10. The executive director of the commission shall inspect each statement filed with the commission under this Act within ten days after the date it is filed. He shall notify a person required to file a statement under this act immediately if:

(a) It appears that the person has failed to file a statement as required by law or that a statement filed by the person does not conform to law; or

(b) a written complaint is filed with the commission by any registered voter alleging that a statement filed with the commission does not conform to law or to the truth or that a person has failed to file a statement by law.

Section 11. Any person who violates the provisions of Section 3, 4, 5, 6, or 7 of this Act is guilty of a misdemeanor and shall be fined not more than $1,000, if an individual, and not more than $10,000, if a person other than an individual, or imprisoned for not more than one year, or be both fined and imprisoned.

Section 12. Any person who pays compensation to a lobbyist, reimburses a lobbyist for all or part of his expenses, or makes an expenditure to solicit others to lobby, and who fails to file a registration form or to report payment of such compensation or reimbursement or expenditure as required by Section 3 of this Act shall, in addition to any other penalty provided by law, pay to the state an amount equal to three times such compensation, reimbursement, or expenditure.

Section 13. Any person who receives any compensation or reimbursement for activity as a lobbyist and who fails to file a registration form as required by this Act shall, in addition to any other penalty provided by law, pay to the state an amount equal to three times such compensation or reimbursement.

Section 14. The appropriate lower courts of this state shall have original jurisdiction to issue injunctions to enforce the provisions of this Act upon application by any citizen of this state.

Section 15. If any provision of this Act, or the application thereof to any person or circumstance, is held invalid, the validity of the remainder of this Act and the application of such provisions to other persons and circumstances shall not be affected thereby.

Section 16. Any person who is a lobbyist as defined in Section 2(c) of this Act on the day this Act becomes effective shall be considered to have become a lobbyist, for the purposes of Sections 3 and 4 of this Act, on the day this Act becomes effective.

Section 17. This Act shall take effect thirty days after passage into law.

Annotations to Model Lobbying Disclosure Bill

Section 2(a) and (b). The inclusion of administrative action and executive decisions under the lobbying disclosure bill represents an expansion of current legislation on the books. Previously, lobbying was considered by law to be an attempt to influence only legislative decisions, executive decisions being exempt. We consider the inclusion of administrative action crucial. You should certainly include, therefore, Section 2(a), (b), (c), and (f)(1) as written.

Section 2(e). Note the expansive definition of "person." If, for some reason, this bill is used in part only and the part used includes a reference to the term "person" be sure to include this comprehensive definition of "person" in the definitions at the beginning of the bill to which the relevant section is appended. The intent of this extensive definition is to include all possible groups and individuals who may have an interest in influencing legislation or executive decisions. The definition is considered to include, among others, consortiums composed of various corporations, one of which may hire a lobbyist to act on behalf of the group.

Section 2(f). All parts of the definition of lobbyists should remain intact. Deletion of any section will provide a massive loophole through which virtually all special-interest lobbyists will crawl.

Section 2(f)(3). Note that this section includes grass-roots lobbying. Whereas most previous lobbying regulations covered only those who lobbied the legislature or the executive branch in person, we feel it is critical, because of the increased use of the media, to include a provision covering those who spend money for the purpose of influencing executive or legislative decisions from outside the capitol building.

Section 3(a). It is imperative that lobbyists' employers and/ or the person whom the lobbyist represents be required to file reports and under no circumstances be exempt from that requirement simply because their lobbyist files a report. Under the current federal law it is not explicitly required that such employers or groups represented file reports if their lobbyists do so, and as a result many organizations file no reports at all. This makes it exceedingly difficult to trace down the connection between a given industry or firm and its political activities.

Section 3(c)(1–4). If reports are to be meaningful, all four sections must be included. The deletion of any one would strip the bill. If you must make a stand, make it on these four points.

Section 3(d). While quarterly reports are sufficient under normal circumstances, it is important that a supplementary registration form be filed with the state Ethics Commission virtually immediately after the change of information on the previous quarterly report. In this way, you require a person to indicate by submitting a new form any intention to lobby on a new issue. This, coupled with the requirement that new lobbyists register within two days after beginning their lobbying activity, will guard against any mid-quarter commencement of major lobbying activities without the knowledge of the Ethics Commission and, therefore, the public.

Section 8. The inclusion of a state Ethics Commission is central to this model bill. It seems the only reasonable way to insure any nonpartisan, nonpolitical scrutiny of lobbyists' activities. If, however, the inclusion of the state Ethics Commission becomes politically impossible, it is preferable to fall back on supervision by the Secretary of State or the equivalent of the federal Comptroller General to the use of the Secretary of the Senate and Clerk of the House. These latter two tend to be more politically connected with their respective legislative bodies than would be a more detached state official.

Section 9. The commission must retain the power to insist on and make interim reports so that mid-quarter increases in activities by one lobbying group or another may be known to the public as soon as they commence.

Section 9(g). When publishing monthly, quarterly, or annual summaries, the commission must be instructed to separate the reports filed by individual lobbyists from those filed by other "persons." Otherwise, it is virtually impossible, or at least tremendously time-consuming, to sort out which organizations are represented by which individuals.

Section 10(b). This provision grants the citizen access to the state Ethics Commission and by implication requires the commission to act upon his request within a reasonable period of time. Because of the risk of a politicized commission, it is important that individual citizens have the right to file such complaints. Since the commission is required to make open and public reports, it should be possible to apply pressure to a commission if it attempts to bury a written complaint.

Section 14. If an individual who has filed a complaint under Section 11(b) fails to receive satisfaction, he must have recourse to the courts, and this bill must grant him standing in those courts.

Section 15. This is without doubt one of the most critical sections in this bill, and its exclusion would very substantially limit the bill's total effectiveness.

Appendix D: MODEL CONFLICT OF INTEREST BILL

Section 1. The legislature hereby declares that elective office is a public trust, and any effort to realize personal gain through official conduct is a violation of that trust.

Section 2. As used in this Act unless the context requires otherwise:

(a) "business" means any corporation, partnership, proprietorship, firm, enterprise, franchise, association, organization, self-employed individual, and any legal entity;

(b) "business with which he is associated" means any business of which the person or a member of his household is a director, officer, owner, employee, or holder of stock worth $1,000 or more at fair market value, and any business which is a client of the person;

(c) "candidate for public office" means any person who has filed a declaration of candidacy or a petition to appear on the ballot for election as a public official, and any person who has been nominated for appointment to serve as a public official;

(d) "commission" means the state Ethics Commission;

(e) "legislative employee" means any person employed by the legislature or by any of its committees and any person employed by a legislator from funds provided by the state, who receives compensation of $10,000 or more per year.

(f) "public official" means any elected or appointed official or employee of the state, including the executive agencies and the judicial branch, any official or employee of a county, municipality, or other political subdivision, any legislator, and any legislative employee.

Section 3. No public official shall use his official position or office to obtain financial gain for himself, any member of his household, or any business with which he or a member of his household is associated.

Section 4. No person shall offer or give to a public official

266

or a member of a public official's household and no public official shall solicit or receive anything of value, including a gift, favor, service, or promise of future employment, based on any understanding that such public official's vote, official actions, or judgment would be influenced thereby, or where it could reasonably be inferred that the thing of value would influence the public official in the discharge of his duties, or as a reward, or which would cause the total value of such things received from the same person not a member of such public official's household to exceed $100 during any single calendar year.

Section 5. No person shall offer or pay to a public official, and no public official shall solicit or receive, any money in addition to that received by the public official in his official capacity for legislative advice or assistance, or for advice or assistance given in the course of the public official's employment or relating to his employment.

Section 6. No public official shall use or disclose confidential information gained in the course of or by reason of his official position or activities in any way that could result in financial gain for himself or for any other person.

Section 7. No legislator shall accept assignment to or serve on a committee the jurisdiction of which consists of matters of other than a *de minimus* nature in which he or a member of his household or a business with which he is associated has a financial interest. No legislative employee shall accept assignment to, be employed by, or perform services for a legislative committee the jurisdiction of which consists of matters of other than a *de minimus* nature in which he or a member of his household or a business with which he is associated has a financial interest.

Section 8. Unless expressly provided otherwise by law, no person shall serve as a member or employee of a state regulatory commisison that regulates any business with which he is associated.

Section 9. Any public official who, in the discharge of his official duties, would be required to take an action or make a decision that would affect directly or indirectly his financial interests or those of a member of his household, or a business with which he is associated, shall instead take the following actions:

(a) He shall prepare a written statement describing the matter requiring action or decision, and the nature of his potential conflict of interest with respect to such action or decision;

(b) he shall cause copies of such statement to be delivered to the state Ethics Commission and to his immediate superior, if any;

(c) if he is a legislator or legislative employee, he shall deliver a copy of such statement to the presiding officer, who shall cause such statement to be printed in the journal and, upon request, shall excuse a legislator from votes, deliberations, and other action on the matter on which a potential conflict exists; and

(d) if he is not a legislator, his superior, if any, shall assign the matter to another employee who does not have a potential conflict of interest, or, if he has no immediate superior, he shall take such steps as the state ethics commission shall prescribe through rules or regulations to remove himself from influence over actions and decisions on the matter on which the potential conflict exists.

Section 10. No public official and no business with which a public official is associated shall represent a client before any state regulatory department or agency for a fee.

Section 11. No public official and no business with which a public official is associated shall enter into any contract with a state agency which is to be paid in whole or in part out of state funds unless the contract has been awarded through a process of public notice and competitive bidding.

Section 12. No person shall offer or give to a member or employee of a state regulatory commission that regulates a business with which such person is associated, and no member or employee of a state regulatory commission, shall solicit or accept from any such person anything of value, including a promise of future employment or a favor or service, while the member or employee is associated with the regulatory commission. No former member or employee of a state regulatory commission shall serve as a lobbyist or represent clients before such regulatory commission for a period of five years after he leaves such regulatory commission.

Section 13. Within ten days after he becomes a candidate for public office, each candidate shall file a statement of economic interests at the office of the state Ethics Commission.

(a) Each official who receives a declaration of candidacy or petition to appear on the ballot for election as a public official and each official who nominates a person to serve as a public official shall, within two days of such receipt or nomination, notify the state Ethics Commission of the name of each new candidate for public office as defined in section 2(c) of this Act, and the date on which such person became a candidate for the purposes of this Act.

(b) The state Ethics Commission shall notify such official and, in the case of candidates for appointive office, the clerk of the body that will approve or disapprove the nomination, of the name of each candidate who files a statement of economic interests at the office of the commission and of the date on which such statement was filed.

(c) Other provisions of the law notwithstanding, if a candidate for elective public office does not submit a statement of economic interests in accordance with the requirements of this Act within ten days after he becomes a candidate, his name shall not appear on the ballot.

(d) If a person who becomes a candidate for appointive public office by nomination fails to file a statement of economic interests in accordance with the provisions of this Act within ten days after such nomination, the nomination ´shall not be approved or ratified until at least ten days after he has filed such statement of economic interests.

Section 14. No person hired to serve as a public official with compensation of $12,000 or more per year and no person retained by the state on a per diem or consultant basis shall be allowed to take the oath of office or enter upon his duties unless he has filed a statement of economic interests in accordance with the provisions of this Act at the office of the state Ethics Commission.

Section 15. Each current public official who receives compensation of $12,000 or more per year shall file a statement of economic interests in accordance with the provisions of this Act at the office of the state Ethics Commission within sixty days after the effective date of this Act, and shall receive no compensation after such filing deadline until he files such statement.

Section 16. (a) Any statement of economic interests filed under this Act shall be on a form prescribed by the commission, and the person filing the statement shall supply the following information:

(1) the identity, by name, of all offices, directorships, and fiduciary relationships held by him or a member of his household;

(2) the legal description of all real estate in the state in which he or a member of his household has any interest, direct or indirect, including an option to buy;

(3) the name of each creditor to whom he or a member of his household owes monies in excess of $1,000, the category of the amount owed, and the interest rate;

(4) the name of each business, insurance policy, or trust in which he or a member of his household has a financial interest, and the nature and category of the amount of such interest;

(5) the source, by name, and category of the amounts of any income, including capital gains, whether or not taxable, received by him or a member of his household during the preceding year;

(6) a list of businesses with which he is associated that do business with or are regulated by the state and a description of the nature of such business or regulation;

(7) if the individual filing is an attorney, a list of all matters of public record in which the state or any public official or executive agency is a party in which he or any member of a law firm with which he is associated represented a client with a fee of $1,000 or more, the name of each such client, the category of the amount of each fee, and a description of the matter involved; and

(8) if the individual filing is an attorney, a list of all clients of the individual or any law firm with which he is associated whose fees were $1,000 or more during the preceding year, and the category of the amount of each such fee.

(b) Where an amount is required to be reported by category, the individual shall report whether the amount is less than $1,000, at least $1,000 but less than $5,000, at least $5,000 but less than $10,000, at least $10,000 but less than $25,000, or $25,000 or more. An amount of stock may be reported by number of shares instead of by category of dollar value. No provision of this Act shall be interpreted to prevent any person from filing more information or more detailed information than required.

Section 17. Each person who is required to file a statement of economic interests under this Act shall file an updating statement at the office of the commission and on a form prescribed by the commission within one week of any addition, deletion or change in his financial status with respect to which information is required to be supplied under Section 16; provided that, if the person has filed with the commission the description by name, amount, and schedule of payments of a continuing arrangement relating to an item required to be reported under subsection 16(c) or 16(e), an updating statement need not be filed for each payment under such continuing arrangement, but only if the arrangement is terminated or altered.

Section 18. (a) There is hereby created a state Ethics Commission, which shall be composed of five members, not more than three of whom shall be members of the same political party and who shall be appointed by the governor with the consent of the state Senate. No public official shall be appointed to membership on the commission. One of the original members shall be appointed for a term of one year, one for a term of three years, one for a term of five years, one for a term of seven years, and one for a term of nine years, beginning from the date of enactment of this Act, but their successors shall be appointed for terms of nine years each, except that any individual chosen to fill a vacancy shall be appointed only for the unexpired term of the member whom he shall succeed. The commission shall elect one member to serve as chairman of the commission and one member to serve as vice-chairman. The vice-chairman shall act as chairman in the absence or disability of the chairman or in the event of a vacancy in that office.

(b) A vacancy in the commission shall not impair the right of the remaining members to exercise all the powers of the commission, and three members thereof shall constitute a quorum.

(c) The commisison shall at the close of each fiscal year report to the legislature and the governor concerning the action it has taken; the names, salaries, and duties of all individuals in its employ, and the money it has disbursed, and shall make such further reports on the matters within its jurisdiction and such recommendations for further legislation as may appear desirable.

(d) Members of the commission shall, while serving on the business of the commission, be entitled to receive compensation at a rate of $50 per day.

(e) The office of the commission shall be in or near the state capital, but it may meet or exercise any or all its powers at any other place in the state.

(f) All members, officers, agents, attorneys, and employees of the commission shall be subject to the provisions of law prohibiting political activity of state employees.

(g) The commission shall appoint an executive director to serve at the pleasure of the commission. The executive director shall be responsible for the administrative operations of the commission and shall perform such other duties as may be delegated or assigned to him from time to time by regulations or orders of the commission. However, the commission shall not delegate the making of regulations to the executive director.

Section 19. It shall be the duty of the commission:

(a) to prescribe forms for statements required to be filed by this Act, and to furnish such forms to persons required to file such statements;

(b) to prepare and publish a manual setting forth recommended uniform methods of reporting for use by persons required to file statements required by this Act;

(c) to accept and file any information voluntarily supplied that exceeds the requirements of this Act;

(d) to develop a filing, coding, and cross-indexing system consonant with the purposes of this Act;

(e) to make the reports and statements filed with it available for public inspection and copying during regular office hours, and to make copying facilities available free of charge or at a charge not to exceed actual cost;

(f) to preserve such reports and statements for a period of ten years from date of receipt;

(g) to prepare and publish, from time to time, summaries of the statements received;

(h) to prepare and publish such other reports as may seem appropriate;

(i) to provide for wide public dissemination of summaries and reports;

(j) to make investigations with respect to statements filed under the provisions of this Act, and with respect to alleged failures to file any statement required under the provisions of this Act and, upon complaint by any individual, with respect to alleged violations of any part of this Act;

(k) to report suspected violations of law to the appropriate law enforcement authorities;

(l) to issue, upon request, and publish advisory opinions on, the requirements of this Act, based on a real or hypothetical set of circumstances;

(m) to prescribe and publish rules and regulations to carry out provisions of this Act.

Section 20. Any person who violates the provisions of Sections 3, 4, 5, 6, 7, 8, 9, 10, 11, 12, 14, or 17 of this Act is guilty of a felony and shall be fined not more than $10,000 or be imprisoned for not more than five years, or be both fined and imprisoned.

Section 21. Any person who violates the provisions of sections 3, 4, 5, 6, 10, 11, or 12 of this Act shall, in addition to any other penalty prescribed by law, pay into the treasury of the state a sum of money equal to three (3) times the financial gain resulting from such violation.

Section 22. The penalties prescribed in this Act do not limit the power of either house of the legislature to discipline its own members or impeach a public official, and do not limit the power of agencies or commissions to discipline officials or employees.

Section 23. The circuit courts of this state shall have jurisdiction to issue injunctions to enforce the provisions of this Act upon application by any citizen of this state.

Section 24. If any provision of this Act, or the application thereof to any person or circumstance, is held invalid, the validity of the remainder of such Act and the application of such provisions to other persons and circumstances shall not be affected thereby.

Section 25. This Act shall take effect upon passage into law.

Annotations to Model Conflict of Interest Bill

Section 2(e). The $10,000 figure is somewhat arbitrary; the intention is to exclude secretaries from the definition, but to include all persons who do research or might have a substantive input to legislation.

Section 2(f). It makes little sense to prohibit some public officials from profiting from their position while allowing others to do so. Thus, the definition of "public official" should be as broad and inclusive as the state Constitution permits.

Section 3. This section is a general statement, which will serve to cover blatant abuses not covered by any other specific section.

Section 4. This section prohibits many sophisticated forms of bribery. Any changes made in the language of this section should be examined very carefully to make sure that they do not make the entire section meaningless. The prohibition of gifts from one person worth more than $100 during a single calendar year in the last clause is intentional, because such gifts may quite possibly influence legislative or administrative action.

Section 5. In a few state legislatures, representatives and senators are actually in the employ of people who hire them for lobbying. Such a situation is intolerable, since such legislators will find it very difficult to represent the public interest. In many other legislatures, members who are attorneys receive exaggerated retainers, which the client pays for the purpose of influencing their legislative judgment. The same devices can also be used to influence administrative officials or officials of other governmental units, and should therefore be completely prohibited.

Section 6. This paragraph is intended to prohibit real estate and other kinds of speculation by a public official who has inside knowledge.

Section 7. In many state legislatures, bankers run the banking committee, highway contractors run the roads and bridges committee, and legislators connected with other special interests run the committees that deal with their interests. Such a practice allows legislation in the public interest to die in committee with no chance for consideration on the floor of the legislature, where the public interest might prevail. This section of the model bill would prohibit legislators and legislative employees who have financial interests in a major part of the committee's jurisdiction from being in a position to frustrate the public interest.

Some persons will argue that these members are needed on the committees in which they have special interests because of their particular expertise in the subject matter. Our response is that expertise will not be lacking if such committees are allowed to hire adequate numbers of skilled staff members.

Section 8. Administration of the laws should also serve the public interest, rather than special private interests. This section will prohibit "hiring the fox to guard the chicken coop."

Section 9. This is the major operative section to prevent the personal interest of a decision-maker from influencing official government actions. With regard to subsection (c), some state legislatures now have rules than provide that a statement not be printed if the legislator abstains or is excused from voting. We believe that the reasons for failure to vote, whether they be absence, other business, or a potential conflict of interest, should be a matter of public record so that each legislator is responsible to his constituents for the performance or lack of performance of his duties.

Section 10. When a public official represents a client before a state regulatory department or agency, many people assume that his position gives the client more weight with the decision-making group. In some instances this is no doubt true. In any event, it is highly undesirable for a legislator or other public official to gain clients merely because of his official position.

Section 11. A public official is obviously in a better position to negotiate highly profitable contracts with public agencies than the average private individual. Those highly profitable contracts in effect amount to a theft from the state. This section would prohibit privately negotiated contracts involving public officials (by allowing public officials to enter into contracts only after competitive bidding).

Section 12. This section is intended to break up the "sweetheart" relationships that exist between the regulators and the regulated in many states.

Section 13. The people have a right to know of a candidate's financial interests before a decision is made as to whether he is to become a public official.

Section 14. The figure of $12,000 in this section and in Section 15 is again somewhat arbitrary, but is intended to include all persons who will be in a position to influence public policy.

Section 15. This section provides for the filing of financial statements by persons who are already public officials when the Act becomes effective.

Section 16. The list of items required to be filed appears to be long and complicated, but we believe every single one of these kinds of financial interests must in fact be disclosed so that the people will have all data necessary to judge whether or not their public officials are behaving ethically. Investments in municipal, state, or federal bonds are not required to be reported, nor are sums in savings accounts. The value of economic interests is required to be reported by *category* of value, so that it will be very difficult for a person to estimate the exact net worth of a particular public official.

Section 17. The statement of economic interest is of worth to the public only if it is up to date. This section requires such updating.

Section 18. This section creates an independent state Ethics Commission composed of private citizens to administer and enforce the act, and specifies some of the procedural aspects of the commission's operations. While we believe the concept of an *independent* commission is crucial, should a compromise be necessary, it is better to do so by giving enforcement capacity to the state equivalent of a comptroller general or to the Secretary of State, not to appointees of the legislature itself.

Section 19. Particularly important among the duties the commission must have if it is to be an effective representative of the public interest are (e), (g), (i), (j), and (m). The wording of (j) is particularly crucial, since it provides for the commission to investigate citizens' complaints about alleged violations.

Section 20. Violation of the public trust is a very serious matter, so it is our belief that violation of any section of this act should be a felony.

Section 21. In addition to the criminal penalties, it is important that a public official who makes money from the state illegally be required to reimburse the state for the amount plus damages.

Section 23. This citizen standing provision is essential. If you must make a stand, make it here. Such citizen standing provides a check against a stacked or ineffective Ethics Commission and guarantees the citizen the right to press for satisfactory action on suspected violations.

Section 24. Inclusion of this or similiar wording will ensure that the entire purpose of the statute will not be gutted by a court decision that part of the Act violates the state or national Constitution.

Section 25. Because this is a matter so vital to the proper operation of government, it should take effect as soon as possible.

Appendix E: MODEL CAMPAIGN FINANCE BILL

Section 1. As used in this Act, unless the context requires otherwise:

(a) "broadcasting station" has the same meaning as in section 315 (f) of the Federal Communications Act of 1934;

(b) "candidate" means an individual who has taken affirmative action to seek nomination or election to public office;

(c) "commission" means the state Elections Commission;

(d) "contribute," "contribution," "expend," and "expenditure" means any advance, conveyance, deposit, distribution, transfer of funds loan, payment, gift, pledge, or subscription of money or anything of value, and any contract, agreement, promise, or other obligation, whether or not legally enforceable, to make a contribution or expenditure, in support of or in opposition to any candidate, political committee, or measure; but do not include services by speakers, writers, publishers or others for which no compensation is asked or given;

(e) "election" means any general, special, or primary election and any convention or caucus of a political party held to nominate a candidate;

(f) "measure" means any proposal submitted to the people for their approval or rejection at an election, including any proposed law, act or part of an act of the legislature, revision of or amendment to the Constitution, local, special, or municipal legislation or proposition or ballot question;

(g) "person" means an individual, corporation, association, firm, partnership, committee, club, or other organization or group of persons;

(h) "political committee" means a combination of two or more individuals, or a person other than an individual, the primary or incidental purpose of which is to support or oppose any candidate or measure or to influence the result of an election;

(i) "political treasurer" means an individual appointed by a

278

candidate or political committee as provided in Section 2 of this Act;

(j) "public office" means any national, state, county, municipal, school or other district, precinct, ward, or political party office or position that is filled by the voters;

(k) "special election" includes a referendum, initiative, or recall election.

Section 2. (a) Each candidate and political committee shall appoint a political treasurer and certify the full name and complete address of the political treasurer to the state Elections Commission.

(b) A candidate or political committee may remove his or its political treasurer. In case of the death, resignation, or removal of his or its political treasurer before compliance with all obligations of a political treasurer under this Act, such candidate or political committee shall appoint a successor and certify the name and address of the successor in the manner provided in the case of an original appointment.

(c) No contribution shall be received or expenditure made by or on behalf of a candidate or political committee (1) until the candidate or political committee appoints a political treasurer and certifies the name and address of the political treasurer to the state Elections Commission; and (2) unless the contribution is received or expenditure made by or through the political treasurer of the candidate or political committee.

Section 3. (a) The political treasurer of each candidate and political committee shall keep detailed accounts, current within not more than seven days after the date of receiving a contribution or making an expenditure, of all contributions received and all expenditures made by or on behalf of the candidate or political committee that are required to be set forth in a statement filed under this Act.

(b) Accounts kept by the political treasurer of a candidate or political committee may be inspected, before the election to which the accounts refer, by an employee of the state Elections Commission who is making an investigation pursuant to section 18 (j) of this Act.

(c) Accounts kept by a political treasurer shall be preserved by him for at least one year after the date of the election to which the accounts refer or at least one year after the date the last supplemental statement is filed under Section 7 of this Act, whichever is later.

Section 4. A political treasurer shall not accept a contribution of more than $100 from a political committee not in this state unless the contribution is accompanied by a written statement setting forth the full name and complete address of each person who contributed more than $25 of the contribution and certified as true and correct by an officer of the contributing political committee.

Section 5. A person required to file a statement under this Act shall file a statement that conforms to law and to the truth.

Section 6. (a) The political treasurer of each candidate and the political treasurer of each political committee shall file with the state elections commission:

(1) not more than forty days and not less than thirty days before the date of an election in which the candidate or political committee is involved, a statement of all contributions received and all expenditures made by or on behalf of the candidate or political committee during the period beginning as provided in subsection (b) of this section and ending on the fortieth day before the date of the election;

(2) not more than ten days and not less than five days before the date of an election in which the candidate or political committee is involved, a statement of all contributions received and all expenditures made by or on behalf of the candidate or political committee since the fortieth day before the date of the election; and

(3) not more than thirty days after the date of an election in which the candidate or political committee is involved, a statement of all contributions received and all expenditures made by or on behalf of the candidate or political committee during the period beginning as provided in subsection (b) of this section and ending on the 10th day after the election.

(b) The period referred to in subsection (1) of this section begins:

    (1) for a general or special election, on the 11th day after the date of the preceding primary election;

    (2) for any other election, on the day that a treasurer was first appointed under Section 2 of this Act, or, for a continuing political committee, on the day following the period included in the last report filed.

(c) Each statement required by this section shall be signed and certified as true and correct by the political treasurer required to file it.

Section 7. (a) If a statement filed under paragraph (3) of subsection (a) of Section 6 of this Act shows an unexpended balance of contributions or an expenditure deficit, the political treasurer of the candidate or political committee shall file with the state Elections Commission:

    (1) not more than thirty days after the deadline for filing the statement under paragraph (3) of subsection (a) of Section 6 of this Act, a supplemental statement of contributions and expenditures; and

    (2) every sixty days after the deadline for filing the first supplemental statement, and additional supplemental statement of contributions and expenditures; such supplemental statements shall continue to be filed until the account shows no unexpended balance of contributions or expenditure deficit.

(b) Each supplemental statement required by this section shall be signed and certified as true and correct by the political treasurer required to file it.

(c) If a candidate wins nomination, supplemental statements under this section need not be filed with respect to the nomination campaign by the political treasurer of a political committee supporting the candidate, if such political committee continues to function in support of such candidate in the campaign for the general or special election, or by the political treasurer of such candidate.

Section 8. If no contribution is received or expenditure made by or on behalf of a candidate or political committee during a period described in Section 6 or 7 of this Act, the political treasurer of the candidate or political committee shall file with the state Elections Commission, at the time required by such section of this Act for the period, a statement to that effect. Each statement shall be signed and certified as true and correct by the political treasurer required to file it.

Section 9. Not more than thirty days after the date of an election, each individual who makes expenditures in a total amount of $50 or more in support of or opposition to any one candidate, political committee, or measure other than by contribution to a candidate or political committee shall file a statement of the expenditure with the state Elections Commission.

Section 10. (a) A statement filed under Section 6, 7, or 9 of this Act shall set forth:

(1) under contributions, a list of all the contributions received, including the full name and complete address of each person who contributed an aggregate amount of $25 or more, and the amount contributed by that person (the statement may list as a single item the total amount of contributions of less than $25 each obtained in similar fashion, but shall specify in each case how such contributions were obtained);

(2) under expenditures, a list of all expenditures made, showing the amount and purpose thereof. Each expenditure in the amount of $25 or more shall be vouched for by a receipt or canceled check or an accurate copy thereof. A statement filed under paragraph (1) or (2) of subsection (a) of Section 6 of this Act may list the total amount of expenditures of less than $25 each by category without showing the exact amount of or vouching for each such expenditure. Anything of value paid for or contributed by any person shall be listed as both an expenditure and a contribution.

Section 11. Each newspaper, periodical, broadcasting station, direct mailing company, printer, and advertising agency that accepts expenditures from a political treasurer shall, not more than ten days and not less than seven days before an election, and again not more than thirty days after an election, file with the clerk of the state elections commission a statement listing the amounts paid and obligations incurred by each candidate, political committee, or political treasurer with respect to such election. Such statement shall be signed and certified as true and correct.

Section 12. (a) No person other than a candidate or a member of such candidate's immediate family shall make, and no political treasurer shall solicit or accept, any contribution that will cause the total amount contributed by such person in support of such candidate or in support of or opposition to a measure, including contributions to political committees supporting such candidate or supporting or opposing such measure, to exceed, with respect to a single election, the lesser of (1) $10,000; or (2) one cent times the total population of the state, district, or other area within which the election is held, provided that the limit shall not be less than $100.

(b) No candidate or member of a candidate's immediate family shall make any contribution that will cause the total amount contributed by such persons to the political treasurers of the candidate and all political committees supporting the candidate to exceed, with respect to a single election, five times the limit specified in subsection (a) of this section.

(c) Any person found guilty of violating subsection (a) or (b) of this section shall, in addition to any other penalty prescribed by law, pay to the state a sum equal to three times the amount he contributed in excess of the amount permitted by such subsection.

(d) If any person is found guilty of violating subsection (a) or (b) of this section, each political treasurer who received part or all of the contribution(s) that constituted the violation shall pay the amount received from such person to the state.

Section 13. (a) No corporation, partnership, or other business entity shall pay or contribute, or offer, consent, or agree to pay or contribute, directly or indirectly, any money, property, free service of its officers or employees, or other thing of value to any political party, candidate, political committee or political treasurer, or to any person for the purpose of influencing an election.

(b) Any corporation, partnership, or other business entity that violates this section shall be fined not less than $1,000 and not more than $10,000 and shall pay to the state a penalty equal to three (3) times the value of the illegal payment or contribution; and, if a domestic corporation, partnership, or other business entity, in addition to such fine and penalty, it may be dissolved; and, if a foreign or nonresident corporation, partnership, or other business entity, its right to do business in this state may be declared forfeited.

(c) Any officer, partner, employee, agent, or attorney or other representative of a corporation, partnership, or other business entity who shall aid, abet, advise, or participate in a violation of subsection (a) of this section shall be fined not less than $100 nor more than $5,000 or imprisoned not more than five years, or be both fined and imprisoned.

(d) Any person who knowingly accepts a payment or contribution made in violation of subsection (a) of this section shall be fined not more than $1,000 or imprisoned not more than one year, or be both fined and imprisoned.

(e) If a political treasurer is offered or receives a payment or contribution made in violation of subsection (a) of this section, he shall take such action as the state Elections Commission shall prescribe through published regulations, but in no event shall he retain such payment or contribution or permit it to be used to benefit any candidate or political committee.

Section 14. No newspaper, periodical, or other supplier of materials or services shall require a candidate or political committee to pay a higher charge than the normal charge it requires other customers to pay for comparable materials and services.

Section 15. (a) No political treasurer or combination of political treasurers shall make or authorize any expenditure that will cause the total amount expended in support of a candidate or in support of or opposition to a measure to exceed, with respect to a single election, ten cents times the total population of the state, district, or other area within which the election is held or $1,000, whichever is more.

(b) No political treasurer shall make or authorize any expenditure that will cause the total amount expended for the use of broadcasting stations in support of a candidate in a primary or other election for any office of this state or of a political subdivision thereof to exceed the amount which would be determined for such primary or other election under Section 104(a) (1) (B) or 104(a) (2) (B), whichever is applicable, of the Federal Campaign Communications Reform Act if such primary or other election were an election for federal elective office or nomination thereto. For the purposes of this section, a political party nominating convention shall be considered to be a primary election.

(c) The provisions of Section 315(d) of the Federal Communications Act of 1934 shall apply to any primary or other election for any office of this state or of a political subdivision thereof.

Section 16. The Secretary of State shall cause one certified copy of each report or statement filed with him under Section 309 of the Federal Campaign Communications Reform Act to be delivered to the state Elections Commission within twenty-four hours of the time he receives such report or statement.

Section 17. (a) There is hereby created a state Elections Commission which shall be composed of five members, not more than three of whom shall be members of the same political party and who shall be appointed by the governor with the consent of the state Senate. No person who has, within the previous five years, served as a public official or political party officer shall be appointed to membership on the commission. One of the original members shall be appointed for a term of one year, one for a term of three years, one for a term of five years, one for a term of seven years, and one for a term of nine years, beginning from the date of enactment of this Act, but their successors shall be appointed for terms of nine years each, except that any individual chosen to fill a vacancy shall be appointed only for the unexpired term of the member whom he shall succeed. The commission shall elect one member to serve as chairman of the commission and one member to serve as vice-chairman. The vice-chairman shall act as the chairman in the absence or disability of the chairman or in the event of a vacancy in that office.

(b) A vacancy in the commission shall not impair the right of the remaining members to exercise all the powers of the commission, and three members thereof shall constitute a quorum.

(c) The commission shall at the close of each fiscal year report to the legislature and the governor concerning the action it has taken; the names, salaries, and duties of all individuals in its employ and the money it has disbursed; and shall make such further reports on the matters within its jurisdiction and such recommendations for further legislation as may appear desirable.

(d) Members of the commission shall, while serving on the business of the commission, be entitled to receive compensation at the rate of $50 per day.

(e) The office of the commission shall be in or near the state capital, but it may meet or exercise any or all of its powers at any other place in the state.

(f) All members, officers, agents, attorneys, and employees of the commission shall be subject to the provisions of law prohibiting political activity of state employees.

(g) The commission shall appoint an executive director to serve at the pleasure of the commission. The executive director shall be responsible for the administrative operations of the commission and shall perform such other duties as may be delegated or assigned to him from time to time by regulations or orders of the commission. However, the commission shall not delegate the making of regulations to the executive director.

Section 18. It shall be the duty of the commission:

(a) to prescribe forms for statements and other information required to be filed by this title, and to furnish such forms to persons required to file such statements and information;

(b) to prepare and publish a manual setting forth a prescribed uniform system for accounts for use by persons required to file statements by this Act;

(c) to accept and file any information voluntarily supplied that exceeds the requirements of this Act;

(d) to develop a filing, coding, and cross-indexing system consonant with the purposes of this Act;

(e) to make statements and other information filed with it available for public inspection and copying during regular office hours, and to make copying facilities available free of charge or at a charge not to exceed actual cost;

(f) to preserve such statements and other information for a period of ten years from date of receipt;

(g) to prepare and publish summaries of the statements received;

(h) to prepare and publish such other reports as it may deem appropriate;

(i) to provide for wide public dissemination of summaries and reports;

(j) to make investigations with respect to statements filed under the provisions of this Act, and with respect to alleged failures to file any statement required under the provisions of this Act, and, upon complaint by any individual, with respect to alleged violations of any part of this Act;

(k) to report suspected violations of law to the appropriate law enforcement authorities;

(l) to issue upon request, and publish, advisory opinions upon the requirements of this Act, based on a real or hypothetical set of circumstances;

(m) to prescribe and publish rules and regulations to carry out the provisions of this Act.

Section 19. The executive director of the commission shall inspect each statement filed with the commission under this Act within ten days after the date it is filed. He shall notify a person required to file a statement under this Act immediately if:

(a) upon examination of the official ballot, it appears that the person has failed to file a statement as required by law or that a statement filed by the person does not conform to law; or

(b) a written complaint is filed with the commission by any registered voter alleging that a statement filed with the commission does not conform to law or to the truth or that a person has failed to file a statement required by law.

Section 20. Within three months after the date of each election, the executive director of the commission shall examine each statement filed with the commission under this Act and, referring to the election, determine whether the statement conforms to law and to the truth. Such examination shall include a comparison of reports and statements received by the commission pursuant to sections 6, 7, 8, 9, 11, and 16 of this Act. The commission may require any person to answer in writing and under oath or affirmation any question within the knowledge of that person concerning the source of any contribution. Failure to answer a question under oath or affirmation as required by this section is a misdemeanor.

Section 21. (a) The name of a candidate shall not be printed on the official ballot for a general or special election if:

(1) the political treasurer of the candidate fails to file any statement referring to such election that he is required to file under Section 6(a) (1) of this Act; or

(2) the political treasurer of the candidate or of any political committee that supports the candidate fails to file any statement referring to the nomination of such candidate that he is required to file under this Act.

(b) A vacancy on an official ballot under this section may be filled in the manner provided by law, but not with the name of the same candidate.

Section 22. No certificate of election shall be granted to any candidate until his political treasurer has filed the statements referring to the election he is required to file under Section 6 of this Act.

Section 23. Any person who violates the provisions of Section 2, 3, 4, 5, 6, 7, 8, 9, 10, 11, 12, 14, or 15 of this Act is guilty of a misdemeanor and shall be fined not more than $1,000 if an individual and not more than $5,000 if a person other than an individual, or imprisoned for not more than one year, or be both fined and imprisoned.

Section 24. The circuit courts of this state shall have jurisdiction to issue injunctions to enforce the provisions of this Act upon application by any citizen of this state.

Section 25. If any provision of this Act, or the application thereof to any person or circumstance, is held invalid, the validity of the remainder of this Act and the application of such provisions to other persons and circumstances shall not be affected thereby.

Section 26. This Act shall take effect 30 days after passage into law, and the first reporting period for any existing candidate or political committee shall start on the effective date of this Act.

Annotations to Model Campaign Finance Bill

Section 1(d). Note the expansive definitions of the terms "contribute," "contribution," "expend," and "expenditure." These terms are intended to apply to not only monies spent supporting or opposing candidates, but also monies spent in support or opposition of measures and issues of various kinds.

Section 1(e). Note that the definition of special election includes initiative, referendum, and recall. See Section 1(k).

Section 1(g). The definition of "person" must be sufficiently broad to include not only individuals but all other possible groups and organizations involved in either making or receiving contributions and making or receiving expended monies. Be cautious, with respect to the term "person" and to other defined terms, that, if you use only a section of this bill for some reason, you include definitions of used terms at the beginning of the bill to which the section is appended. The failure to do so may substantially distort the intent of the section used.

Section 1(h). "Political committee" as defined here includes committees established to support not only individual candidates or issues but also the political parties themselves. Be certain that the language you use in defining "political committee" ensures the inclusion of parties as well as committees established to support specific candidates or issues.

Section 1(j). Defining "public office" is a touchy problem. What was intended was to include such offices as school board member, city council member, state legislator, etc., but not to include offices held in membership organizations, however broad, or whatever impact such offices may have on the public. Therefore, president of the local union or of the Junior Chamber of Commerce does not fall under this definition.

Section 1(k). See the discussion of 1(e).

Section 2(c) (2). This provision makes the candidate responsible for attempting to control the unauthorized expenditure of funds on his behalf. Too often in the past, political committees have spent substantial sums in support of or opposition to a given candidate while the prime beneficiary of their action has denied any association with them and, therefore, avoided any responsibility for their actions or expenditures. This important section is intended to close that loophole.

Section 3(b). It is important to give employees of the state elections commission access to the accounts of a political candidate or committee prior to the election so that the commission may act intelligently and, where appropriate, make public disclosures prior to the election.

Section 6(a) (1) and (2). If campaign contribution disclosure laws are to have any meaning whatever, they *must* include the requirement that the candidate disclose his expenditures prior to the election so that the voter may evaluate them before voting. At least one such reporting date must be well in advance of the election. Section 6(a) (1) guarantees this. Likewise, it is important that another reporting date be as close to the election as reasonably possible while still permitting time to distribute disclosed data. This second date is important to pick up what are frequently substantial contributions and expenditures in the final weeks of a campaign that would not have been disclosed in the earlier report. Section 6(a) (2) accomplishes this.

Section 8. This merely assures a complete record of the income and expenditures of all political candidates, even if they receive no funds. It requires that they indicate in a legally binding manner the absence of receipt of funds. This is important.

Section 10. Note the requirement for reports of both contributions and expenditures. The contribution paragraph, Section 10(a), requires a statement listing full name and address of persons whose aggregate contribution equals or exceeds $25.00. The use of the word "aggregate" is important here as it avoids the possibility of having a contributor give great numbers of $24.00 contributions, thereby avoiding the need to report. The final sentence in the expenditure paragraph is quite important because it brings into the picture all contributions other than monetary, and in some campaigns these may be of substantial value.

Section 11. This section provides a check against the reporting of expenditures by political treasurers. A substantial percentage of many campaign expenditures goes to the media, so this check is a useful one.

Section 12. This ceiling on campaign contributions is sufficiently high to allow individuals to make reasonable contributions and for individuals to make some use of personal wealth while at the same time making it unlikely that for most elections a candidate may be effectively bought by a single interest. All four subsections of this section must be maintained. The burden of responsibility is placed in Section 12(c) and (d) on both the donor and the political treasurer, who is likely to have been involved in the solicitation of the donated funds.

Section 13. This guards against the use of corporate or business monies to influence elections. This prohibition is consistent with those included in federal legislation as well as in some existing state law.

Section 14. This prevents the print media from gouging candidates and further escalating already high campaign costs by preventing them from charging higher than normal rates for services rendered.

Section 15. This section sets a ceiling on campaign expenditures based on a formula similar to that used in the newly passed federal campaign finance bill. It does guarantee the opportunity to spend at least $1,000, thus protecting a candidate for office in a small population area from being unduly handicapped by the formula.

Section 15(b). The somewhat wordy language of this section is necessary in order to make state law conform to federal statute. As now written, the federal Campaign Communication Reform Act limits expenditures on broadcast media to six cents times the total population of the potential constituency. Much of the escalating cost of campaigns in recent years has been in the area of broadcast media, and much of that money spent has been on short, high-cost spots, too brief to argue an intelligent case and only of sufficient length to confuse or deceive the public.

Section 17. Only by the establishment of an independent elections commission can reasonable objectivity be assured. It is important to make a stand in favor of the establishment of such a commission and not fall back to the much less desirable options of having some state political appointee or politicized group oversee the regulations in this bill.

Section 17(g). The commission must be guaranteed the opportunity to have a full-time executive director and staff to perform their mandated tasks. This is not a part-time job.

Section 18(e). The commission must be required to publicize the data it receives from political treasurers.

Section 18(j) and (k). It must be a duty, not just an option, of the commission to investigate suspected violations and to report those violations to appropriate law enforcement authorities.

Section 19(b). This provision grants the individual citizen access to the commission and requires the commission to respond to and evaluate written complaints filed by citizens. This is a very important check on the operations of the commission, and any attempt to delete this section can be viewed as a desire to substantially weaken the total bill.

Sections 21 and 22. These sections prevent the candidate from deriving benefit from his illegal act.

Section 24. This may be the most important section in the bill. It grants citizens standing in court to fight for the enforcement of the provisions of this bill. If you make a stand on anything, make it here. Be certain that when you adjust this bill to conform to the needs of your particular state you guarantee the citizen not only the right to courts of original jurisdiction, but to appellate courts as well.

Section 25. After having fought hard for the adoption of this bill, you would hardly want to see the entire bill overturned because one provision may be overturned in court. This section provides protection against such an eventuality.